DIAGNOSTIC
TEACHING
OF READING

DIAGNOSTIC TEACHING OF READING

RUTH STRANG

Emeritus Professor of Education, Teachers College, Columbia University

The Peter Sandiford Visiting Professorship for 1968–69

The Ontario Institute for Studies in Education

SECOND EDITION

McGRAW–HILL BOOK COMPANY

New York   St. Louis   San Francisco   London   Sydney   Toronto   Mexico   Panama

89147

DIAGNOSTIC TEACHING OF READING

Library of Congress Catalog Card Number: 72–77560

07–062002–4

567890   KPKP   7987654

PREFACE

In the discussion of reading problems, we often hear the words *identifica-tion, appraisal, diagnosis,* and *evaluation.*

Identification determines a student's reading status. It is a first step to-ward grouping pupils either within a class or in separate sections. Without identification of some kind, individualization of instruction is impossible. Many schools have not gone far beyond the process of identification.

An *appraisal* of a student's reading ability gives a more complete positive picture of his reading status and development. It emphasizes his potential in relation to his performance; it helps him to set attainable goals.

Diagnosis puts more emphasis on defining the nature of the individual's reading difficulties and the conditions causing them. Diagnosis is also con-cerned, however, with positive factors on which one may build. Even a tentative diagnosis gives the teacher a sense of direction and confidence in working with the individual. Without diagnosis, the teacher may miss im-portant areas, may overemphasize others.

Evaluation stresses the desirability and worth of the reading instruction. It not only ascertains the progress that has been made toward specified objectives but also asks questions such as: "Are the changes that are being effected worthwhile?" "What values have they to the students and to society?" Evaluation looks beneath certain obvious or superficial results of reading instruction. For example, suppose a student brings his reading rate up to 400 words per minute. Looking at the student's improvement in rate, the teacher who evaluates this change may ask: "What purpose did the increase in speed of reading serve?" "At what cost has speed been gained?" "What has happened to the reader's habit of reflective thinking?" "How much strain or tension was involved?" "How much does such rapid read-ing contribute to his personal development?"

Appraisal, diagnosis, and evaluation have much in common. All involve (1) getting facts about the individual and his reading, (2) synthesizing and interpreting these facts, (3) arriving at hypotheses that are modified as new information is obtained, and (4) using the understanding gained to help students improve their reading.

Diagnosis is never an end in itself; it is only a means to more efficient learning. Gaining an understanding of the student's reading proficiency and difficulties takes time, but it also saves time. It saves time by enabling the teacher to focus his attention on the specific help the student needs, thus avoiding trial and error and unnecessary instruction and practice.

In this book diagnosis is viewed as an intrinsic part of teaching. Most of the information a teacher gains about a student's reading is not recorded; it is used immediately in helping the student to improve. The more familiar a teacher is with factors that may influence a student's reading development, the more alert he will be to note their presence as he works with individuals and with groups.

Another important emphasis is on student's self-appraisal. Diagnostic information is for the student as well as for the teacher or reading specialist. Increasing proficiency in self-appraisal is a major goal throughout school years.

The introduction gives a brief background of principles and points of view and an overview of diagnostic information, its sources, and its synthesis.

Part One presents procedures such as observation, group tests, written reports, essays, and informal inventories that can be used with groups. These methods may also be used with individual cases. Other procedures, described in Part Two, are designed to be administered individually.

This revision puts still more emphasis on the role of the teacher in diagnosis and on diagnosis and effective teaching as a continuum. It reviews more thoroughly recent research on the correlates and causes of reading development and difficulties and describes some of the more recently developed diagnostic instruments. At the request of students, more case data and descriptions of remedial procedures have been included, although the focus of the book is primarily on diagnosis. To avoid making the book unwieldy, key references are included in the bibliography for further study. Instead of a description in the Appendix of a few reading tests, the theme of the book has been reinforced by suggesting diagnostic patterns including observation, informal tests, standardized group tests, and individual tests of reading and mental abilities.

This book should give the beginning teacher (1) a developmental rather than a problem approach to the teaching of reading, (2) a feeling for the complexity of the process of learning to read, (3) a description of practical methods of appraisal leading to improvement in reading, and (4) an increased perception of children's struggles with reading difficulties. In the past, too many children have suffered from the "flaw focus" or fault-finding approach.

For the experienced teacher of reading, the book should serve as a source of principles, diagnostic procedures, and materials essential in making decisions about the improvements needed by a class or by individuals. As a reminder of a philosophy and psychology that sometimes becomes dim in the press of multiple duties, this book may also be useful.

The detailed descriptions of procedures and record forms suggested for teachers should be equally useful to the reading consultant or clinician. Unless the specialist's recommendations are practical enough to be carried out under classroom conditions, much of his diagnostic study is wasted. In addition to its value to teachers and reading specialists, the book should also be helpful to principals, psychologists, and guidance workers.

The author owes much to a number of people: to the students whose lively participation in the author's courses in the diagnosis of reading difficulties at Teachers College, Columbia University, and at the University of Arizona over a period of many years has helped to identify and clarify important questions and problems; to Dr. Rachel Burkholder, who for the past five years was co-instructor in the course in diagnosis of reading development and difficulties; to Dorothy Maxson, Marjorie Cameron, Betty Fry, and many other teachers who contributed descriptions of creative teaching and case work procedures; and to Dr. Barbara Bateman, Dr. John Carrol, Dr. Theodore Clymer, Dr. Samuel Kirk, Dr. Constance McCullough, Dr. Helen Robinson, Dr. George Spache, and many others whose publications have contributed to the author's understanding of the role of diagnosis in the teaching of reading.

Ruth Strang

CONTENTS

GROUP METHODS

Chapter One

INTRODUCTION

Inability to read is recognized as the most important single cause of school failure. It is also related to other problems, since children may respond to this handicap in devious ways. Many give up trying to do the impossible tasks assigned. Some become emotionally disturbed, others express their frustration in delinquent behavior.

Estimates of the frequency of reading disabilities vary greatly depending upon the definition, the population sampled, the tests used, the statistical methods employed, and the investigator's interpretation. In general, estimates range from 10 to 25 percent of the school population. According to M. D. Vernon (1960),[1] the amount of severe, permanent backwardness in reading has not been accurately reported.

Diagnosis underlies prevention as well as remediation of reading difficulties. It is the basis for a diagnostic curriculum, that is, a curriculum based on diagnosis. Appropriate instruction stems from and is interwoven with accurate and pertinent diagnostic information. Accordingly, the factors significantly related to reading development and difficulties should be familiar to teachers as well as to reading specialists.

PRINCIPLES UNDERLYING INSTRUCTION

Many principles apply to both diagnosis and teaching and serve as a guide to teachers and clinicians:

1. Determine where a child is functioning, start instruction at or slightly below that point, and help him to progress as far and as fast as he can toward his potential reading ability.

[1] Parentheses refer to publications listed in the References at the end of each chapter.

3

2. Success has a tonic effect; nothing succeeds like observed success. Too often the retarded reader has become convinced that he is too dumb to learn to read. Members of his family may have told him so. Teachers have become exasperated when he did not respond to their best efforts. He has demonstrated his inability to himself on reading material that was too difficult for him. His embarrassment and sense of failure are intensified when his classmates shout out the words that he stumbles over and the teacher calls on another student who reads the passage fluently and with accurate comprehension. He needs the experience of success. In general, success is more conducive to learning than failure, reward more than punishment, praise more than blame.

3. Respect for the pupil increases his self-esteem and self-confidence. If the teacher listens intently to the student and shows that he understands how he is thinking and feeling, he thus conveys his respect and genuine concern for the pupil as a person. On the other hand, self-esteem is *not* usually developed by superficial reassurance. For example, if the teacher says, "Now don't worry about your reading. It doesn't matter so much," the student who is very much concerned about his reading may feel, "The teacher doesn't understand. If she did, she would know that it *does* matter."

4. Learning takes place in a relationship. In conveying a warm, friendly feeling and positive regard, the teacher's manner and actions speak louder than his words. When the teacher's face lights up at the student's successful performance, or when he takes the trouble to find an interesting book or to make suitable exercises that will help the student improve, then the student knows that the teacher cares. If a student seems antagonistic or resistant, the teacher should not take this attitude personally; it may stem from previous coercion by parents and teachers and from many an unpleasant reading experience. Children respond differently to apparently similar approaches. One may love a certain teacher, while another hates him. One may reject kindness as weakness in discipline, while another may respond to it in an almost miraculous way. Criticism may motivate one student to do better, while it completely discourages another. Praise and recognition may embarrass some, motivate others. Consequently, the teacher constantly tries to discern what the situation means to a particular individual.

5. There is no substitute for skillful instruction based upon an analysis of the learning process. By analyzing the steps in a given learning task, programmed instruction has made an important contribution to teaching. Learning tasks should be presented in a sequence from simple to complex, from concrete to abstract, that the student can follow; then they should be reviewed, applied immediately, and overlearned if permanent retention is necessary.

6. Fundamentally, success in teaching reading relates to the dynamics of the situation. There should be an atmosphere of children learning and growing. In the small reading group or individual conference, the student is free from his classroom associations with failure, free from the teacher's disapproval and the ridicule of classmates.

7. Successful teaching of retarded readers depends also on discovering what makes them tick. This cannot be done through a direct question, "What is your reading problem?" They want to forget it. They often are ingenious in diverting attention from it. The teacher needs to be alert to pick up the indirect and incidental clues to the difficulties that they reveal in their discussion, conversation, written work, and other behavior.

These principles of teaching also have implications for diagnosis and remediation. The problem is to translate the theory of learning into principles of teaching, and principles of teaching into practice.

DIAGNOSIS AND THE BROAD VIEW OF READING

Every promising path to improvement in reading demands an understanding of both the reading process and the reader. Viewed as communication, the reading process involves the abilities (1) to decode or decipher the author's printed words, (2) to associate them with meaning gained through the reader's firsthand experience and previous reading, and (3) to express the ideas thus acquired through speaking, drawing, writing, or other verbal or motor responses. The broad view of reading includes an understanding of what constitutes effective reading, what contributes to effective reading, and what interferes with effective reading.

Techniques of diagnosis vary with our theories of reading. If we think of reading as a visual task—seeing clearly the printed words—then we will focus on visual screening tests and eye examinations. These reveal some defects that prevent reading proficiency or cause discomfort and thus decrease an individual's satisfaction in reading.

If we think of reading primarily as word recognition, then our appraisal procedures will test auditory and visual perception and discrimination, skill in using sound-symbol association to pronounce unfamiliar words, and facility in anticipating and checking their meaning by the context.

If, however, we think of reading as getting the meaning of the selection (and what could be more futile than merely pronouncing words without knowing what they mean?), then we must ascertain the student's comprehension of what the author is trying to communicate. We question students on what they have read. We may also use tests, both standardized and informal, some calling for free or composition-type, creative responses; some testing comprehension by means of objective exercises.

If we view reading as more than the literal comprehension of the author's thought, if we include the idea of reading between the lines and beyond the lines, then we must further expand the diagnostic procedure. We will find out whether the student can make inferences and generalizations based on the selection, draw conclusions, interpret literature, appreciate literary excellence, and sense the author's mood, intent, and purpose. It seems impossible to say where reading ends and thinking begins, impossible to separate the two processes.

If our concept of reading embraces the reader's use of the material read, our diagnostic procedure becomes still more complicated. We are then concerned with how effectively the student uses ideas gained from reading in conversation, discussion, committee or individual reports, creative writing, drawing, and other modes of expression and communication. His purpose in reading largely determines his rate and method of reading.

If we go further and recognize that reading ought to change the individual's ideas, feelings, attitudes, and behavior, then we have set ourselves a truly difficult task. There are no standardized tests to measure these outcomes of reading. We must resort to informal methods which depend largely upon observation, interviews, and introspective reports from the students. Difficult as it is, however, this kind of diagnosis should be attempted, for one of the two main objectives of teaching reading is personal development through reading.

To represent the broad view, diagnosis must be comprehensive. To be dynamic, it must yield understanding of the forces at work within the individual and the situation; forces that are attracting or repelling him. Such diagnosis recognizes the role played by the individual's previous experiences, his specific goals, preferably self-determined, and his progress toward these goals.

TWO APPROACHES TO DIAGNOSIS

There is some controversy about the best approach to diagnosis. One is the clinical-medical intensive diagnosis prior to treatment. This school of thought advocates obtaining as much relevant information as possible before beginning to work with the individual. The teacher or clinician gathers data from existing records; interviews parents and the student; administers, scores, and interprets intelligence and achievement tests. Before attempting any remedial work, he reviews, interprets, and synthesizes this information. This approach is similar to the directive or counselor-centered approach in counseling. It is used, of course, when reading cases are referred to a clinic for diagnosis.

There are advantages to this approach. It may detect crucial factors on which to begin working. Obtaining a fairly complete, initial understanding of the individual assures greater accuracy in selecting reading materials and procedures pertinent to the case. It may avoid waste of time due to following unproductive leads. It may deter the teacher or clinician from doing or saying something detrimental.

On the other hand, there are possible disadvantages in prolonged preliminary diagnosis. An individual who is eager to improve his reading tends to become impatient if he must spend several hours without receiving any apparent help. Moreover, a person who is anxious about his reading and has feelings of inferiority about himself is likely to have these feelings intensified as he fails to answer the increasingly difficult questions on standardized tests; he may feel more strongly than ever that something must be seriously wrong with him. The skillful examiner can minimize these disadvantages, but he cannot eliminate them entirely. Another objection to the routine preliminary diagnosis is that some of the information obtained may not be relevant to the case, while other information of special or unique importance to the case may not be obtained.

When diagnosis is made while working with the student, the forward movement is guided by the feedback from each previous step taken singly or in combination. If, on the other hand, the diagnostic information is obtained by hours of preliminary testing and interviewing, it does not have the benefit of the intuitions and hypotheses that emerge, are revised, and are tested in the process of working with the individual.

In the other approach the teacher or clinician starts with the reading problem as the student presents it and begins immediately to help him solve it. While observing and giving instruction, the teacher learns about the student's approach to reading, the skills he has mastered, and those in which he is still deficient. If the worker feels the need for additional information, he may obtain it from an intelligence test, a reading test, a home visit, or other sources. Thus diagnosis and instruction have a recip- rocal relationship.

By beginning to work on an immediate problem, the teacher meets the expectation of the individual who comes for help on his reading difficul- ties. By combining diagnosis with instruction, there is no gap between obtaining information and using it. The student has the satisfaction of accomplishing something, of making some progress in every period. The experience of success motivates him to try harder. Since reading abilities are interrelated, improvement in one tends to give greater proficiency in others. Moreover, this approach invites self-appraisal; it encourages the student to take the initiative in solving his own reading problems, for he works along with the teacher in diagnosing his strengths and deficiencies. Thus the individual takes more responsibility for his own learning and develops an objective, hopeful attitude toward his strengths and limitations.

A disadvantage of this second approach, as was already implied, is the danger of treating symptoms and neglecting underlying disabilities that are blocking progress.

To some extent, the two approaches can be combined. There is no rea- son why a diagnostic test given according to directions should not be used immediately to give a student insight into his reading difficulties. There is no reason why instruction should not lead to further diagnosis of the difficulties recognized. For example, difficulty in word recognition may suggest the need for an eye examination or tests of visual and auditory discrimination and memory. Any approach which uncovers and meets an individual's needs almost simultaneously has a decided psychological ad- vantage. The proportion of each approach depends largely on the com- plexity of the reading problem and on the level on which the teacher or clinician is working. The success of each approach depends largely on his understanding of the causes and correlates of reading achievement.

LEVELS OF DIAGNOSIS

Diagnosis may be made on different levels of comprehensiveness, psycho- logical depth, and competence. On the first or symptom-surface level, reading performance is described: strengths and weaknesses in vocabulary, word recognition, sentence and paragraph comprehension, and related abilities. This kind of information may be obtained during classroom in- struction and from informal and standardized tests; it is used immediately to develop or reinforce strengths and to minimize or correct weaknesses. But information about a student's reading performance is not enough; an understanding of how he acquires certain knowledge and skills is also necessary.

On a second level, clues to conditions that may be influencing an individual's reading performance may be observed in the classroom, on the playground, and in interviews. A general passivity or low energy level may be preventing a student from putting forth optimum effort. A meager speaking vocabulary, imprecise articulation, immature sentence structure, and other inadequacies in verbal communication would interfere with accurate decoding and interpretation of printed material. Anxiety may interfere with thinking. Habits of work may result in intermittent effort, a tendency to give up when the work becomes difficult, a lack of concern for accuracy. Such conditions may be at the root of a student's retardation in reading.

A third level of diagnosis focuses on the abilities systematically involved in the reading process from intake to output through the steps of reception, perception, differentiation, association, retention, and retrieval leading to motor, visual, or vocal output. In such a differential diagnosis of correlates, specific abilities and deficiencies can be detected as a basis for remedial instruction.

A fourth level of reading diagnosis is concerned with other mental abilities underlying success in reading. These abilities are measured by subtest scores on the Stanford-Binet Intelligence Test (Valett, 1964) or on the Wechsler Intelligence Scale for Children (WISC) (Deal, 1965) (see Chapter 11). They include visual memory and association and the more subtle and pervasive aspects of memory and reasoning. If these underlying abilities were determined early and then developed by practice on exercises somewhat similar to those in the tests, the child should show improvement in reading.

A fifth level of diagnosis related to reading improvement involves clinical analysis of personality and values. Such techniques as figure drawing, incomplete sentences, the Rorschach technique, the Thematic Apperception Test (TAT), and other projective techniques may supplement, confirm, or contradict impressions gained from observation. In some cases they may indicate the individual's need for psychotherapy preliminary to or concomitant with reading instruction.

A sixth level of diagnosis requires a neurological examination of possible brain damage. However, definite correlations of brain pathology with inability to learn readily, to retain, and to recall what is read have not been established (Cohn, 1964). "Remediation must still be planned largely on the basis of observed behavior" (Bateman, 1965, p. 168). These cases of severe reading disability are comparable to a chronic illness requiring long-term treatment.

A seventh diagnostic level or approach is based on introspective-retrospective reports. The student is encouraged to describe his process in reading selected articles. While giving instruction, teachers may ask children how they arrived at the pronunciation of an unfamiliar word, the meaning of a word they had not been taught, or the thought of a sentence or paragraph. If they have made an error in pronunciation or meaning, the teacher may ask them to explain their difficulty (see Chapter 5).

Teachers and clinicians will work on their levels of competency and with reference to the complexity of the reading problems with which they are dealing. The classroom teacher may work on the first, second, and seventh levels. By appraising the student's present reading performance and his responses to the methods and materials of instruction, the teacher will obtain from his daily contacts clues of conditions that are favorable or unfavorable to the student's progress; he will gain understanding of how the individual acquires certain knowledge and skills. The special reading teacher may use any of the techniques described except the neurological examination and projective techniques, which require special training. The latter may be in the repertory of the reading clinician. By using the team approach, the depth of diagnosis and treatment needed in individual cases may be provided.

COMPREHENSIVE DIAGNOSTIC PATTERN

The first step is to describe in detail the student's reading performance: What phonic skills does he possess? What method of word attack does he consistently use? How large is his sight vocabulary? How well does he read orally? How quick and accurate is his comprehension in silent reading? What difficulties does he encounter? What errors does he make?

The second step is to determine so far as possible his reading potential and whether there is a discrepancy between his reading performance and his mental and chronological age.

The third step is to discover the specific abilities and conditions that underlie his reading performance. His lack of phonic skills, for example, may be due to deficiencies in auditory or visual discrimination, memory, or closure; to failure to integrate auditory and visual impressions; and to other factors. Lack of motivation and outgoingness may decrease the psychological energy that the individual applies to any aspect of learning.

> On the basis of the information gathered in the preceding three steps an hypothesis is formulated which must be both precise and comprehensive. It must take into account all the relevant factors and yet be so precise that it leads directly to remedial planning (Bateman, 1965, p. 172).

The teacher may follow these steps in an informal and incidental way; the clinician, in a more precise and systematic way.

RELATION OF DIAGNOSIS TO REMEDIATION

Diagnosis should lead directly to the improvement of reading through the reinforcement of strengths and the correction of difficulties discovered. No gap should intervene between diagnosis and remediation. Bateman (1965, p. 171) shows this relationship in a schematic representation of the diagnostic-remedial process. Remedial work begins on the reading performance level, i.e., with the specific difficulties indicated by the diagnostic hypothesis. If the individual does not respond to this direct attack on his

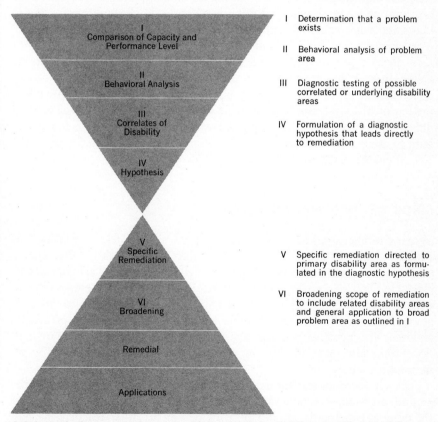

I   Determination that a problem exists

II   Behavioral analysis of problem area

III   Diagnostic testing of possible correlated or underlying disability areas

IV   Formulation of a diagnostic hypothesis that leads directly to remediation

V   Specific remediation directed to primary disability area as formulated in the diagnostic hypothesis

VI   Broadening scope of remediation to include related disability areas and general application to broad problem area as outlined in I

A Schematic Representation of the Diagnostic-Remedial Process (Barbara Bateman, "Learning Disabilities: Yesterday, Today, and Tomorrow," *Exceptional Children*, 31:171, December, 1965.)

reading deficiencies, attention must be given to the correlates and causes that may be blocking progress in reading. After these conditions have been made more favorable, the reading skills acquired could be applied more broadly to different kinds of reading.

Some teachers and specialists seem to have little regard for the appropriateness of their remedial procedures to the diagnostic findings. One reading program uses games with all the students; another employs nothing but the kinesthetic approach; another finds in group therapy the cure-all of reading problems; still another gives all classes tachistoscopic training regardless of individual differences.

There are several reasons for this failure in relating treatment to diagnosis. One is that the disproportionate amount of time spent on diagnosis and record keeping leaves little time for differentiated instruction. A second reason is that the processes are often carried on by different persons, neither of whom understands what the other is trying to do. A third explanation is that some single cause of reading difficulty is overemphasized.

A fourth reason for the ineffectual use of diagnostic information is its inadequacy. Most quantitative data tell little about the child as a person, about the specific nature of his retardation, or about the dynamics of the difficulty. An astute teacher could obtain more immediately useful information of this kind simply by asking a child to read paragraphs of varying difficulty, to demonstrate his comprehension of them, and to try to explain both his successful and his unsuccessful responses (Dolch, 1951, pp. 124–125; Sheldon, 1958, pp. 545–546).

KINDS OF INFORMATION NEEDED

When a teacher is asked, "What do you know about Dick?" a ninth-grade student in his class, he is likely to say something like this: "Oh, Dick's an average boy. He causes no trouble," or "He's a disturbing element in the class. He's better in arithmetic than in reading." A more perceptive teacher may observe that, although Dick has a speech defect, he wants to talk and always has something to say. Another teacher, with a positive approach to children, may perceive primarily the things Dick does well and report that he is especially good in drawing and that she has used this ability to increase his self-esteem.

Dick's homeroom teacher has obtained facts about the boy's home background, attendance, school marks, test results, and educational plans from the cumulative records. By talking with one of his other teachers, he has learned that Dick was a poor reader, fidgeted a great deal, did not do his work, misspelled many words, wrote in a cramped hand, and was absent a great deal. He was given a buddy to help him, but this did not work out very well because the pair disturbed other children, and Dick let his buddy do the work for him. It was significant that Dick was quite different on the playground; there he entered into the activities with enthusiasm.

In a half-hour interview with Dick after school, his reading teacher gained these additional tentative impressions and bits of information. Although he looked healthy, he had moved to this city because of persistent colds. His mistakes on a vocabulary test, such as calling *hurt* for *hunt*, suggested the possibility of poor visual acuity. His poor memory and dull facial expression raised questions about his mental ability. He mentioned that his father was out of work; this and other incidental comments suggested possible anxiety or tension in his home. Here were a number of leads that a teacher might use in working with Dick.

In his daily observation and contacts with Dick, the teacher can obtain information of the following kinds:

How he approaches reading tasks

How well he reads at present

How he attacks unfamiliar and difficult words

What his concept of reading is

How he feels about reading

How he responds to help

What his specific difficulties are

What enjoyment or satisfactions he gets from reading

What progress he is making

What he reads voluntarily

How much time he spends in reading

What his reading interests are

Why he reads

How far he can go in reading—what his reading potential is

How quickly he can learn

What home and school conditions are favorable to his reading development

What conditions seem to be causing his reading difficulty

Which of these conditions can be modified

Information of this kind can be grouped under three headings: reading performance, reading potential, correlates and causes.

Reading performance

In observing Dick's oral reading, the teacher would note his enunciation, his ability to recognize words in the basic sight vocabulary, his method of attack on unfamiliar words, his phrasing and attention to punctuation, his fluency, and his comprehension and interpretation of the selection read aloud.

When Dick reads silently, the teacher notes whether he can comprehend better than when he reads orally and why. Perhaps because of his speech defect or emotional difficulties, he becomes too embarrassed to concentrate on the meaning when he reads aloud.

His comprehension of the selection is shown by his ability to summarize or outline what the author said—to get the main ideas of a passage and the subordinate details, to distinguish essential details from those that are incidental or unimportant.

Comprehension also requires ability to see relationships such as comparisons, contrasts, and time sequences; to read between the lines and to sense the author's tone, mood, or intention in writing the material; and to evaluate—agree or disagree intelligently with the writer. Comprehension, as broadly defined, includes the ability to read beyond the lines, applying the author's ideas to one's present and future life and problems; to project oneself into the situations described and decide how one would have acted and why. Comprehension of descriptive passages in literature requires ability to imagine or picture what the printed word describes.

A thorough appraisal of Dick's reading status also includes information on his proficiency in the use of the dictionary, index, and other location-of-information skills. Can he locate sources of information in the library? After he has found a book or article on the topic, can he scan it to obtain the specific information he needs? After he has found the facts, can he analyze, synthesize, and communicate them? Does he know how to read graphs, maps, and tables?

Reading potential

To gain understanding of Dick's reading potential, the teacher would need help from the psychologist or reading specialist. The three groups of abilities that Holmes (1961, pp. 111–122) found to have greatest weight in reading speed and power were (1) intelligence as measured by Thurstone's Primary Mental Abilities Test, (2) linguistic abilities, and (3) listening comprehension or auding.

MENTAL ABILITY AND LEARNING CAPACITY   Other things being equal, the less intelligent child will have the greater difficulty in reading. He is more likely to lack curiosity, which is basic to good reading. He lacks the reasoning ability to see essential relations in complex sentences. His lack of reading ability limits his acquisition of information, and this in turn makes it more difficult for him to put meaning into what he reads.

Learning capacity and learning rate are important aspects of intelligence that are often neglected in a diagnostic study. There are simple tests of learning capacity, such as that included in the Durrell-Sullivan Reading Capacity and Achievement Tests (1937–1945). However, more valuable evidence can be obtained by the clinician as he works with a case and by the classroom teacher as he observes students' responses to his instruction and keeps dated samples of their work.

THE PERCEPTUAL-CONCEPTUAL CONTINUUM The individual's sensory impressions are invested with meaning and organized into perceptions and then into concepts which are basic to still larger thought patterns. In beginning reading the ability to copy forms, perceptual speed, visual and auditory memory and closure, classification and concept formation are frequently better indicators of reading potential than abilities as measured by intelligence tests. Dick may have had initial perceptual deficits, or he may still have difficulty in auditory or visual discrimination, memory, or integration.

LINGUISTIC ABILITIES Fluency and precision in speech, superior oral vocabulary and sentence patterns, "word sense," and familiarity with both colloquial and literary expressions are prognostic of success in reading. These abilities often are taken for granted. Children from homes where English is correctly spoken acquire correct language patterns naturally; children from foreign language backgrounds and illiterate homes require special linguistic instruction and much verbal association with English-speaking children and adults.

LISTENING COMPREHENSION Ability to comprehend by listening (sometimes called auding) is another indication of potential reading ability. If an individual comprehends a passage read aloud much better than he comprehends a comparable passage that he reads silently, the prognosis for improvement in his reading is favorable. For prognostic purposes, tests of listening comprehension are being recommended in addition to individual intelligence tests (see Chapter 11).

Correlates and causes

Dick, like most people, has unrealized reading ability. His potentialities exceed his achievement. Such discrepancy between capacity and performance may be due to his lack of interest, his attitudes toward himself and toward reading, inner conflicts, or other factors.

INTERESTS   In addition to learning about Dick's favorite subjects, his general interests, and his reading interests, the teacher may obtain more objective information about his family's reading habits and the way Dick uses his leisure time. Does he have books available at home? Does he borrow books from the school and public libraries?

ATTITUDES   Even more important than this factual information are the student's self-concept and his attitudes and feelings about his reading. Does he see himself as a person who can read better, or has he become so discouraged that he thinks of himself as unable to learn to read? If Dick has a reading handicap, what need does it serve? What satisfaction does he get from being a retarded reader? Why does he hold on to his handicap? Why does he resist learning to read?

His method of coping with his reading difficulty often stems from his attitudes. Does he try to cover it up by aggressive or annoying behavior? Does he withdraw into a world of fantasy in which he is the best reader in the class? Does he withdraw from the whole situation by playing truant?

EMOTIONAL DIFFICULTIES   Emotional freedom to learn is essential to success in reading. Various fears may lurk behind many plausible explanations of reading retardation. Is the student afraid of growing up, afraid to compete with more able readers, afraid of making mistakes (Walters and others, 1961, pp. 277–283)? There are many emotional disturbances that may be involved in cases of serious retardation.

VALUES   The individual's value system underlies his attitude toward himself and his reading. What are his purposes in reading? Are they immediate—to win the approval of his parents, teachers, or classmates; to enjoy using his mind; to satisfy his curiosity; to learn how to make or do something? Does he also have long-term goals such as college entrance or vocational success?

PHYSICAL FACTORS   Of special importance in a child's early reading development are prenatal and birth conditions, visual and auditory defects, lack of motor and eye-hand coordination, general immaturity, low energy level, endocrine disturbances, and malnutrition. Signs of these physical defects may be observed by the teacher. He may suspect visual and auditory difficulties if the child holds a book too near or too far from the eyes, if he pays no attention unless he is looking directly at the speaker, if he loses his place and skips lines in reading. Some of these visual factors are described in Chapter 9. Neurological, chemical, and glandular conditions have been receiving increased emphasis.

HOME AND SCHOOL CONDITIONS   These have a very important bearing on the pupil's reading development. The education of the parents and their expectations of the child influence his school achievement. In homes where there is little conversation or where a foreign language is spoken, there is usually little opportunity for the child to develop a meaningful vocabulary or to master common English language patterns. Children who have learned to think verbally and express themselves fluently naturally have the advantage in learning to read.

Children need opportunities to learn. Unfavorable school conditions and inferior instruction are responsible for considerable failure in reading. For some children, reading may have been introduced before they were physically, mentally, or socially ready to learn. The teacher's skill and the prevalent teacher-student relations may either facilitate or block a child's growth in reading.

The parent-child and sibling relationships that prevail from infancy also exert a strong influence on the child's reading development. Peer relations, especially during adolescence, play a prominent role in students' achievement. In many peer cultures (Coleman, 1962, pp. 4–7), popularity, athletics, and extraclass activities are more important to the students than scholarship. A significant negative relationship exists between peer prestige status and reading achievement status (Porterfield and Schlichting, 1961, pp. 291–297).

The research findings on each of these aspects are inconclusive (Hartup, 1968). M. D. Vernon (1960) pointed out many difficulties in interpreting and using research generalizations and conclusions of this kind. For example, surveys show that poorer readers tend to lack concentration, persistence, and emotional stability. But surveys do not show the extent to which these factors exist in poor readers and whether they are the cause or the effect of difficulty in reading. It has been reported that size of school, urban locality, and socioeconomic status all correlated positive with reading achievement. But unless intelligence is excluded, these results may merely show that the more intelligent children who have higher reading achievement live in better class neighborhoods and attend larger schools (Vernon, 1960, p. 147).

Despite the contradictions in generalizations and conclusions, research findings do alert the diagnostician to relationships that may exist. They help him understand the factors and diagnostic patterns that may be pertinent in a given group or in an individual.

SOURCES OF INFORMATION

Some procedures can be used with an entire class, others must be administered individually. An overview of these procedures may be helpful at this point.

Group procedures

These include the following:

1. Observation day by day, a basic technique by means of which the teacher may gather much information about the student's manifest reading achievement, attitudes, and interests.

2. Interest inventories and questionnaires. The unstructured type of inquiry often yields more significant results than one that consists only of specific questions.

3. The reading autobiography gives clues to the individual's reading development and the genesis of his difficulties, as well as revealing his present attitudes, interests, satisfactions, and dissatisfactions.

4. The daily schedule throws light on the student's interests and the pattern of his daily activities, including reading of different kinds.

5. The Dolch Basic Sight Word Test is useful to ascertain whether the student can recognize the most common words in one quick glance.

6. Informal reading tests should include at least two types of questions: those calling for a creative or free response, such as "What did the author say?" and short-answer or objective questions on different aspects of reading. Informal tests can be used in a testing-teaching-self-appraisal procedure.

7. Standardized group intelligence and achievement tests give clues to the individual's level of ability and achievement in comparison with those of his peers. Subtest scores and analysis of the student's responses yield additional information.

8. Listening comprehension tests are useful in determining reading potential.

9. Classroom projective-type tests include incomplete sentences, in-

complete stories, the draw-a-person technique, and free response to selected pictures. These techniques, used by a clinically trained person, yield clues to feelings and relationships that may cause reading difficulties.

Individual procedures (see Chapter 10)

1. Visual screening tests.
2. Diagnostic reading tests (see Appendix).
3. Tests of visual and auditory perception, discrimination, and closure: Frostig, Wepman, Illinois Test of Psycholinguistic Ability, and others.
4. Individual intelligence tests.
5. Individual reading inventories.
6. Interviews with the student and with his parents. In interviews that encourage introspection, we may learn much about the individual's reading process and the intricate ways in which he arrives at the meaning of printed material.
7. Individually administered projective techniques presenting unstructured situations that evoke unique responses.
8. Case conferences on individual cases.

Combination of procedures

The following table shows some sources of information and the kind of information that can be obtained from each.

Sources, methods, and instruments	Kinds of information obtained	What was learned about an individual student, Dick
1. School records	Scores on previous intelligence and achievement tests; school marks in all subjects; family size, economic and social background, language spoken, visual, auditory, and general health information; attendance; change of schools.	Dick is the oldest of seven children. His family is of low-middle socioeconomic status; white, Irish and German extraction. Poor English, but no foreign language is spoken. Kuhlmann-Anderson IQ 110; no recorded health problems; good attendance at the same school. Dick has done consistently poor work through the first year of high school.

Sources, methods, and instruments	Kinds of information obtained	What was learned about an individual student, Dick
2. Classroom observation of students engaged in oral reading, in group discussion, and other classroom activities	Success in completing a given assignment; oral and silent reading performance; indications of attitudes toward reading, school, and himself; interests; relations with other students; speaking vocabulary and sentence structure; uses made of reading; changes in attitudes, points of view, and behavior.	Dick seems to make no real effort to learn new and difficult words. He glides over them and does not stop to analyze or remember them. Even after the teacher has pointed out obvious errors in spelling, Dick makes the same errors again. On the same page he will spell a word both correctly and incorrectly. Other pupils choose him in games. Woodworking in his favorite subject.
3. Interest inventories and questionnaires	Reading interests and other interests.	Dick's main interest is sports. He checked several reading interests but may just have thought this was the thing to do.
4. Reading autobiography and other introspective reports	Family reading habits, his own past and present reading interests, his analysis of his reading difficulties.	The family does little reading; Dick has read little in the past. At present he says he enjoys reading books on aviation.
5. Daily schedule	How he spends his time: in outdoor activities, TV, movies, chores, part-time work; alone, with friends, with family; kinds and amount of reading.	Most of Dick's free time was spent playing outdoors. After supper he usually watched TV. During the days recorded he did no voluntary reading.
6. Dolch Basic Sight Word Test	Sight recognition of basic words, words that he needs to study.	Dick failed to recognize at sight about one-fourth of the Dolch basic vocabulary.
7. Informal tests and group reading inventory	The free or creative-type response yields information about the pupil's approach to reading and inferences as to how his mind works when he reads. The short-answer or multiple-choice questions give understanding of other aspects of comprehension.	Dick could not read independently books above sixth-grade level. He picked out a few scattered ideas but saw no relation or sequence among them. He was able to identify most of the main ideas and supporting details in the multiple-choice ques-

Sources, methods, and instruments	Kinds of information obtained	What was learned about an individual student, Dick
		tions. He made no application of the ideas to his own life.
8. Standardized reading tests	Different tests yield different kinds of information: speed of reading easy material, speed-comprehension ratio, special vocabulary in each subject, sentence and paragraph comprehension, ability to use index and reference material.	On the subtests as reported on the Iowa Silent Reading Test, Dick's vocabulary, sentence meaning, and directed reading seem to be very poor. He used the index well but slowly, had surprisingly high ability to get the main idea of a paragraph. His total reading score was at the 33d percentile.
9. Listening comprehension tests	Relation between listening comprehension and silent reading comprehension on comparable material.	Dick comprehended much better when he listened than when he read.
10. Diagnostic spelling test	Grade level of spelling ability, kinds of errors made.	Dick's spelling is about sixth-grade level; he is not word-conscious.
11. Classroom projective techniques, e.g., incomplete sentences, pictures	Attitudes toward self, family, and clues as to emotional conflicts, worries, etc.	Dick gave repeated indications of fear of failure and dislike of school.

SYNTHESIS AND INTERPRETATION OF INFORMATION

From the information collected about Dick, we learn that his achievement is more than two years below his grade placement, yet he is intelligent enough to be a better reader. Why is there this discrepancy between his reading performance and his mental ability? The problem is long standing; he has been a poor reader from the first grade to the freshman year of high school. His continued lack of success may account for his fear of failure and his dislike of school. These, in turn, result in decreased effort. The two central factors in this case seem to be lack of effort and ineffective instruction in reading. He seems to make no real effort to analyze, learn, or remember new words. Why is this? There are a number of possible explanations:

1. He may not have acquired word recognition skills.

2. He may not have learned to apply the word recognition skills he had learned.

3. He may be deficient in visual or auditory discrimination or other underlying abilities needed for word recognition.

4. He may resent having to read aloud and feel embarrassed by his inadequacy.

5. He may have no interest in the reading material and little or no interest in reading itself or in the curriculum. His preferred activities are sports and TV.

6. His lack of effort may be tied up in some way with his family relationships. If Dick identifies with a father who does little reading and who may have a disparaging attitude toward reading and toward education in general, Dick may assume a similar attitude. Little information has been given on family relationships that may be influencing his fear of failure and dislike of school. If his anxiety about his reading is intense, it may interfere with rather than stimulate greater effort.

7. Lack of affection and intellectual stimulation during infancy and early childhood may have resulted in a persistent passivity with respect to verbal learning.

These are some speculations about the causes of Dick's lack of effort which might be explored in the order given above.

The hypothesis that an unsuitable curriculum and poor instruction might account for Dick's deficiencies in reading is suggested by his lack of interest and effort. The fact that he comprehends better when he listens to a story than when he reads it suggests that he has the ability to get the meaning of a verbal communication. By the time he reached high school he may also have acquired a knack of answering objective questions without even reading the selection.

Since school health examinations leave much to be desired, Dick should have his eyes tested by a competent ophthalmologist. Tests of visual and auditory discrimination and memory may detect deficiencies that underlie word recognition skills. An informal reading test would enable the student and teacher to explore specific difficulties in reading comprehension and reasons for them.

But since Dick's sense of failure is keen and his previous instruction in reading probably inadequate, it would seem wise to attack the reading problem directly and specifically, using material that had meaning for him, that dealt with things he needs and wants to know and which were related to his life. The reading teacher would go through every step of the process with him: reading the headings, recalling what he already knows about the topic, and jotting down some questions that the selection would answer. Together they would read each sentence in the first paragraph to get its meaning and its contribution to the main thought of the paragraph. They would systematically use context clues, syllabication, and other structural analysis and phonetic analysis if useful, and the dictionary when necessary to pronounce and get the meaning of unfamiliar words. They would note which procedures helped him to learn best.

In this way Dick would learn to read a number of selections successfully. He would also become aware of the reading skills he needed to acquire. As he diagnosed his difficulties with the teacher and saw more clearly his reading problems, he would welcome specific practice exercises if needed. He would also have had the experience of acquiring knowledge that was important to him. While working with him on his immediate reading problems, the teacher would gradually find out more about the causes of his lack of effort and his reading difficulties.

PRINCIPLES OF DIAGNOSIS

Diagnosis should have a developmental emphasis

Traditionally, diagnosis has had a pathological connotation. It has focused too exclusively on what the individual cannot do, rather than on what he does under particular conditions. Focusing attention on the reader's deficiencies may affect unfavorably the teacher's attitude toward the child and the child's attitude toward himself. Labels like *dyslexia* (which merely means "inadequate reading ability") and *strepho-symbolia* (meaning "twisted symbols") alarm many parents and may increase the child's anxiety about himself and his reading.

Diagnosis should be continuous

The initial impression is modified by each contact with the individual as the teacher or clinician gains new understanding of his reading problem.

Diagnosis is interwoven with teaching

There is a reciprocal relationship between diagnosis and teaching. While teaching, the teacher obtains diagnostic information; in teaching, he uses the information he has obtained.

Diagnosis includes consideration of the ecological as well
as of the personal factors related to reading disability

In the past, diagnosis of reading problems tended to neglect conditions in home, school, and neighborhood that might be giving rise to the reading problem. Having recognized the influence of these environmental factors, the teacher or clinician may try to change *them* rather than to focus his attention on changing the individual directly.

Early diagnosis of crucial importance

If deficits or detrimental conditions are not recognized and corrected, many children experience years of failure not only in reading but in other school subjects. If the teacher expects them to use reading skills they have not developed, if he takes for granted experiences they have never had, they are faced with failure. Continued failure contributes to a concept of themselves as persons who cannot learn to read.

Diagnosis recognizes the multiple causation of reading disability

Instead of merely listing causes and correlates, the attempt should be made to describe the relationship or pattern. Often there is a central factor from which others stem. Although an initial cause may have precipitated a reading difficulty, it seldom continues to exist singly; other difficulties follow in its train. For example, an eye condition that makes fusion difficult and results in a blurred image may cause initial difficulty in the visual perception of words, which in turn may cause difficulty in reading, which may lead to emotional disturbance.

Diagnosis underlies prevention as well
as remediation of reading difficulties

Accordingly, the factors found to be significantly related to reading development and difficulties should be familiar not only to reading specialists, but also to teachers who want to prevent the occurrence of reading disabilities in their classes.

APPLICATION TO READING PROBLEMS

Procedures for working with pupils on their reading should stem from the understanding we have gained about them. Otherwise there is no justification for spending time on diagnosis. Information such as that described in this chapter gives the teacher or clinician clues to the individual pupil's reading development or difficulty.

This information is often used in what has been called the client-centered or student-centered approach to reading problems. The teacher or clinician feels his way as he works with the individual. He offers opportunities for the person to explore the situation and present himself in his own way. The teacher notes and responds to any expressions of interest and to other learning clues. Activities in which the student takes initiative facilitate learning, whereas required drill may increase his sense of failure or his resistance to authority.

Descriptions of the treatment of several children extremely unresponsive to reading instruction will illustrate this approach. Max liked to work with tools as much as he disliked reading. The first thing he noticed when he came into the room was a workbench on which were nails and a hammer. After some general conversation the teacher said, "We need a bookcase. Could you make one for us? I'll help all I can, but I'm not good at making things." They spent the first period making the bookcase. This accomplishment gave Max a friendly feeling toward the room and the teacher. Such a fine new bookcase needed books in it. To find appropriate books Max had to look over the pile that had been donated by parents. He could read some words and, with the help of the pictures, he selected those he thought his classmates would like to read. There were several books that interested him particularly. During his reading period he asked for help in learning to read them. Thus the reading instruction, stemming from another interest, began.

David was extremely apathetic. He made no response to the teacher's friendliness. He showed no interest in the picture books. He did not accept the teacher's invitation to help her erase the board. The first thing that aroused a flicker of interest was the typewriter. "Would you like to write your name on it?" the teacher asked. He chose a sheet of paper and typed his name, picking out and naming each letter carefully. This was the beginning of a book to which he added stories each period that he came for special help. Typing was an opening wedge to teaching.

Charles was belligerent about reading. He would have none of it. If the teacher continued the pressure that his parents and previous teachers had been putting on him, she would only intensify his resistance. She decided to play a waiting game and follow any leads he gave her. Seeing some paper and crayons, he began to draw. That was all he did for two periods. No words were introduced until he suggested that one picture ought to have a name. Then he printed the title he wanted to give it. This was the beginning of his picture dictionary. In this case it was fortunate that the teacher knew Charles had been nagged incessantly about his reading. Thus she avoided intensifying his rebellion. If he had been the sort of child who had been allowed to do as he pleased and had known no standards or firmness, the situation might have demanded quite a different approach; he may have needed to be made to do what he was capable of doing.

Stanley responded to vocabulary games. He showed much satisfaction in the growing pile of words that he could define and pronounce correctly and the increasing number of sentences he built. He was stimulated by objective evidence of progress.

These cases illustrate only a few of many possible approaches through interests, permissiveness, reasonable pressures, games, systematic instruction in word recognition or other needed reading skills, team learning, stories, practice exercises, and the like. A versatile approach that uses materials and methods in a flexible manner has been found to be most successful. The teacher uses information gathered about each student both prior to and during the teaching periods to maintain a continuous sensitivity to his needs and to his receptivity to learning.

CONCLUDING STATEMENT

Diagnosis is as complex as the reading process itself. The causes of reading difficulty are subtle and difficult to uncover. Often there is no clear line of demarcation between the causes and the effects of reading deficiency; it is sometimes hard to tell which is cause and which is effect.

On the basis of the information gained, the clinician makes inferences and formulates hypotheses leading to recommendations. As he gains new information he is constantly making new and always tentative formulations. The teacher goes through the same process in a less comprehensive, systematic way. Against his background of understanding of the student the teacher often makes immediate use of the information he has gained.

Without some diagnostic information, individualization of instruction is impossible. Diagnosis is a basic tool in providing for individual differences. Without such understanding, the teacher cannot help each pupil realize his potential reading ability.

Diagnosis should gear in with treatment. Finding out what is wrong should lead, as soon as possible, to doing something constructive about it.

SUGGESTED PROBLEMS: PRACTICE AND DEMONSTRATION [2]

1. What specific applications of teaching principles can you make to diagnostic procedures?

[2] In these sections throughout the text the suggestions are directed to students taking a course in the teaching of reading or to teachers in service. They may also be adapted, through demonstrations and discussions, to college teachers of such courses and to workshops and institutes for experienced teachers.

2. Give diagnostic information on a case and show how a teacher may use it in the classroom situation.

3. Dramatize an interview between a reading specialist and a teacher who has referred a reading problem to him. The specialist presents the results of his diagnostic study; the teacher and specialist together plan a program of remedial work for the student.

4. Review research on the value of intelligence tests and listening comprehension tests in predicting reading achievement.

5. Summarize the diagnostic information in several case studies of reading difficulty and tell how it was obtained.

6. Obtain estimates from different sources of the percentage of reading cases in which there is emotional involvement, then discuss the possible reasons for such marked differences.

7. Make a chart showing common elements and differences in emphasis in the processes of identification, appraisal, diagnosis, and evaluation.

REFERENCES

BATEMAN, BARBARA: "Learning Disabilities: Yesterday, Today, and Tomorrow," *Exceptional Children*, 31:167–177, December, 1965.

————: "Learning Disorders," *Review of Educational Research*, 36:93–119, February, 1966.

COHN, ROBERT: "The Neurological Study of Children with Learning Disabilities," *Exceptional Children*, 31:179–186, December, 1964.

COLEMAN, JAMES: "Teen-agers and Their Crowd," *The PTA Magazine*, 56:4–7, March, 1962.

CONANT, JAMES BRYANT: *Recommendations for Education in the Junior High School Years*, Educational Testing Service, Princeton, N.J., 1960.

DEAL, MARGARET: "A Summary of Research Concerning Patterns of WISC Subtest Scores of Retarded Readers," *Journal of the Reading Specialist*, 4:101–111, May, 1965.

DOLCH, EDWARD W.: "Testing Reading with a Book," *Elementary English*, 28:124–125, March, 1951.

DURRELL, DONALD D., and HELEN BLAIR SULLIVAN: *Durrell-Sullivan Reading Capacity and Achievement Tests*, two levels: grades 2.5–4.5, Primary; grades 3–7, Intermediate (Form A of Primary Test and Intermediate Reading Capacity Test, Forms A and B of Intermediate Achievement Test), Harcourt, Brace & World, Inc., New York, 1937–1945.

HARTUP, WILLARD W.: "Early Education and Childhood Socialization," *Journal of Research and Development in Education*, 1:16–29, Spring, 1968.

HOLMES, JACK A.: "Personality Characteristics of the Disabled Reader," *Journal of Developmental Reading*, 4:111–122, Winter, 1961.

PORTERFIELD, O. V., and H. F. SCHLICHTING: "Peer Status and Reading Achievement," *Journal of Educational Research*, 54:291–297, April, 1961.

SHELDON, WILLIAM D.: "Teacher Must Diagnose," *Education*, 78:545–546, May, 1958.

SPACHE, GEORGE D.: "Integrating Diagnosis with Remediation in Reading," *The Elementary School Journal*, 56:18–26, September, 1955.

VALETT, R. E.: "A Clinical Profile for the Stanford-Binet," *Journal of School Psychologists*, 2:49–54, 1963–1964.

VERNON, M. D.: "Symposium: Contributions to the Diagnosis and Remedial Treatment of Reading Difficulties," *British Journal of Educational Psychology*, 30:146–154, June, 1960.

WALTERS, RICHARD H., and others: "A Study of Reading Disability," *Journal of Consulting Psychology*, 25:277–283, August, 1961.

SUGGESTED READINGS

BOND, GUY L., and MILES A. TINKER: *Reading Difficulties, Their Diagnosis and Correction*, 2d ed., Appleton-Century-Crofts, Inc., New York, 1967.

BRYANT, N. D.: "Some Principles of Remedial Instruction for Dyslexia," *The Reading Teacher*, 18:527–572, April, 1965.

"Contributions to the Diagnosis and Remedial Treatment of Reading Difficulties; Symposium," *British Journal of Educational Psychology*, 30:146–179, June, 1960; 31:79–105, February, 1961.

DIEDERICH, PAUL B.: "Design for a Comprehensive Evaluation Program," *School Review*, 58:225–232, April, 1950.

FIGUREL, J. ALLEN (ed.): *Challenge and Experiment in Reading, International Reading Association Conference Proceedings*, vol. 7, Scholastic Magazines, Inc., New York, 1962.

———: *Vistas in Reading, International Reading Association Conference Proceedings*, vol. II, part 1, Proceedings of The Eleventh Annual Conference, International Reading Association, Newark, N.J., 1967.

HAFNER, L. E. (ed.): *Improving Reading in Secondary Schools*, The Macmillan Company, New York, 1967.

HARRIS, ALBERT J.: "Diagnosis of Reading Disabilities," *Conference on Reading*, University of Pittsburgh, Pittsburgh, 1960, pp. 31–37.

———: *How to Increase Reading Ability*, 4th ed., David McKay Company, Inc., New York, 1961.

HOLMES, JACK A.: "The Substrata-factor Theory of Reading: Some Experimental Evidence," *International Reading Association Conference Proceedings*, vol. 4, Newark, Del., 1960, pp. 115–121.

INTERNATIONAL READING ASSOCIATION: *World Congress Proceedings (Paris)*, International Reading Association, Newark, Del., 1966.

MC CULLOUGH, CONSTANCE M.: "Changing Concepts of Reading Instruction," in *Changing Concepts of Reading Instruction, International Reading As-*

sociation Conference Proceedings, vol. 6, Scholastic Magazines, Inc., New York, 1961, pp. 13–22.

MECKEL, HENRY C.: "Evaluating Growth in Reading," in *Reading in the High School and College,* National Society for the Study of Education, 1948, chap. 12, part 2.

OLSON, WILLARD C.: "Reading as a Function of Total Growth of the Child," in *Reading and Pupil Development,* Supplementary Educational Monograph no. 51, The University of Chicago Press, Chicago, 1940, pp. 233–237.

ROBINSON, H. ALAN (ed.): *Reading: Seventy-five Years of Progress,* Supplementary Educational Monograph no. 96, The University of Chicago Press, Chicago, 1966.

ROBINSON, HELEN M.: *Why Pupils Fail in Reading,* The University of Chicago Press, Chicago, 1946.

ROSWELL, FLORENCE, and GLADYS NATCHEZ: *Reading Disability: Diagnosis and Treatment,* Basic Books, Inc., Publishers, New York, 1964.

RUSSELL, DAVID H.: "Evaluation of Pupil Growth in and through Reading," in *Reading in the Elementary School,* Forty-eighth Yearbook of the National Society for the Study of Education, The University of Chicago Press, Chicago, 1947, chap. 14, part 2.

SPACHE, GEORGE D.: *Toward Better Reading,* The Garrard Press, Champaign, Ill., 1963.

STRANG, RUTH: "Evaluation of Development in and through Reading," in *Development in and through Reading,* Sixtieth Yearbook of the National Society for the Study of Education, The University of Chicago Press, Chicago, 1961, pp. 376–397.

————: "Controversial Programs and Procedures in Reading," *The School Review,* 69:413–428, Winter, 1961.

VERNON, M. D.: *Backwardness in Reading,* Cambridge University Press, New York, 1957.

WILSON, ROBERT M.: *Diagnostic and Remedial Reading for Classroom and Clinic,* Charles E. Merrill Books, Inc., Columbus, Ohio, 1967.

Chapter Two

THE ROLE OF THE TEACHER IN DIAGNOSIS

Any teacher can gain an understanding of his students that will help him to reinforce their desirable attitudes and competencies and to develop those which they lack. He need not wait for a specialist to give him diagnostic information; it is available to him in his daily work. According to Lytton (1967) an adequate basis for preventive and for remedial teaching is provided by a continuous analysis of students' classroom behavior. He found that teachers trained to detect individual differences have been as accurate in selecting retarded readers for remedial education as were group tests yielding IQs and AQs (accomplishment quotients). Haring and Ridgway (1967) likewise concluded that a battery of diagnostic tests does not predict as effectively as does trained teacher observation of the individual child.

Such teachers diagnose as they teach. They note individual pupils' reading performance. In their daily contact with children they also gain an understanding of *how* the individual acquires certain reading skills and *why* he makes certain errors. In diagnostic teaching, reading difficulties are recognized, understood, and, as far as possible, remedied. This should be an intrinsic part of the teaching process.

To obtain diagnostic information the teacher observes, listens, gives informal tests, and uses available standardized test results. He may make a case study of a particularly baffling problem.

> It is only through working with an individual child who has a reading problem that a teacher truly learns *how* to teach reading. Every teacher of reading should have such an experience, for it is through teaching individual children to read that teachers gain insight into the intricacies of reading instruction. Such work makes any teacher a better teacher of reading (Cutts, 1964, p. 97).

As the teacher collects information about the student, he interprets, synthesizes, and uses it to help him improve his reading. Recognizing the individual's present powers, he tries to adjust the curriculum and his teaching procedures to the child's competencies, needs, and interests at the moment.

Instruction is guided by the student's own evolving curriculum and by the teacher's knowledge of a psychological sequence of reading skills. (For a comprehensive chart of sequential development of reading abilities see Strang, McCullough, and Traxler, 1967, pp. 131–144.) As the teacher continues to appraise the student's progress and to work with him on his reading improvement, he obtains additional information that suggests to both student and teacher further methods and materials to be employed. Thus diagnosis and teaching are fused into a single process.

The teacher also works indirectly through the environment, which he often can manipulate so that the student will be successful. With the younger children, he will work with parents in creating a more favorable home environment.

UNDERSTANDING GAINED INCIDENTALLY

Much understanding is gained incidentally. For example, when the principal assured Pat and another first grader that he had not accused them of walking on the grass, Pat said to her boy friend, "Percy, we are exonerated." In response to the teacher's question, "What is the opposite of *tame?*" another first-grade child said, "Ferocious." Both children gave indications of an unusual speaking vocabulary for their age. General diagnostic signs of reading difficulty that teachers observe are:

A dislike of school and especially of reading.

Frequent absence for no good reason and other evasive methods of avoiding failure.

Apparent effort, but lack of learning.

Frequent wrong answers, showing lack of comprehension of the selection read.

Immature sentence structure and inaccuracy of descriptions.

Signs of fatigue, in one case the result of a 4:00 A.M. newspaper route.

A casual remark such as, "Now I'll find out who in the class likes me." This may indicate the child's concern about his social relations.

A child may also reveal his personal feelings and interests in the accounts of his own experience or in his stories and poems.

UNDERSTANDING GAINED DURING A READING LESSON

The teaching of any story or article offers opportunities for an informal kind of diagnosis. The following description of a reading lesson shows ways in which the teacher can learn about the student's vocabulary knowledge, his reading habits, his comprehension of the selection, his specific difficulties, and the background of experience that he brings to his reading.

Obtaining understanding

In orienting students to a selection, the teacher encourages them to talk about experiences they have had which are relevant to the story. He notes background knowledge that they bring to the interpretation of the selection. The extent and quality of their speaking vocabulary, sentence structure, and speech habits also become evident. This preliminary discussion may indicate the need to enrich the students' previous experience with pictures, explanations, or descriptions of the author and the setting. Before reading the selection, the teacher may help students set up a target or purpose for reading and discuss the unfamiliar words and concepts that they will encounter.

While the students are reading silently, the teacher will note that some seem to be reading rapidly with interest and attention. Others read slowly and show signs of difficulty—inattention, frowning, lip movements. A few ask questions that indicate the particular difficulties they are having. The poor readers usually are easily distracted. Their resistance to distraction is an index of their reading proficiency and their interest in the book.

The group discussion that follows the silent reading will give additional information: How well have individual students accomplished their purposes for reading the selection? Were they able to comprehend the selection accurately and easily? Did they comprehend what the author said? Did any of them make creative comments and applications? Did they profit by the instruction given? How did they answer the question, "How might you apply this story to your own lives or to the world today?" Class discussions also give clues as to students' ability to learn from listening. In some discussions they spontaneously give information about family reading habits, their favorite TV programs, and other home conditions.

To obtain more specific information about their vocabulary and word recognition and comprehension skills, the teacher may ask individual students, while the others are still reading, to read a paragraph aloud, to state its main thought, to give the meanings of certain words in context, and to point out relationships or sequences.

If the teacher allows ample time for reading the selection, some students will finish before the time is up. How do they spend their free time? What initiative and self-direction do they show in finding something worthwhile to do? Some may begin reading another book; others may draw an illustration or write a poem or story suggested by the selection.

Using understanding

The teacher may use information of this kind immediately or later in planning individual and group instruction. He will vary individual assignments as to length and difficulty. To help each student progress at the rate and on the level appropriate for him, the teacher may use multilevel material such as The Science Research Associates Reading Laboratories (Science Research Associates, Chicago). To students who have similar difficulties he will give instruction and practice in small groups. To meet the needs of all students, he will draw on his reservoir of instructional procedures, materials, and ideas for creative activities. For the able learners he will provide some challenging books in different fields, plays for dramatized reading, and opportunities to prepare and present special reports and programs.

For poor readers the teacher will supply study guides, books, and other reading materials that are on their level. They need much easy supplementary reading to give practice in basic sight vocabulary and in the use of word recognition skills in context. Interesting books also serve as an incentive to acquire the reading skills that they need. To obtain additional practice, they may play vocabulary and word recognition games such as those published by the Garrard Press, Champaign, Illinois. Poor readers especially enjoy participating in choral reading and taking minor parts in the dramatized reading of plays. In interest groups, they can contribute to the study of special topics or problems by reading and reporting on a simple book, even a picture book. Motivated by a need to find out, a retarded reader sometimes makes sense out of material that the teacher thinks is too difficult for him. He uses clues the teacher may not recognize and puzzles out meanings in ways known only to himself.

The most seriously retarded readers cannot comprehend the texts provided for their grade. For these students the teacher may present orally the science and social studies content that is too difficult for them to read. He may make his presentation more vivid by the use of audio-visual aids. The students then dictate the main points, which the teacher will write on the board and type for them to read. In the stories they write or dictate, they often disclose their personal feelings and interests as well as vocabulary, sentence structure, and sense of sequence. If special reading classes are available, the teacher will refer these students for special instruction.

Diagnostic teaching becomes a process of continuous adjustment to individual pupils. The teacher accepts a bright student's comment, but gives special recognition to another student who needs encouragement. He may offer help to a student who is on the verge of frustration, but leave another who needs to develop independence to arrive at the solution himself. By adjusting the difficulty of his questions to the ability of his students, he challenges the gifted and helps the slow, shy individual to gain self-confidence. He helps the student to view mistakes as an opportunity to identify his errors and to learn how to correct them.

Understanding individual differences

In any class, many kinds of reading behavior may be noted:

1. Charles, age nine, tries to escape any type of reading. When he is called upon to read, he excuses himself by saying that he has not studied the lesson. During silent reading periods he stares at the page, but makes no effort to read. He likes to go to the library just to look at the pictures in books. The teacher reinforces his reading interest of the moment, which may eventually lead to other interests. By adjusting the length and difficulty of the reading selection to Charles's present ability, the teacher avoids confronting him with a task too difficult and complicated for him even to attempt. A certain degree of difficulty and novelty attracts attention; too great a degree of either causes anxiety or frustration or withdrawal.

2. Sue, age twelve, does not like to read aloud for fear of making a mistake. While reading, she frequently clears her throat. Words of encouragement work like magic. With students like Sue who show extreme lack of confidence in their reading ability, the teacher avoids making value judgments. Instead, he might ask, "How did you get the main thought this time?" or "How might you use a better method next time?"

3. Karen, age twelve, signs up for all school activities and then backs out or forgets. She displays much assurance and is inclined to brag often. In her reading she guesses wildly. Before Karen starts to read, the teacher may suggest several things to look for. When she makes a generalization, the teacher may ask her to state the ideas that support it. As the child learns to read more thoughtfully and deliberately, she will become less impulsive.

4. Mike, age eleven, will not read of his own accord unless the assignment is very simple. If the work is a little difficult and he does not

get help immediately, he slams his book down with, "Oh, I can't do that." In silent reading he mutters continually. He is a discipline problem and often in trouble for bullying the smaller children. But he likes to help the teacher, and if he is kept busy enough, he does not get into trouble.

5. Randy, age nine, is apathetic toward reading. He does not even wish to have stories read to him. When the other children read, Randy looks off into space. His attitude toward reading is changing now that the teacher is reading with him alone.

6. Fred, age seven, is always squirming in his seat, playing with his ears, and daydreaming. He talks in such a soft voice that he can hardly be heard. When reading, he gives up at the slightest error. Fred was retained in first grade, and this seems to bother him very much.

7. Cathy, age seven, is inclined to daydream during reading periods, but makes an effort when called upon. She often substitutes a story of her own, which may or may not have anything to do with what the group is reading. She is so successful in other things that she is not concerned about her failure in reading.

Having noted conditions that seem to be interfering with students' progress in reading, the teacher may say or do something to reinforce their strengths and overcome their weaknesses. He would reward Sue's successful attempts, insist on Karen's substituting systematic word attack for guessing, and give Mike much easy reading material before gradually increasing its difficulty.

BUILDING READINESS FOR READING

Early identification of children with learning disabilities and the correction of remediable deficits will make the teaching of reading much easier for first-grade teachers. At home, at nursery school, at kindergarten and beginning first grade, parents and teachers can provide games that will develop eye-hand coordination, facility in the use of language, visual and auditory perception, discrimination, and memory. Practiced in a natural setting, these skills become immediately functional (Haring and Ridgway, 1967; Early, 1962). Reading aloud to children acquaints them with the sound of language and introduces them to the delight that books may give. Providing them with varied experiences and talking with them build their speaking vocabulary of meaningful words. In a reading environment, they acquire a love of books and an eagerness to learn to read. If these experiences have been lacking during preschool years, they may be supplied to some extent in the kindergarten or at the beginning of the first grade.

The first-grade teacher may diagnose the child's readiness to learn to read informally and by the use of a readiness test such as the Metropolitan Readiness Tests, 1965 revision (Harcourt, Brace & World, Inc.), and the Lee-Clark Reading Readiness Test, 1962 revision (California Test Bureau). Dykstra (1966) concluded that thirty minutes of testing in addition to the teacher's day-to-day observation would give an adequate diagnosis of readiness. The diagnosis of readiness at any age level makes possible a good match between the child's development and the reading task. A good match, in turn, results in intrinsic satisfaction in the experience.

TEACHERS MAY FAIL, TOO

Often diagnostic information is acquired too late. It was only after several weeks that a classroom teacher realized fifteen-year-old Dan needed special help. In his silent reading assignments and on tests he was always the last to finish. As the weeks passed, his scholastic standing decreased and his misbehavior increased. One day when the teacher, after an enthusiastic introduction of "The Great Stone Face," asked the class to read it silently, she saw that Dan was the only student not reading. His head was on his desk. The teacher quietly moved to his desk and touched him on the shoulder. "Dan, won't you try? It's a wonderful story."

"Are you kidding," he replied, almost in tears. "Do you know how long it would take me to read one page? I wouldn't finish it before the others had read all twenty pages."

It was not until then that the teacher checked the school records. Although average in intelligence, his grades in the academic subjects were low, and his reading score still lower. The teacher had not realized that the boy's apparent indifference, restlessness, attention-seeking behavior, lethargy, withdrawal, slow performance, and disheveled appearance all signaled for help. He did get help, but much too late.

UNDERSTANDING GAINED IN A SPECIAL READING CLASS

A period with a special reading class in a junior high school further illustrates how the teacher may gather information about individual students while teaching. According to group reading tests, the boys in this class were three or more years below their seventh-grade placement. Each boy was given a copy of the third-grade *Reader's Digest Skill Builder* to read. When they had finished the story, the teacher discussed it with them.

One boy, whom we shall call Bert, apparently had comprehended very little of it. Although he spoke glibly, he had little to communicate. When later asked individually to read a few paragraphs aloud, he stopped at every word of more than three letters. When asked if he did much reading, he merely shrugged his shoulders. When sports were mentioneod, he showed a little more interest. When asked if he liked animals, he became excited and took from his pocket two photographs of bears taken by his brother who had a job feeding animals at the zoo. Although Bert was enthusiastic about animals, he showed no interest in reading books or articles about them.

Near the end of the period Bert asked if they could do the *Reader's Digest* exercises next week. He told the others that he had got 100 percent on the SRA Reading Laboratory's Power Builder Test. Actually, the teacher discovered, he had left the spaces blank and filled in the correct answers by consulting the scoring key; then he had proudly claimed to have scored 100 percent.

He was very slow in all his reading and was extremely restless. He distracted others by his wisecracks and useless questions.

It became obvious in this single period that Bert could not comprehend second-grade material, that he needed to build up his basic sight vocabulary and acquire effective word recognition skills. He revealed his need to succeed in the group by making wild guesses and by copying the answers so that he could boast about getting 100 percent. His tension showed in restlessness and nail biting.

Using the understanding gained from this preliminary appraisal, the teacher planned to help Bert build a basic sight vocabulary and acquire word recognition skills so that he could achieve some real success. He could get this practice through drill on sound-letter associations, through reading easy material, and through a variety of games and activities that would also help to relieve his physical tension. The teacher planned to interest him in keeping a record of the words he learned so that he could see his progress. As he acquired sufficient reading ability, she would provide animal stories he might enjoy if he could read them without frustration. Since recognition in the group was so important to him, the teacher planned to teach him the skills needed to participate successfully in some group activity such as reading a few lines in a play. If Bert did not respond to this instruction in reading skills in which he was deficient, the reading teacher would move to a deeper level of diagnosis.

UNDERSTANDING GAINED THROUGH
INDIVIDUALIZING INSTRUCTION

In one fifth-grade class the last twenty minutes of each reading period was used for free reading. Pupils kept a record of their reading by writing on a card a few sentences telling what the story was about. Since this requires the ability to summarize, which is a difficult skill to master, the teacher demonstrated and went through the process with them several times.

She noticed one boy frowning over his card when he had just finished a simple story. He hesitated for quite a while as though he did not know what to write; then he started copying parts of the first page word for word. The teacher sat down with him and asked him to tell her what happened in the story. She led him along with such questions as "What happened first? Then? What happened at the end?" She also asked other questions to test his comprehension of details. His general comprehension was good. It became clear to him that the story had four main parts or happenings. The teacher asked him to think of one sentence that would tell what happened in each part. Once he sensed the structure of the story, he was able to write several sentences telling what happened. All he needed was instruction and practice in telling a story in sequence.

While members of the class are independently reading suitable interesting books of their own choice, the teacher has time for individual conferences. In these conferences she may ask the student to read a paragraph or two aloud. She first notes and approves something the student does well or better than he did before. Then she may analyze a task which the student needs to improve and go through the process with him. With another student, the teacher may spend his ten-minute conference in finding out how well he has comprehended the selection and in helping him to discover ways of improving his comprehension. With a student who can read but does not, the teacher may spend the time introducing this reluctant reader to a book that he may be persuaded to read outside of class.

Sometimes the teacher may give a larger amount of time to an individual student whose lack of improvement is baffling. Group methods have not reached him. For example, Alice, an apathetic, slow-learning girl, seemed to have only one interest—her dog Blackie who had died. She still felt very sad about it. "Blackie was my best friend," she said. As she told about Blackie, the teacher wrote the story, typed it, and gave it to her to read. Alice found little difficulty in reading her own language patterns and words whose meaning she already knew. This experience encouraged her to make a book about the care of dogs. She visited a friendly veterinarian who gave her some firsthand information as well as a pamphlet on selecting, feeding, and caring for dogs. As Alice read this pamphlet aloud, the teacher observed:

Which words Alice knew at sight.

How she attacked the pronunciation of unfamiliar words.

Whether she understood the meaning of certain words and phrases: "Substantiating your claims" she explained as "showing the reasons for your claims"; "grooming the dog," as "making the dog look nice."

How quickly she learned and how permanently she remembered the meaning of the new words she was being taught.

Whether she could get the main thought of paragraphs.

What her attitude was toward reading.

How spontaneously she was able to express her feelings.

In the individualized reading periods the teacher may also uncover sudden changes in a child's performance that call for further study. A third grader, Patty, previously at the top of her class, seemed overnight to go rapidly downhill. She appeared to pay attention in class, but her expression and her responses gave the impression that her thoughts were elsewhere. The teacher observed her behavior and work habits to see if there might be something in the school situation that was disturbing her. There were no signs of visual, auditory, or nutritional problems. The teacher did not think the child's difficulty stemmed from her home, which was one of the best. However, from a home visit the teacher learned that Patty's mother was going to have another child and that Patty was afraid something might happen to her mother. After the baby arrived and the mother returned home well and happy, Patty's work again reached its former superior quality.

An individualized reading program gives teachers more time to synthesize information from a number of sources. For example, it became apparent to a first-grade teacher that Jack was not reading up to his capacity. He tested in the average range on the Lorge-Thorndike Intelligence Test and above average on the Metropolitan Reading Readiness Test. He could recognize all the Dolch Basic Sight Vocabulary and always received 100 percent on his phonics worksheets. When the vowel sounds were introduced, Jack was delighted to find that he could read and spell new words by inserting the short vowel sound, for example, h-t, hat; c-n, can. But he could not read from the first-grade book.

After eliminating possible visual and emotional causes of his difficulty and closely observing his oral reading, the teacher came to the tentative conclusion that Jack could not transfer the phonics skills he had learned in isolation to the reading of the printed page. On the basis of this hypothesis the teacher, with the cooperation of the boy's parents, presented all new words to him in context. In reading each story he systematically used his word attack skills to pronounce the unfamiliar words. The teacher helped him only with the words he could not figure out for himself. His progress was amazing.

DIAGNOSIS AND INSTRUCTION IN READING ON THE FIRST DAY OF SCHOOL

One teacher described her method of gaining an understanding of a middle-class fifth-grade group on the first day of the school year. Beforehand she gets information about each child that is available on his cumulative record: his achievement as measured by tests and school marks, and any outstanding physical, emotional, social, or learning problems that might need her special attention.

On the first day she asks pairs of children to interview each other and then introduce their partner to the class. Thus she learns their interests, linguistic abilities, speech difficulties, and poise. To assist her in remembering names and faces she asks each child to fill out a card with his name, address, family composition, main interests and hobbies, favorite TV programs, the books he has read during the past year, and his educational plans. The pupils usually enjoy writing the answers to the question, "If you had three wishes, what would they be?" These cards form a convenient basic information file for each class.

In their first reading lesson the teacher selects a story from one of their fifth-grade books. They read it silently. She asks questions to check their understanding of the story. She also notes how well they express their ideas: Can the rest of the class understand what they are saying? Are the ideas well organized? Which students are eager to answer? Which seem too shy to speak up? Which seem to be paying no attention at all?

By reading a short story or article aloud to the class, the teacher tests their listening comprehension and ability to discuss the selection.

From these informal diagnostic methods the teacher gains initial understanding of individuals who need special attention because of reading deficiencies or because the average work of the grade may not be stimulating to them.

VALUES OF TEACHER DIAGNOSIS

Without these kinds of understanding, the teacher may either neglect practice and instruction on skills badly needed or give unnecessary instruction. He may also unwittingly reinforce an undesirable response as, for example, when he accepts and apparently approves word calling, i.e., without comprehension, or when he tells the student the meaning of a word he could have solved himself if he had used his newly acquired word recognition skills. There is a nice balance between the extremes of "accentuating the positive" and insisting upon "errorless learning."

The information obtained in appraising the progress of individual students can also be used in evaluating the reading program as a whole. Is it balanced? Does it use the best features of various methods and materials as they are appropriate, e.g., drills from a phonic system if they are needed by some children and wide, challenging reading for the able learners? Are combined instruction and appraisal an essential part of the program?

CONCLUDING STATEMENT

There is a reciprocal relationship between diagnosis and teaching. The teacher analyzes each behavioral objective into steps, beginning with the student's concrete experience and leading into the more complex and abstract process of reading.

As he teaches, he notes which children progress easily and which encounter difficulty at certain stages. He may ask successful students to describe their methods of learning so that others may apply them; e.g., how did they manage to pronounce a word? how did they come to know its meaning? how did they get the author's thought so clearly?

For those who have special difficulty the teacher provides special instruction individually or in small groups. While the class as a whole is working independently, the teacher holds conferences with individuals in the most private part of the room to obtain more specific diagnostic information and to help them with their immediate reading problem.

The teacher has in mind characteristics and conditions that influence individual students' reading achievement: mental alertness; learning capacity; listening comprehension; visual and auditory acuity and discrimination; previously acquired reading abilities; needs, interests, and attitudes toward themselves and toward reading. He is aware of conditions and attitudes in the home and community that affect the child's interest and effort.

Too many teachers think that they must depend upon test results. It is better to select a few reliable instruments that the teacher can interpret and apply than to administer many tests whose results are poorly interpreted and used unwisely. Many teachers underestimate the diagnostic possibilities of their day-by-by contacts with students. Many do not realize that they themselves are the most important influence on students' reading achievement.

Fortunately, the teacher does not bear the entire burden of helping a student improve his reading. Administrators, counselors, librarians, and other staff members all make some contribution to the diagnosis and remediation of reading difficulties and to the appraisal of students' progress in reading (Early, 1962, pp. 1–6). The teacher is the most important member of a team that is concerned with making better readers and better persons.

SUGGESTED PROBLEMS: PRACTICE AND DEMONSTRATION

1. With a new class use the method of having pairs of students interview each other and report to the group what they have learned about the other's interests, background, need to improve his reading, etc. What kinds of understanding of individual students may a teacher gain from this procedure? Consider their use of language, organization of ideas, social sensitivity, poise, feelings of inferiority, interests, hobbies, purpose, personal relations, and other items.

2. Describe different classroom situations; point out the kind of information about pupils that may be obtained in each, and tell how the teacher might use it.

3. How can a teacher obtain diagnostic information from individual students and also keep the other students profitably engaged in independent study?

4. Write a detailed report of your work with an individual case and show how understanding of the person grew as treatment proceeded.

5. If you had a student who did not respond to the best individual instruction you could give him, what help could you obtain?

6. How would you refer a child with a baffling reading problem for special services?

7. What is the responsibility of the specialist for reporting back on the case to the teachers?

REFERENCES

BOND, GUY L.: *The Coordinated Phases of the Reading Study*, progress report presented at the Annual Conference of the International Reading Association, Dallas, Tex., May, 1966.

BURNETT, RICHARD W.: "The Diagnostic Proficiency of Teachers of Reading," *The Reading Teacher*, 16:229–234, January, 1963.

CAPOBIANCO, R. F.: "Diagnostic Methods Used with Learning Disability Cases," *Exceptional Children*, 31:187–193, December, 1964.

CUTTS, WARREN G.: *Modern Reading Instruction*, Center for Applied Research in Education, Inc., Washington, D.C., 1964, p. 97.

DYKSTRA, ROBERT: "Auditory Discrimination Abilities and Beginning Reading Achievement," *Reading Research Quarterly*, 1:5–34, Spring, 1966.

EARLY, MARGARET J.: *Providing Leadership for Secondary Reading Programs*, Council for Administrative Leadership, Albany, N.Y., June, 1962.

HARING, N. G., and R. W. RIDGWAY: "Early Identification of Children with Learning Disabilities," *Exceptional Children*, 33:387–395, February, 1967.

LYTTON, H.: "Follow-up of an Experiment in Selection for Remedial Education," *British Journal of Educational Psychology*, 37:1–9, February, 1967.

STRANG, RUTH, CONSTANCE M. MC CULLOUGH, and ARTHUR E. TRAXLER: *The Improvement of Reading*, 4th ed., McGraw-Hill Book Company, New York, 1967.

SUGGESTED READINGS

AMIDON, EDMOND, and ELIZABETH HUNTER: *Improving Teaching: The Analyses of Classroom Verbal Interaction*, Holt, Rinehart and Winston, Inc., New York, 1966.

ANDERSON, IRVING, and WALTER DEARBORN: *The Psychology of Teaching Reading*, The Ronald Press Company, New York, 1952.

ARTLEY, A. STERL: "Classroom Help for Children with Beginning Reading Problems," *The Reading Teacher*, 15:439–442, May, 1962.

BARBE, WALTER B.: *Educator's Guide to Personalized Reading Instruction*, Prentice-Hall, Inc., Englewood Cliffs, N.J., 1960.

BURNETT, RICHARD W.: "The Diagnostic Proficiency of Teachers of Reading," *The Reading Teacher*, 16:229–234, January, 1963.

BURTON, WILLIAM H.: *Reading in Child Development*, The Bobbs-Merrill Company, Inc., Indianapolis, 1956.

COHN, STELLA M., and JACK COHN: *Teaching the Retarded Reader: A Guide for Teachers, Reading Specialists, and Supervisors*, The Odyssey Press, Inc., New York, 1967.

DE BOER, JOHN J., and MARTHA DALLMAN: *The Teaching of Reading*, Holt, Rinehart and Winston, Inc., New York, 1960.

DE CECCO, JOHN P. (ed.): *The Psychology of Language, Thought and Instruction: Readings*, Holt, Rinehart and Winston, Inc., New York, 1967.

DREIKURS, RUDOLF: *Psychology in the Classroom*, 2d ed., Harper & Row, Publishers, Incorporated, New York, 1968.

ERICKSON, ALLEN: *Handbook for Teachers of Disabled Readers*, Sernoll, Inc., Iowa City, Iowa, 1967.

GAGNE, R. M. (ed.): *Learning and Individual Differences*, Charles E. Merrill Books, Inc., Columbus, Ohio, 1967.

HERBER, HAROLD (ed.): *Developing Study Skills in Secondary Schools*, International Reading Association, Newark, Del., 1965.

HOLT, J.: *How Children Fail*, Pitman Publishing Corporation, New York, 1964.

HUNTER, MADELINE: "When the Teacher Diagnoses Learning," *Educational Leadership*, 23:545–549, April, 1966.

HUXLEY, A.: "Human Potentialities," *Psychology Today*, 1:70, May, 1967.

KEATING, CHARLOTTE M.: *Building Bridges of Understanding*, Palo Verde Publishing Company, Tucson, Ariz., 1967.

KEPHART, N. C.: *The Slow Learner in the Classroom*, Charles E. Merrill Books, Inc., Columbus, Ohio, 1960.

KOTTMEYER, WILLIAM: *Teacher's Guide for Remedial Reading*, McGraw-Hill Book Company, New York, 1959.

MC DONALD, ARTHUR S. (ed.): "Research for the Classroom: Using Standardized Tests to Determine Reading Proficiency," *Journal of Reading*, 8:58–61, November, 1964.

MEARNS, HUGH: *Creative Power*, 2d rev. ed., Dover Publications, Inc., New York, 1958.

MOUSTAKAS, CLARK E.: *The Authentic Teacher: Sensitivity and Awareness in the Classroom*, Howard A. Doyle Publishing Company, Cambridge, Mass., 1966.

RATHS, L. E., A. JONAS, A. ROTHSTEIN, and SELMA WASSERMAN: *Teaching for Thinking, Theory, and Application*, Charles E. Merrill Books, Inc., Columbus, Ohio, 1967.

ROBINSON, H. ALAN, and SIDNEY J. RAUCH (comps. and eds.): *Corrective Reading in the High School Classroom*, Perspectives in Reading no. 6, International Reading Assoiation, Newark, Del., 1966.

ROBINSON, HELEN M.: *Corrective Reading in Classroom and Clinic*, Proceedings of the Annual Conference on Reading no. 79, The University of Chicago Press, Chicago, 1953.

RUSSELL, DAVID: *Children Learn to Read*, Ginn and Company, Boston, 1961.

——— and others: *Reading Aids through the Grades*, Teachers College Press, Columbia University, New York, 1956.

SANDERS, NORRIS: *Classroom Questions: What Kinds?* Harper & Row, Publishers, Incorporated, New York, 1966.

SPACHE, G. D.: "Diagnosis of Reading Problems in the Classroom," *Education Digest*, 26:47–49, November, 1960.

STAUFFER, RUSSELL (ed.): *The First Grade Reading Studies: Findings of Individual Investigations*, International Reading Association, Newark, Del., 1967.

STRANG, RUTH, and DOROTHY BRACKEN: *Making Better Readers*, D. C. Heath and Company, Boston, 1957.

TINKER, MILES A., and CONSTANCE M. MC CULLOUGH: *Teaching Elementary Reading*, Appleton-Century-Crofts, Inc., New York, 1962.

TOWNSEND, AGATHA: "Research and the Classroom Teacher," *The Reading Teacher*, 18:591–594, April, 1965.

TYLER, FRED (ed.): *Individualizing Instruction*, Sixty-first Yearbook of the National Society for the Study of Education, The University of Chicago Press, Chicago, 1962.

WALLACH, M., and N. KOGAN: "Creativity and Intelligence in Children's Thinking," *Transaction*, 4:38–43, January–February, 1967.

WITTY, PAUL (ed.): *Development in and through Reading*, Sixtieth Yearbook of the National Society for the Study of Education, The University of Chicago Press, Chicago, 1961.

WOLFE, DON M.: *Language Arts and Life Patterns*, grades 2–8, The Odyssey Press, Inc., New York, 1962.

ZINTZ, MILES V.: *Corrective Reading*, William C. Brown Company, Dubuque, Iowa, 1966.

Chapter Three

OBSERVATION IN THE CLASSROOM

An elementary school teacher who stays with his class four hours a day for over 150 days has a total of about six hundred hours of possible time for observation. If he has fifty pupils in his class (which, heaven forbid!), theoretically he would have twelve hours to devote to each pupil. Of course he must spend some of his time in giving instruction to the class as a whole. But even then he may be noticing how the class and certain individuals in it are responding to the instruction. A teacher readily identifies a student who has reading difficulties: he often looks away from his book; he tries to avoid reading; he gets better marks in subjects that do not require reading. Sometimes he comprehends what he hears better than what he reads. As the teacher observes more closely, he discovers specific difficulties in visual and auditory acuity, perception, discrimination, and memory; in vocabulary, word recognition, comprehension, and logical thinking. From further observation in the classroom and from interviews, he may infer that certain emotional difficulties are interfering with the student's achievement in reading. It seems possible that most teachers can develop greater skill in understanding their pupils through observation, specific and objective.

Observation is a basic technique (Cronbach, 1960; Strang, 1953; Thorndike and Hagen, 1961; Withall, 1960). It is employed every day by every teacher. It does not require extra time or materials. Day by day the teacher observes pupils in his classes as they engage in learning all the language arts.

Teachers and clinicians should have (1) a background knowledge of behavior and of conditions frequently associated with reading achievement, (2) techniques of accurate, insightful observation, and (3) ability to under-

47

stand the behavior they have observed. The traditional diagnostic approaches have focused too exclusively on pathological conditions and on what an individual *cannot do* rather than on what he actually *does* under certain conditions. Teachers' observations usually have the same tendency.

With training in methods of observation, teachers learn to observe behavior involved in classroom learning tasks. From an experiment in training teachers in forty-eight kindergarten classes, Haring and Ridgway (1967) concluded (1) that the teacher plays a key role in the early identification of children with learning disabilities and (2) that even a battery of tests does not predict as effectively as does teacher observation of the individual child. Trained teachers who observe and respond appropriately to pupils' reading strengths and difficulties bridge the gap between diagnosis, classroom teaching, and remedial work.

Most of the teacher's observations are never recorded; they are used immediately or at the first opportunity to help the student. For example, a child hesitates over the initial sound of an unfamiliar word. The teacher says, "What other words do you know that begin with the same letters?" Thus the child identifies the initial sound of the word. This clue may enable him to pronounce the word. As a check on the correctness of his pronunciation, the teacher asks, "Does the word you pronounced make sense in the sentence?"

LIMITATIONS OF OBSERVATION

Although individual teachers' appraisals of a child's reading development are often remarkably accurate, not all teachers have the training, intuition, or experience that would enable them to make a reliable evaluation (De Hirsch and others, 1966). And while observation is excellent for gaining understanding of the way a student reads, it does not directly tell us why he reads this way. From our observation we can only make inferences about the causes of the student's reading failures or successes. To guide the student in improving his reading, we need inferences or hypotheses based on a number of observations plus all the other relevant information that is available.

As safeguards against misinterpreting recorded observations, four principles should be kept in mind:

1. Since the student is always changing and growing, an observation that was made last year may not describe his present reading performance.

2. A teacher can observe only a small part of a student's total be-

havior. On the basis of such limited information the teacher can make only tentative generalizations about the student's reading.

3. Observations made by a teacher may tell more about the teacher than about the student. What the teacher sees may be influenced by his beliefs and biases, by his interest in the children observed, and by a subtle expectancy of a child's success or failure. His first impression of the student, his philosophy of education, and many other factors may color what he sees. What he looks for may be only what is already in his mind. It is therefore very important that the teacher understand the reading process and common causes of reading difficulty, and that he be receptive to what the child is trying to communicate through his behavior.

4. Ideally, observations should be interpreted in conjunction with interview, test, and other data. However, observations often are the only data that are available at the moment, and sometimes action should not be deferred.

OPPORTUNITIES FOR OBSERVATION

The classroom is a normal situation in which conditions are significant for the child. The teacher's opportunity to make many observations over a long period of time enables him to recognize typical behavior and temporary deviations from that behavior. In his role as teacher, his observations are unobtrusive; they do not alter the behavior observed. The teacher's observation and appraisal are a regular part of classroom procedure.

Any test administered individually, whether an oral reading test, an informal reading inventory, or a standardized individual intelligence or achievement test, offers excellent opportunities to see how an individual's mind works. One child will impulsively guess at the meaning and pronunciation of a word; another will use a trial-and-error approach instead of reasoning. One child may refuse to give any answer unless he is sure he is right, while another will glibly give answers to questions about which he has no knowledge. The individual's responses may also indicate disturbed thinking and disclose attitudes and values (Cronbach, 1960).

DETAILED ANALYSIS OF CLASSROOM SITUATIONS

Teachers are daily confronted with many common classroom situations in which they may gain much understanding of their students' reading

(Wright, 1959). A detailed analysis of these situations serves as a guide to observation; it alerts the teacher to significant reactions which he might not otherwise notice. We may either start with the situation and describe the kind of understanding we can obtain from it, or start with the kind of understanding we need and indicate the situations in which such understanding can be obtained.

The analyses on the following pages show kinds of information that may be significant for students' progress in reading (see Chapter 1). This information often raises the question "Why," which can be answered only by further observation and conversation with the student. Such understanding may be obtained in different classroom situations. To save space we have run the items on the same line; however, it would be easier for the teacher to select the items he wants to observe and record each one on a separate line, e.g.:

Language abilities

Vocabulary		*Sentence structure*		*Speech*	
Meager	_____	Incomplete sentences	_____	Distinct	_____
Rich	_____	Simple sentences	_____	Inaudible	_____
Accurate	_____	Complex sentences	_____	Monotonous	_____
Incorrect	_____			Expressive	_____
				Defects	_____

Oral report periods

In kindergarten and the lower grades and in oral English periods in the upper grades, students are offered many opportunities to relate their experiences. At the teacher listens, he learns about their vocabulary and language patterns, their interests and personality traits. Glimpses of home conditions also are frequently revealed.

In making and giving oral reports individually or in a small group, the students may show their interest in certain topics; their acquaintance with sources of information; and their ability to evaluate and compare sources, extract relevant information from them, organize it, and report it effectively. Observation of the audience gives indication of the speaker's effectiveness and of the audience's ability to listen and evaluate tactfully the reports given.

Specific observations:

Vocabulary: meager _____, rich _____, accurate _____, incorrect _____, words mispronounced _____
Sentence structure: incomplete sentences _____, simple sentences _____, complex sentences _____; says little _____, is very voluble _____
Imagination: creative _____, bizarre _____

Organization: events recounted in proper sequence _____, well organized _____, disjointed _____, repetitive _____

Sense of humor: enjoys humor _____, makes others laugh _____

Intelligence: is alert mentally _____, sees relations _____, solves problems _____, learns slowly _____

Interest: wholehearted _____, indifferent _____, apathetic _____

Personality: self-confident _____, shy _____, socially poised _____, embarrassed _____, tense _____, hostile _____

Family relations and background: affectionate home relations _____, unhappy home _____

Relations with parents: constructive _____, detrimental _____

Relations with siblings: congenial _____, rivalrous _____

Peer reactions: interested _____, friendly _____, sympathetic _____, uninterested _____, critical _____

Appearance: happy _____, sad _____; well dressed and well groomed _____, poorly dressed _____, inappropriately dressed _____, disheveled _____

Listening to the teacher read a story

Note degree of interest evoked: keenly interested _____, eager to talk about it _____, indifferent _____, bored _____

Comprehension: accurate _____, detailed _____, inadequate _____

Students reading aloud

This situation gives the teacher opportunity to observe each student's word recognition skills, pronunciation, phrasing, and expression. One can quickly detect word callers by asking several searching questions on the selections they have read. The student may also reveal his attitude toward reading and toward himself as a reader. It will be evident whether he approaches reading with enjoyment, indifference, dislike, anxiety, resistance, or hostility.

Dramatized reading of a story or play shows still more clearly the student's ability to read aloud with expression, to bring out appropriate feeling and meaning, to interpret clues of character, and to evoke the interest of the audience.

Types of observations:

Familiarity with phonics: _____

Method of word attack: sounds out words _____, uses syllabication _____, tries to analyze structure _____, uses context clues _____

Word recognition problems: skips words _____, reverses letters, words, phrases _____, substitutes words _____, guesses wildly _____

Rate of reading: appropriate to material _____, too slow _____, too rapid _____

Substitutions yield valuable clues. If the student substitutes a word that makes sense in the sentence, we may infer that he is reading for meaning. If, however, the word he substitutes makes no sense, we may infer that he is merely pronouncing words with little concern for the meaning of what he reads. The teacher should also note what kinds of words cause the student difficulty. Are they short common words such as those in the Dolch basic vocabulary, or longer words; words within his experience or words foreign to him? It is also important to observe how he goes about getting the meaning of unfamiliar words.

Phrasing: reads word by word _____, reads in phrases or other thought units _____, loses place easily _____, reads clearly and with expression _____

Closure: cannot blend sounds _____, has difficulty in supplying missing letters, words, sentences _____

Sequence: difficulty in retelling story in sequence _____, following series of directions _____, remembering order of letters _____, of words _____

Comprehension: recognizes basic vocabulary at sight _____, gives good answers to questions _____, gives irrelevant answers _____, sees relationships and sequences of ideas _____, can recount or discuss what he has read _____, shows originality in interpretation _____, relates reading to experience _____

Attitudes: volunteers to read orally _____, reads only when called upon _____, appears to enjoy reading orally in audience situations _____, reads aloud to others in free time _____, makes excuses to avoid reading aloud

Reaction of classmates to student's oral reading: are eager to have him read _____, show interest _____, attention wanders _____, are restless _____, are disinterested _____, rudely interrupt _____

Silent reading in library, free-reading, and study periods

The student's choice of books in a free-reading or library period may show his reading interests and level. His behavior during the period indicates his silent reading habits and power of concentration. In addition to the specific observation, teacher or student may make an attention-distraction chart. Such a chart may make the students more aware of the time they are wasting. Of course, it would be necessary for the students to have a chance to discuss what goes into their attention-distraction charts. Were they just idly daydreaming, or were they staring into space while pondering thoughts evoked by their reading? If they were distracted, what caused it? Was the book too hard? Were they thinking about tonight's party?

Types of observations:

Approach to books: does not enjoy books or pictures _____; leafs through many books _____, chooses quickly _____; looks first at chapter titles and/or table of contents _____, pictures _____, printed pages _____; tends to choose small books _____, large books _____, one kind of book _____, a particular author or series _____; is rather uniform in choices _____, chooses a variety of books _____; chooses books at his own age level of interest _____, below _____, above _____; takes books home often _____, seldom _____, never _____; reads them through _____; can discuss what he has read _____; returns books on time _____, undamaged _____; asks for books he does not find on shelves _____; is unable to find any book of interest to him _____

Uses library just to look at magazines _____; reads little of newspapers except the sports page and "funnies" _____; always carries a big stack of books home _____; asks for permission to take a new book home over the weekend _____

Can locate sources of information _____, uses index _____, table of contents _____, finds suitable material _____, makes useful notes on relevant material _____

When a new book is distributed, receives it enthusiastically _____, groans and shows other signs of rejection _____, turns pages aimlessly _____, systematically examines book _____, asks questions about book _____

Voluntary reading: does no voluntary reading _____, reads more than required _____, includes a variety of material _____, makes clear, original, thoughtful comments on reading _____, shows depth of appreciation beyond his grade level _____

Visual habits and posture: frowns _____, blinks often _____, squints _____, rubs or wipes eyes _____; holds book at average distance _____, too close _____, too far _____; has good general posture _____, complains of headache _____

Uses reference tools such as glossary and dictionary: freely _____, seldom _____, never _____, effectively _____, as an excuse for leaving seat (as evidenced by attitude, approach, results) _____; independently _____, with assistance _____

Reads by himself _____, talks to others _____; if the latter, in cooperative study _____, as a disturbance _____

Amount of work completed: about same as classmates _____, noticeably more _____, noticeably less _____; if assignment is completed early, goes on to more of the same _____, stops and is idle _____, does something else _____, related (such as drawing pictures to illustrate the story) _____, unrelated _____; disturbs others _____

Asks for teacher's help _____

Group instruction and discussion

The teacher will observe that some students "catch on" quickly while others need to have an explanation repeated several times. The student who learns quickly should not have to mark time while the slow learners gain sufficient comprehension to go on. Sometimes, in a question or comment, a quiet student will reveal undetected ability. In response to a picture or incomplete story, a student may show exceptional originality.

Interaction in the group also may be observed. A great deal of learning takes places as a result of group interaction. Students may stimulate and encourage one another to read better; they may share their most effective reading methods, recommend stories they have liked, and otherwise facilitate each other's learning. On the other hand, interaction in some groups may be detrimental to growth in reading. Many retarded readers have told of being embarrassed when classmates shouted out the words they did not know, laughed at their mistakes, or made fun of the easy books they were reading. The bright child who enjoys reading may suffer in equal measure from an anti-intellectual spirit.

In informal discussions, students may show what they are learning through television, radio, and part-time work and indicate its relevance to what is going on in school. The teacher who is receptive will be able to enter at least a small part of his students' world and see where reading fits into it.

Types of observations:

Attitudes: eager to participate _____, interested _____, indifferent _____, withdrawn _____

Work habits: works well alone, _____, with others _____

Thought habits: follows sequence of story or discussion _____, organizes thought well _____, recognizes cause and effect relations _____, summarizes well _____, does not understand questions or directions or the significance of what is said _____, is confused in his thinking _____

Learning capacity: quick to catch on _____, needs to have directions or questions repeated _____, asks searching questions _____, relates ideas _____

Oral expression: expresses thought clearly in well-constructed sentences _____, uses words accurately _____, has good enunciation _____, uses a wide range of oral vocabulary _____, is halting _____, is incoherent _____

Discussion techniques: contributes relevant facts _____, analyzes the situation _____, shows breadth of information _____, listens to others and builds on what they have said _____, does not participate _____, makes irrelevant comments _____

Creativity: is inventive _____, shows imagination _____, is intellectually curious _____, shows maturity of interests _____, shows little or no originality _____

Personal involvement: tense _____, noncommittal _____, nervous and ill at ease _____, self-conscious _____; enjoys discussion _____, listens well but contributes little _____, applies vicarious experience to himself _____, displays wholehearted participation _____

Quality of comprehension: accurate _____, well-organized _____, factual _____, inaccurate _____, incoherent _____, creative _____
Whole observer _____, part observer _____

Other activities during the day

Types of specific observations:

Positive attitudes: toward school _____, toward reading _____, toward self _____, toward parents _____
Negative attitudes: toward school _____, toward reading _____, toward self _____, toward parents _____
Difficulty in physical activities: in sports and games _____, in coordination _____

Favorite school subjects: _____
Subjects disliked: _____
Best friends: younger _____, older _____, brighter _____, duller _____

Significant events in the student's past: _____

Some teachers may think this detailed analysis of observation in classroom situations is bewilderingly complex. Others may think it is "much ado about nothing." Obviously, a teacher cannot observe all the items about every student. But if he is familiar with kinds of understanding of students' reading that a teacher may gain during the school day, he becomes more alert to significant responses that individual students may make.

Observation during play periods

Observation of children on the playground may yield helpful information about psychomotor abilities related to the reading achievement especially of younger children. It is easy to spot the children who are lacking in motor and eye-hand coordination and those who exhibit "directional confusion" (inability to discriminate right from left parts of the body). Less important is observation of lateral preferences, which are no longer considered of much significance in reading disability. The incidence of inconsistency in hand and eye preferences changes with age—around 42 percent for six-year-olds and only 18 percent for seven-year-olds.

On the playground a child's interest in sports, the quality of his participation, leadership, and initiative, the tendency to get into trouble, and the rejection or acceptance by classmates may all be indirectly related to his reading achievement.

Tape recordings of spontaneous conversations of children in groups yield valuable information on proficiency in vocabulary, sentence structure, and logical thinking. Most useful is an observation and analysis of the setting in which children experience success or failure in various reading tasks.

Observation over a period of time

Joe, a third-grade boy, comes from a non-English-speaking home. He is just beginning to read with difficulty at a primer level. His speaking vocabulary is meager; his enunciation, poor; his sentences, incomplete and poorly organized. When he reads orally, he stumbles over basic sight words in the Dolch vocabulary. He lacks word attack skills. His substitution of wild guesses for the words he does not know suggests that he is not reading for meaning. In relating a story, he relies heavily on the pictures.

During a free-choice reading or library period, Joe resists teacher guidance in selecting appropriate books. He chooses books that are too difficult for him and merely goes through the motions of reading them. Whenever possible, he avoids reading and prefers to draw pictures during reading time.

Listening in a group situation is one of Joe's main problems. He is restless and seems preoccupied, listens only part of the time, and is easily distracted. His work habits are poor, and he often disturbs others.

Both the teacher's observation and the results of psychological tests indicate more mental potential than he is demonstrating. He can see relationships and answer inference questions. If he is given individual atttention, his comprehension is much better.

His background of experience is quite different from school experiences, and there are emotional problems in the home. His failure in reading, together with home problems, has made him tense and anxious and lacking in self-confidence. The amazing thing is that although he has had so little success in his past reading experiences, he seems willing and determined to overcome his deficiencies.

Since he responds so well to individual attention, even a few minutes of the teacher's exclusive attention would be helpful. In these brief individual conferences, the teacher could stress his good qualities and evidences of progress, and give him specific instruction in pronouncing English words that cause special difficulty. In class the teacher could use choral reading and dialogues to give him fluency in speaking a selection before he attempts to read it. Encouraging verbal interaction with English-speaking children on the playground and in class would increase his facility in speaking English.

Observation of children with severe reading disability

The teacher's classroom observation is important in the initial screening of problems referred to as "developmental lag," "minimal brain damage," or "sensorimotor immaturity." The following clues may alert the teacher to possible neurological deficits:

Extreme difficulty in learning to read and spell

Awkwardness in finger and hand movements, difficulty in coloring between lines, inability to copy a simple geometric form

Difficulty in balancing, in riding a two-wheeler or a skateboard, in skipping or hopping

Reversing letters or numerals: reading *was* for *saw*, *12* for *21*

Hyperactivity, short attention span

Apparent anxiety and insecurity about school

Many kinds of behavior measured by standardized tests can be observed by the classroom teacher if he knows what to look for. For example, the teacher can observe day-by-day kinds of responses measured by the Illinois Test of Psycholinguistic Abilities (see Chapter 10). Among those most closely related to reading development are understanding the significance of what he hears, reproducing and identifying what he has been shown and relating it to his past experience; seeing similarities, completing missing parts of a sentence or figure, retelling a story in sequence, and duplicating and remembering a sequence of numbers or forms presented to him orally and visually. Having recognized a difficulty or deficit, the teacher can give the child practice in that kind of ability.

If such difficulties are observed in preschool, kindergarten, and early in first grade, they might be corrected by games and other activities that children enjoy: skipping to music, jumping rope, playing hop scotch, finding missing elements in pictures, playing "Simon Says," etc. Practice in auditory discrimination and memory is given by tapping two rhythms and asking the child to tell whether they were the same or different, asking him to repeat interesting sentences, letting him watch a simple experiment and tell what happened. First-grade children who have not developed tactual, motor, visual, and auditory discrimination and integration need special practice. For them activities such as have just been suggested are not just play; they are essential to success in learning to read.

Observation of interaction between student and teacher

Since the influence of teacher behavior on children's spontaneous, cooperative, and self-initiated behavior and on their learning and achievement has been demonstrated by a number of research studies (see Anderson, 1939, 1954; Withall, 1960; Flanders and Havumaki, 1960; Moustakas and others, 1956), we should observe not only the individual student or teacher, but also the interaction between them. In this way teachers can gain an understanding of the effect of their behavior and methods on students' attitudes and efforts. They can see the results of their words and action. By observing interaction among students, the teacher can gain insight into the influence of peer relations and values.

Observation varies in breadth and depth. Separate observations of behavior and errors become more meaningful when grouped into patterns. For example, omission of one or more words may be related to inability to comprehend and that, in turn, to inability to recall the author's ideas. Repetition of words or parts of words becomes more meaningful when it is seen as a way of stalling for time while trying to pronounce a different word or to relate an idea to the first part of the sentence.

The observed behavior is not so important as the motivation and sequences that lead up to it. It is possible to observe clues to the individual's cognitive style in reading. In other words, what is his thinking process in various types of reading—why and how does he arrive at certain responses? Such understanding can be obtained only by a person who is able to think and feel with another individual and to sense why he is acting as he does at a given moment.

EXAMPLES OF OBSERVATION DURING AN INDIVIDUALIZED READING PERIOD

Sixth-grade boys were reading books of their own choice during an individualized reading period. Bruce, a large boy who was repeating the grade, laughed out loud as he was reading *Rufus M.* by Eleanor Estes. Most of the other students paid no attention to him; a few of his immediate classmates looked up, some annoyed, some amused. Occasionally he smiled to himself. It was almost four minutes before he turned the page. His lips were moving as if he were pronouncing each word to himself. In the second period he was still struggling through his book; he had completed two-thirds of it, still reading in the same slow way.

This observation raises questions about the meaning of Bruce's behavior: Did he really appreciate the humor of the book, or was his loud laughter an attention-getting device? Do his classmates tolerate, ignore, or reject him? What are the causes of his slow reading—lack of a basic sight vocabulary? Inability to apply the word recognition skills he has been taught? Poor reasoning ability? Failure to use his knowledge of sentence structure to get meaning? Overemphasis on phonics that has led to persistence of the habit of sounding out every word? Further observation and conversation with Bruce are necessary to answer these questions.

Mack, the slowest student in the group, sat with the open book he had chosen, *Kidnapped,* looking into space. He did not get beyond page 9. He had previously read and enjoyed a simplified version of *Treasure Island* and wanted to read another book by the same author. But this time he had got hold of the original edition and could not understand it. Once in a while he roused himself and tried hard to read it, but made little progress. He seemed glad when the period ended. Next time he chose an easy, new, illustrated book and enjoyed looking at the pictures. This observation made the teacher realize the importance of helping Mack choose a book that he could read independently without frustration. A too difficult book might destroy his recently acquired interest in reading and his effort to improve.

John had selected *Robinson Crusoe.* He squinted and grimaced as he read. He told the teacher he had a headache. He said he often got a headache when he read in school. Although he said he had been to an eye doctor who told his mother there was nothing wrong with his eyes, in view of these signs of visual discomfort the teacher decided to ask the school nurse to make a follow-up of his eye examination. The teacher also recognized that John's inability to read the books that his friends were reading might account for symptoms he had observed.

These examples illustrate a few kinds of understanding that a teacher may gain from observation. They also show the limitations of observation alone; one needs additional information to interpret most observations.

RECORDING OF TEACHER OBSERVATIONS

Although most teachers' observations are not recorded, some systematic recording of the most significant student behavior is useful to the teacher, the student, the parent, and the student's next teacher.

The recording may take either of two forms: (1) dated observations of individual students or anecdotal records that are recorded and then may be collected in each child's cumulative record folder and summarized periodically or (2) a checklist. The checklist may be used for a single pupil or as a record for the entire class. A checklist may contain some blank spaces for recording additional observations or explaining items checked.

A checklist record form

A checklist type of guide to observation in the classroom may be judged by these criteria:

1. It is organized around classroom situations with which the teacher is confronted.
2. Its items refer to specific behavior that can be observed rather than to generalizations or inferences about behavior.
3. It provides space to add further observations, impressions, and insights.
4. It is selective; i.e., it does not contain so many items that it becomes unwieldy.

The following directions for using this form of record are suggested:

1. The teacher will have one of these checklist forms for each student. He will include the most significant kinds of observations that may be made in different classroom situations (see pages 50–55).
2. In each of the situations described, the teacher will record his observations of each student's performance. For example, it is Mary Jones's turn to tell about her weekend. The teacher takes Mary's checklist from the pile, listens and observes as Mary gives her report. He makes these comments on it: "Mary spoke very clearly and distinctly. I liked the way she told about each event in her weekend in just the order in which it happened—what happened first, next, and last. You were all interested in her story, weren't you? There was one new word she used that we can all learn to pronounce correctly. . . ." As the teacher summarizes the good points and the criticisms, he makes a tally on Mary's record as follows:

Speech	Language patterns	Reaction of peers
1 ____ Distinct, clear	1 ____ Good organization	1 ____ Interested

In the blank space provided, the teacher may write the word that Mary mispronounced and his impression of progress she has made.

By putting the first tally to the extreme left and the tallies for each subsequent observation a little further to the right, the teacher can get some indication of the student's progress.

In each period the teacher will not attempt to record his observations of all the students. Instead he will focus his attention on a few students and record his observations on their records. Thus, in time the teacher may systematically accumulate observations of behavior significant for reading improvement. In some instances it may be easier for the teacher to jot down his observations on a scratch pad and tally them later on the checklist.

If, as suggested, the teacher calls attention to or asks the students to point out the individual's strengths, he will reinforce the good reading habits of the other students. If he gives instruction in an error noted, as when the teacher taught the pronunciation of a new word, the entire class profits by the analysis of one student's performance.

In addition to this immediate use, the checklist serves as a periodic appraisal of a student's progress. The teacher may go over the record with the student, who thus becomes more aware of his reading goals, the progress he is making toward them, and the practice he needs to correct certain faults or deficiencies. Such a record, passed on to the next teacher, supplies a wealth of initial understanding of the students in the new class.

Various checklists have been developed. A one-page form that is remarkably concise and at the same time cumulative and comprehensive in its coverage of significant diagnostic information was developed by Newman and is published by Science Research Associates. It includes (1) a scale of recreational reading fluency from readiness to high sixth grade, (2) a rating scale of interest in pleasure reading, (3) three estimates of voluntary reading, (4) titles of favorite books, and (5) results of academic aptitude and achievement tests.

A much more detailed checklist based on an analysis of reading skills, beginning with the readiness level and continuing with one page for each grade through sixth, is published privately by Barbe, 3124 Harriet Road, Silver Lake, Cuyahoga Falls, Ohio. Each grade level includes details on vocabulary, word analysis, comprehension, and oral reading.

As a guide to high school students' own analysis of their reading development, Ellen Thomas, Reading Consultant of the University of Chicago Practice School, has prepared a unique series of sheets that invite students to explore their educational and vocational plans as these may affect their reading performance, their purpose in coming to a reading class, their present reading interests. This first page is followed by a checklist of skills that they want to improve. Having thus set their goals, tentatively, they may obtain more information from standardized and informal tests. On the basis of their test results they list the reading areas and skills which they would like to improve. The students also estimate the amount of time they can devote to practice outside of class and other values they would like to gain from the class. This analysis is made in the form of a letter to the instructor. The students are then provided with a form having three columns: (1) skills to be improved, (2) practices to do, and (3) record of results. In the column "Practices to Do" the teacher suggests practice material and effective ways of using it. These forms, which may be adapted to the elementary school, encourage students' initiative in planning and carrying out their own reading programs.

To aid in the diagnosis of emotionally disturbed children, Llorens and others (1964) made a comprehensive list of primary, cognitive, perceptual, and motor correlates of behavior. They also included and evaluated tests used to measure these functions and suggested training procedures.

A global approach

What might be called a "global approach" is another possible way of recording observations, plus interpretation, plus recommendations. It describes the most significant aspects rather than checking separate items.

This method is most effective when used by an experienced person, one who has gone through the process of specific analysis many times and is thoroughly familiar with the detailed guide to observation. He should also be skillful in seeing relationships and drawing inferences from the observed behavior. Such a person can sense the central factor and the related factors that are affecting the student's responses.

For example, the teacher might write about Mary Brown's oral report: "Mary speaks clearly and distinctly. This ability and her sense of sequence in reporting her stories help her to hold the attention of the class. She likes to use new words but does not always pronounce them correctly. We shall encourage her to listen carefully to new words and to be precise in her pronunciation of them."

INTERPRETATION OF OBSERVATIONS

The most difficult part of the technique of observation is interpreting what one sees. For example, it is easy to observe that a poor reader wants to read aloud at every opportunity and attempts to answer questions that are too difficult for him, but what is the motive underlying this observed behavior? Is it family pressure to be an outstanding student? Desire for attention? An inaccurate self-appraisal? Or is there some other explanation?

Manifestations of inattention may indicate language difficulty, visual or auditory defects, resistance to authority, inner conflicts, lack of immediate as well as long-term goals, or failure to recognize one's need for the knowledge and skills that are being taught—to mention only some of the many possible interpretations.

Ideally, interpretation should be attempted only after a number of observations have been made, and then it should be supplemented by interviews and other sources of information. Actually, however, an experienced teacher, against the background of his accumulated impressions, often may use a single observation as the basis for giving immediate help to a student.

CONCLUDING STATEMENT

There is no substitute for skill in observation. The understanding of students' reading development and difficulties that can be obtained by this technique is pertinent, specific, and often immediately applicable to the instruction being given.

However, the prerequisites for and the limitations of observation should be recognized. First, descriptions of typical behavior can be obtained only by a sufficient number of pertinent, systematic observations. Several observations may indicate merely a temporary deviation from the individual's usual behavior. Second, knowing that the teacher is observing may alter the behavior observed. This is all to the good if observation is a regular part of the school day and motivates the student to do his best. Third, occasionally each student may be placed in essentially the same situation, e.g., oral reading of a given paragraph, which permits comparison with other students doing the same reading task. Observation of the student under natural classroom conditions that are significant to him often elicits diagnostic information most important for practical purposes.

Other sources of information are needed to interpret the facts and to answer questions raised by observation of the students' behavior. What appears to be the same behavior may have different meanings to different students.

Although the teacher uses most of his daily observations immediately in instruction, or merely adds them to his general impression of his students, there are some items significant enough for him to record. The checklist form of record serves both as a guide to classroom observation and as a summary of information he has gained from day to day. The global or descriptive account is the more dynamic form of cumulative record; it is more effective after the teacher has become familiar with the kinds of details that may be most significant. Then he may prefer to write a brief description of the highlights of his observation and interpretation. Both types of records are of value only insofar as they are used in helping students to improve their reading. Neither should become a burden to the teacher or usurp time he might be spending in giving instruction that the student needs immediately. As the student grows older he should increasingly participate in the appraisal of his reading. Tape recordings, sound motion pictures, and video tapes make possible the most precise basis for appraisal of samples of teacher and student behavior and interaction.

There is some research evidence (Haring and Ridgway, 1967) that day-by-day observation by trained teachers who respond appropriately to the information gained may be as effective and more practical than elaborate test batteries. If generally applied, observation so used would diminish the distinction between classroom teaching and remedial teaching. Observation would then become a method of diagnosing the efficacy of teaching methods as well as the abilities, attitudes, and interests of the students.

SUGGESTED PROBLEMS: PRACTICE AND DEMONSTRATION

1. Observe children in any common classroom situation and record significant facts about individual children's reading.

2. Experiment with different methods of recording your observations, e.g., using a checklist for each pupil or jotting down notes which you summarize later.

3. In what situations can you as a teacher record observations of individual children's reading most easily? In what situations can you gain the best impression of the reading ability of the class?

4. How can you use a checklist as a guide to observation?

5. Give examples of the immediate use of observations made by the teacher.

6. Suggest possible interpretations of several observations of students' reading. How would you obtain understanding of the meaning of the observed behavior to the individual through an interview with him?

7. Observe classroom reading situations and record your observations of individual students, either on a checklist form or in a descriptive summary.

REFERENCES

ANDERSON, HAROLD H.: "The Measurement of Domination and Socially Integrative Behavior in Teachers' Contacts with Children," *Child Development*, 10:73–89, June, 1939.

————: "A Study of Certain Criteria of Teaching Effectiveness," *Journal of Experimental Education*, 23:41–71, September, 1954.

CRONBACH, LEE: *Essentials of Psychological Testing*, 3d ed., Harper & Row, Publishers, Incorporated, New York, 1960, pp. 506–538.

DE HIRSCH, KATRINA, JEANNETTE J. JANSKY, and W. S. LANGFORD: *Predicting Reading Failure*, Harper & Row, Publishers, Incorporated, New York, 1966.

DRISCOLL, GERTRUDE P.: *How to Study the Behavior of Children*, Teachers College Press, Columbia University, New York, 1956.

DURKIN, DOLORES: *Phonics and the Teaching of Reading*, Teachers College Press, Columbia University, New York, 1962.

FLANDERS, NED A., and SULO HAVUMAKI: "The Effect of Teacher-Pupil Contacts Involving Praise on Sociometric Choices of Students," *Journal of Educational Psychology*, 51:65–68, April, 1960.

HARING, N. G., and R. W. RIDGWAY: "Early Identification of Children with Learning Disabilities," *Exceptional Children*, 33:387–395, February, 1967.

LLORENS, LELA A., and others: "Cognitive-Perceptual-Motor Functions," *American Journal of Occupational Therapy*, 18:202–208, September–October, 1964.

LYTTON, H.: "Follow-up of an Experiment in Selection for Remedial Education," *British Journal of Educational Psychology*, 37:1–9, February, 1967.

MOUSTAKAS, CLARK E., and others: "An Objective Method for the Measurement and Analysis of Child-Adult Interaction," *Child Development*, 27:109–134, June, 1956.

STRANG, RUTH: *The Role of the Teacher in Personnel Work*, 4th ed., Teachers College Press, Columbia University, New York, 1953, chap. 8.

THORNDIKE, ROBERT, and ELIZABETH HAGEN: *Measurement and Evaluation in Psychology and Education*, 2d ed., John Wiley & Sons, Inc., New York, 1961, pp. 399–421.

WITHALL, JOHN: "Research Tools: Observing and Recording Behavior," *Review of Educational Research*, 30:496–512, December, 1960.

WRIGHT, E. MURIEL M.: "Development of an Instrument for Studying Verbal Behaviors in a Secondary School Mathematics Classroom," *Journal of Experimental Education*, 28:103–121, December, 1959.

SUGGESTED READINGS

ELKIND, DAVID: "Piaget and Montessori," *Harvard Educational Review*, 37:535–545, Fall, 1967.

HARTUP, WILLARD W.: "Early Education and Childhood Socialization," *Journal of Research and Development in Education*, 1:16–29, Spring, 1968.

WILSON, ROBERT M.: *Diagnostic and Remedial Reading for Classroom and Clinic*, Charles E. Merrill Books, Inc., Columbus, Ohio, 1967, pp. 68–79.

Chapter Four

ORAL READING AS A DIAGNOSTIC TECHNIQUE

The modern use of oral reading differs in several ways from the oral reading of a century ago. It is not nearly so common, even in the primary grades. It is used only occasionally in the upper elementary and then mostly in audience situations. In the first grades the main purpose of oral reading is to give the teacher opportunity to study the child's reading. The second purpose is to encourage well-phrased, expressive reading. The third purpose is to give children opportunities to share their enjoyment of a book with others. If the teacher supplements oral reading with introspection, he may learn much about the pupil's reading process.

In the primary grades, where the basic sight vocabulary and word recognition skills are acquired, oral reading is essential as a basis for diagnosis. As the child reads aloud, the teacher notices proficiency and progress as well as errors and difficulties. The latter might go uncorrected in an individualized silent reading program. Classmates, too, learn from other pupils' self-correction of errors in oral reading.

DIAGNOSIS THROUGH ORAL READING IN THE ELEMENTARY GRADES

To obtain a quick general idea of the oral reading ability of a new class, the teacher is justified in asking each child to read a paragraph aloud in turn. In this way he will quickly identify those who read fluently on the grade level, those who have to puzzle out even the basic sight vocabulary, those who have no ready word recognition skills, and those who feel embarrassment and frustration in the reading situation. To avoid causing embarrassment on the part of sensitive students, the teacher will ask them to read only a sentence or two, make an encouraging remark, and plan to analyze their reading in private.

If the teacher has a double-spaced typed copy of the paragraphs to be read, he can quickly mark the errors for each student according to the following code (see also Gray, 1963):

1. Encircle all *omissions* (whole words, syllables, letter sounds, endings, etc.).

2. Insert with a caret (∧) all *insertions*.

3. Underline and write in all *mispronunciations* (writing in the mispronunciations indicates whether the child uses initial-sound clues, shape-of-word clues, or no perceptible clues at all).

4. Draw a line *through* words for which substitutions were made; write in the *substitution*. (Note whether it makes sense, indicating that the child is reading for meaning, or whether it is irrelevant to the context.)

5. Use dotted or wavy line to indicate *repetitions*.

ILLUSTRATION

Spot was ⓐ good dog. He never ran after‸ the boys and girls or automobiles. But Woof ~~was~~ saw a naughty dog. He ran after ~~dogs~~ boys and girls‸ and horses and automobiles, and he barked at ⟨all of⟩ them.

The teacher may add a comprehension check after each paragraph, for example:

1. What is the story about?

2. What kind of dog was Spot?

3. How was Woof different from Spot?

4. Why was Woof a bad dog?

It is best to write each student's answers to the questions because the quality of these answers may vary widely within the limits of correctness.

In a diagnostic oral reading period the teacher is very active—quite different from the teacher who lazily listens as the children stumble through their basic reader.

If the teacher can provide books for independent reading or other worthwhile work for the class as a whole, he can ask the students individually to read aloud to him. This method is obviously superior to having the students take turns reading aloud before the class. Teacher and student can explore the reasons for errors. The student profits not only from gaining insight into his oral reading skills, but also from the morale-building effect of having an adult's exclusive attention. The individual reading inventory and the standardized oral reading tests described in Chapter 10 represent an extended and more precise diagnostic use of oral reading.

Incidentally, the individual conference has been found to be an effective way of preventing and working with discipline problems. The seriously retarded reader usually feels considerable frustration in a reading period (Natchez, 1961, pp. 308–311). As in other frustrating situations, he may react by becoming dependent, aggressive, or withdrawn.

Instruction may follow diagnosis immediately. If a student is weak in word recognition skills, the teacher shows him how to use several methods of word attack; if one does not solve the word, the good reader tries another method until he experiences success in analyzing the word in context. If this instruction is given in the class as a whole or, better, in small "seminar" groups of students having the same difficulties, the other students can listen and learn (Russell, 1959). Everyone in the group should give as close attention to the instruction being given to an individual reader as though it were being given to him personally.

Tests and exercises to develop basic sight vocabulary and psycholinguistic abilities

To supplement the information obtained from the student's oral reading, the Dolch Basic Sight Word Test (1942) may easily be given to any class or subgroup within a class that seems to lack the ability to recognize common words quickly at sight. The test presents 220 words "which make up 70 percent of first readers and 65 percent of second and third readers" (Dolch, 1942). The children circle the one word on each line that is read by the teacher. It is desirable to know how many of these essential sight words the children can recognize immediately and which words they need to study and practice further, preferably in sentences. The Dolch and other vocabulary games (Russell and Karp, 1956; *Good Ways to Strengthen Reading Skills*, 1956; Spache, 1955) are useful for children who need extra practice on this basic vocabulary in order to become more rapid, effective readers. Tachistoscopic methods that expose words for a small fraction of a second give practice in quick recognition of common words. The reading of sentences including the words to be learned acquaints students with the meaning of these words in context.

To find out more about the student's specific word attack skills, the teacher pronounces each test word—*build, danger, tumble*, etc.—distinctly and asks the students to write the letters representing the single or double initial consonant sound and the final sound of each word. The student's knowledge of endings—*s, d, ed, ing*—and the possessive form *'s* may be tested by asking him to separate the root from the endings. His ability to divide words into syllables and to write the two words that make up a compound word can also be tested informally.

A more thorough appraisal is possible with the McCullough Word Analysis Test (1962), which combines phonics with structural analysis. This test also measures the student's understanding of seven rules of syllabication, of prefixes and suffixes, and of how consonant blends and vowel sounds are combined to make a word. Since the test is based on words familiar to fourth graders, it can be used in the fourth grade and above. The teacher gives one part of the test a day. Their errors call children's attention to the aspects of instruction that each particularly needs.

A more elaborate, unified design for studying the psycholinguistic reading development of children has been described by Samuel A. Kirk and James J. McCarthy in an article entitled "The Illinois Test of Psycholinguistic Abilities: An Approach to Differential Diagnosis" in the *American Journal of Mental Deficiency*, 65:399–412, November, 1961. This test consists of five dimensions: (1) auditory and visual stimuli, (2) reception of meaningful visual and auditory stimuli, (3) association of these stimuli with past learning, (4) motor or vocal expression of the ideas, and (5) abilities that help to integrate the other learnings (see Chapter 10). For application of this procedure to slow learners, see Samuel Kirk, "Reading Problems of Slow Learners" in *The Underachiever in Reading*, pages 62–69, compiled and edited by H. Alan Robinson, Supplementary Educational Monograph no. 92, The University of Chicago Press, Chicago, 1962.

Exercises such as many first-grade teachers give children involve some of the abilities measured by standardized tests; they have both diagnostic and practice value. For example, auditory perception, discrimination, and memory were taught by one teacher [1] as follows: The teacher wrote on the board the known word *brown*; the children pronounced the *br* sound at the beginning of the word, then mentioned other familiar words that began with the same sound—*breeze, bring, bridge, broke,* and *brush*. The teacher wrote these words on the board, the children read them and noted that they all began with the same *br* sound as *brown*.

The next step was to have the children discriminate the *br* sound in pairs of words: *rake-break, band-brand, laid-braid, drag-brag*. Each pair was presented orally by the teacher, and the *br* sound was identified by the children. Thus each new sound was combined with letters previously

---

[1] Mrs. Marjorie Cameron, Reading Consultant, Sunnyside School District, Tucson, Ariz.

learned so as to maximize their discriminability and identifiability. Association of sound-letter combinations is facilitated by progressing from the most easily discriminable to the least discriminable forms. This reduction of initial complexity of the reading task is especially important in teaching mentally retarded children (Davy, 1962). Bright children, on the other hand, prefer to be presented with a complex reading situation and to take initiative in selecting their own system of word recognition (Robinson, 1963).

To apply immediately their memory of the *br* sound, the teacher made riddles based on these words, e.g., *breeze, bridge, branch, bracelet*—"Air that is moving is called a _____." In exercises of this kind, not only auditory discrimination but other abilities such as seeing relations, reasoning, and conceptualization are involved.

Ability to recognize phonetic clues for unlocking unknown words, as well as memory and application of the *br* sound, was further tested as follows: The teacher wrote "Jack went for a swim in the brook." The children were asked to try to recognize the underlined word. When a child said "brook," the teacher asked, "Why couldn't it be *lake?*" And the child replied, "Because it doesn't begin with the sound that '*br*' stands for."

Other sentences, such as "You look so much like that boy, I thought you were his brother," offered further opportunity to analyze the child's method of word attack. "Why couldn't it be *cousin?* Why not *bridge?*" This procedure combined the use of initial sounds with contextual clues as a means of unlocking words.

The technique of consonant substitution was taught as another phonetic key to pronouncing new words. In the word *face, gr* was substituted for *f*, and the children read *grace;* the final consonant in *weed* was changed to a *p*, and they read *weep*.

When a child has difficulty in responding to these practice exercises, the teacher gains diagnostic information about his word recognition skills. When a child succeeds in pronouncing an unfamiliar word, the teacher may ask him to describe the method that he used.

In a fifth-grade class Jean was reading a paragraph in the science book. She came to the word *parachute*, which she had never seen before. Thoughtfully she looked at the word, verbalized a bit, and tried to pronounce it: "par-par-a-chute." Then she continued reading the selection. In response to the teacher's question about how she had figured out the pronunciation, she said, "Oh, I just figured that the *a* in the middle of the word had to be a syllable by itself, so I just tried it that way and it worked." By describing her method Jean became more aware of the process that brought success. She also stimulated other children to try a similar kind of word analysis instead of using ineffective methods such as guessing, skipping over the word, spelling it out, or sounding the first letter and saying any word that begins with that sound.

When a child has difficulty in oral reading, he may be backward in sensorimotor and perceptual development. If the school asks him to make discriminations he is not capable of making, this tends to create anxiety, a negative attitude toward school, and avoidance of the very activities in which he needs practice and instruction. His difficulties accumulate. Two possibilities of treatment are (1) to delay reading and writing and (2) to build up the perceptual abilities that he needs for success in reading. A combination of the two is best.

DIAGNOSIS THROUGH ORAL READING IN HIGH SCHOOL AND COLLEGE

The difficulties of high school and college students in basic vocabulary, word recognition skills, phrasing, and expression likewise may be detected in oral reading. Lack of a basic sight vocabulary and efficient word recognition skills often are an explanation of students' slow reading. Poor phrasing may reveal ignorance of language patterns. In some cases, errors in pronunciation may be related to errors in comprehension. Auditory defects may be associated with poor reading, especially in children who have been taught by the phonetic method.

To illustrate the diagnostic use of oral reading on the high school and college level, the four oral reading paragraphs in the Reading Diagnostic Record for High School and College Students (Strang and others, 1952) may be used. Paragraphs A and B are at approximaely fifth- or sixth-grade level of difficulty; paragraph C is approximately college freshman level; paragraph D is from Dewey's *Human Nature and Conduct* and will be comprehended only by the more mature readers. The four paragraphs are as follows:

> READING PASSAGE A   Fear, like anger, stops the flow of the digestive juices. In India a test was once used to tell whether or not a prisoner was guilty of a crime. The man was given a handful of dry rice to put in his mouth. He was told to keep the rice in his mouth a few minutes. If the prisoner had committed a crime and was very much frightened, his saliva would stop flowing and the rice would remain dry. If he was not guilty and had no fear of being punished, his saliva would flow as usual and the rice would be wet.

> READING PASSAGE B   The earth has written its own story. Like all the books in the world, it cannot tell everything. Like all very old books, this

book of the earth has missing pages. In places the words are dim or in a language men have not yet learned to understand. But the book is there— a thrilling story of strange and mysterious things, of living creatures so small they have to be imagined, and of monsters the like of which we shall never see alive. The pages of the book are the layers of rock that lie one on top of another.

READING PASSAGE C   The widespread realization of the importance of "the human factor" is a striking feature of present-day civilization. More and more attention is being paid to psychological characteristics of human beings. In industry we attempt to discover the main temperamental qualities and abilities that influence an individual's adjustment to his job, and we explore the attitudes of employees to working conditions or to their employers. In education we try to guide parents and teachers as to the best means of dealing with children at home and at school, and treat the maladjusted and the delinquent at Psychological and Guidance Clinics.

READING PASSAGE D   Actual social change is never so great as apparent change. Ways of belief, of expectation, of judgment, and attendant emotional dispositions of like and dislike are not easily modified after they have once taken shape. Political and legal institutions may be altered, even abolished; but the bulk of popular thought which has been shaped to their pattern persists. This is why glowing predictions of the immediate coming of a social millennium terminate so uniformly in disappointment, which gives point to the standing suspicion of the cynical conservative about radical changes. Habits of thought outlive modifications in habits of overt action.

The directions to students are simple: "Read the following paragraph aloud as you usually read orally." While the student reads, the examiner records errors by the method already described. He also observes phrasing, intonation, stress, and pauses that indicate the student's understanding of the language structure of the selection. It is easy to detect word-by-word reading, mechanical division of sentences into parts of phrases and clauses, and other evidences of failure to read in thought units. More subtle aspects of expression also should be noted. Performance may cover a range from colorless monotone to the richness of feeling and significance that a great actor gives to every line.

The student's comprehension is first tested by an unstructured, creative-response question, such as "What did the author say?" This free-response question is followed by specific comprehension questions to test the ability to get the main ideas and important details, to interpret, to draw inferences and conclusions, and to explain key words and phrases.

To obtain additional understanding of the relation between the student's oral and silent reading comprehension, the examiner may ask him to read the same paragraph silently.

The student's remarks and expressive movements may reveal his attitudes. The poor reader frequently shows embarrassment at being asked to read orally. He is apologetic and insecure. Occasionally a student seems to exercise no critical judgment; he appears to be content with an exceedingly poor performance. A few students take an objective attitude toward their reading and express interest in the diagnostic procedure.

The student's ability to express in his own words what he has just read orally gives still more information about the way his mind works while reading and communicating what he has read. The wide range of responses to the question "What did the author say?" may be rated from 0 to 5 on a scale such as the following:

Rating	*Response*
0	No response Inability to understand the paragraph: "I never know what I read aloud." "I can't explain." Inability to remember what one has read: "I don't remember."
1	Totally inadequate—vague; gives no idea of the content of the paragraph. Examples: Passage A: "It was an interesting story." Passage B: "You get knowledge from books." Passage C: "Everybody is doing something for human beings." Passage D: "Things change."
2	Very inadequate—very brief, fragmentary, general, or partly inaccurate. Examples: Passage A: "India has a test of guilt." Passage B: "The rocks are pages of a book." Passage C: "That the psychological factor of people is studied." Passage D: "Opinions of people do not change."
3	Inadequate—accurate but too brief; a generalization; one important idea. Examples: Passage A: "Fear stops the flow of saliva." Passage B: "The earth has written its own story." Passage C: "The human factor is important." Passage D: "Habits of thought are hard to change."
4	Adequate—accurate summary of the passage. Examples: Passage A: "Fear stops the flow of saliva. This fact was used in India to tell whether a person was guilty or not." Passage B: "The author has compared the earth to a book. What is found in the layers of rock is compared to the writing in

Rating	*Response*

a book. He feels we can read the history of the world from rock formations."

Passage C: "There is at present an emphasis being placed on understanding the individual by employers, parents and teachers. Maladjusted individuals are being studied in clinical situations."

Passage D: "Attitudes remain and are harder to change than the more outward aspects of culture."

5   Superior—relationship of main points and details summarized somewhat creatively. Examples:

Passage A: "Anger and fear stop the digestive juices. A recognition of this fact caused the rice test to be used in India as a test of guilt. A man suspected of a crime was given a mouthful of dry rice. If the rice became moist it showed lack of fear and he was judged guiltless."

Passage B: "The author compared the geology of the earth (its rock formations) to the pages in a very old book—some of them missing, and others not entirely clear."

Passage C: "We are becoming increasingly interested in the individuality of people. In industry attempts are being made to understand the factors of the adjustment of the individual to his job. In education we cooperate with parents in the study of children through psychological and guidance clinics."

Passage D: "Ways of belief and judgment are not easily modified after they have taken shape. There is always a lag between social change and popular thought—that is, institutions change but people's attitudes change more slowly."

The student's attempts to summarize these paragraphs give insight into his ability to comprehend and communicate what he has read. Some students who are able to identify statements as false or true and to answer multiple-choice questions correctly cannot coherently express an author's thought in their own words. Other students who make no errors in pronunciation and read fluently reveal, when checked for comprehension, that their reading has been little more than word calling and that they have not learned to read with the intent to understand, remember, and communicate.

This type of free or creative response, unlike the questions in the usual standardized test, is purposely unstructured so as to reveal more about the student's unique and habitual approach to reading. Does he pick out a few scattered details or the main ideas? Does he try to condense the author's thought into a short, succinct statement? Does he comprehend the author's whole pattern of thought? Does he enhance the author's thought by reflection and reference to his own experience? The rating of 3 may be obtained by a student who habitually makes a terse, precise summary. Such a response is often appropriate, and the student should be commended for this ability. At the same time, it should be pointed out that ratings of 4 and 5 are given for more complete and creative summaries. Information of this kind could also be obtained by having the group read the paragraphs silently.

To obtain more comprehensive diagnostic information, a wider variety of paragraphs should be used. These would include poetry, other types of literature, and selections from each of the content fields.

If time permits, the teacher may give instruction after the student has read and responded to the paragraphs. In the first paragraph the structure is clear-cut: the topic sentence, followed by a block of illustration:

> Fear and anger stop digestion.
>
> A test of guilt in India illustrates this generalization.

In the second paragraph, the main idea is again found in the first sentence. The topic sentence is followed by statements of limitation. The word *but* signals a contrast. In the last sentence the main idea is reinforced:

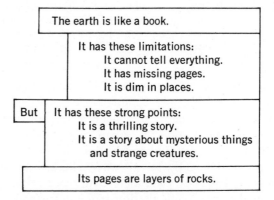

> The earth is like a book.
>
> It has these limitations:
>   It cannot tell everything.
>   It has missing pages.
>   It is dim in places.
>
> But It has these strong points:
>   It is a thrilling story.
>   It is a story about mysterious things and strange creatures.
>
> Its pages are layers of rocks.

In the third paragraph, the first two sentences express the main idea. The remaining two sentences give illustrations of it:

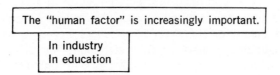

> The "human factor" is increasingly important.
>
> In industry
> In education

The fourth paragraph requires detailed analysis of each sentence. The first sentence is the topic sentence. The next two explain the two main concepts contrasted in the first sentence. The next sentences support the main idea, and the last sentence repeats the main idea in different words.

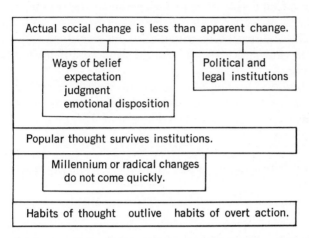

Instruction in sentence and paragraph structure is basic. In simply written paragraphs of a traditional pattern, the main idea can be quickly recognized. In paragraphs packed with ideas, such as D above, one must analyze the contributions made by each sentence to the structure of the thought. Other paragraphs would lend themselves to an analysis of the purposes for which the paragraphs were written and the various kinds of relationships expressed in the paragraphs, such as cause and effect, sequence of ideas, comparison or contrast.

CONCLUDING STATEMENT

In the primary grades children comprehend printed words when they pronounce words whose meaning is already familiar to them. For this reason any opportunity for children to read aloud enables the teacher to appraise their comprehension of the sentences as well as their word recognition skills. Observing children as they read aloud may also give clues to word calling, to fluency as compared with word-by-word reading, and to interest and attitude toward reading. In an audience situation, proficiency in skills of interpretation is indicated by the reaction of the audience to the child's reading as well as by direct observation of the reader.

In the primary grades, oral reading is an important diagnostic procedure; the teacher is far from being a passive listener when the child reads aloud. In the upper grades, the teacher's observation of the student in situations in which he needs to read aloud yields important understanding of his phrasing and interpretation of the passage, his attitude toward reading and toward himself, and the audience's response to his reading. To test his comprehension of factual material, he should be asked both an unstructured question and specific, searching questions concerned with vocabulary, sentence and paragraph structure, and higher levels of interpretation and critical reading.

Standardized oral reading tests, which are described in Chapter 10, aid the teacher in appraising an individual's oral reading more precisely and with reference to the performance of others of his age and grade.

SUGGESTED PROBLEMS: PRACTICE AND DEMONSTRATION

1. In what ways may a teacher quickly obtain information about the oral reading of each new student without causing embarrassment to the poor reader?

2. Record a pupil's reading of a paragraph orally. Play it back and mark the errors he makes as suggested in the first section of this chapter. Do this several times until you have gained proficiency in the technique. Make an interpretation of the pupil's oral reading and recommendations for helping him to improve.

3. Make an analysis of your own oral reading of each of the four paragraphs on pages 72–73 and your response to the question. "What did the author say?" Rate your answers on a 5-point scale from totally inadequate to superior.

4. Analyze the task of oral reading from the standpoint of the desire to communicate, basic speaking abilities, and skills in interpreting a selection to an audience, e.g.:

    Chooses appropriate selection for reading aloud

    Reads selection silently with comprehension

    Assumes proper posture for reading to audience

    Wants to share his enjoyment of a selection with an audience

    Articulates words clearly

    Phrases selection in thought units

    Reads with appropriate emphasis and expression

    Makes mental images of descriptive passages

    Accepts audience reaction graciously

REFERENCES

BUSWELL, GUY T.: *Non-oral Reading: A Study of Its Use in the Chicago Public Schools*, Supplementary Educational Monograph no. 60, The University of Chicago Press, Chicago, 1945.

DAVY, RUTH A.: "Adaptations of Progressive Choice Method for Teaching Reading to Retarded Children," *American Journal of Mental Deficiency*, 67:274–280, September, 1962.

DOLCH, E. W.: *The Basic Sight Word Test*, The Garrard Press, Champaign, Ill., 1942.

GRAY, WILLIAM S.: *Gray Oral Reading Test*, The Bobbs-Merrill Company, Inc., Indianapolis, 1963.

LANCASTER, LOUISE: *Introducing English: An Oral Pre-reading Program for Spanish-speaking Primary Pupils*, Houghton Mifflin Company, Boston, 1966.

MC CULLOUGH, CONSTANCE M.: *McCullough Word Analysis Test*, Ginn and Company, Boston, 1962.

NATCHEZ, GLADYS: "Oral Reading Used as an Indicator of Reactions to Frustration," *Journal of Educational Research*, 54:308–311, April, 1961.

ROBINSON, H. ALAN: "A Study of the Techniques of Word Identification," *The Reading Teacher*, 16:238–242, January, 1963.

RUSSELL, DAVID: *Listening Aids through the Grades: One Hundred Ninety Listening Activities*, Teachers College Press, Columbia University, New York, 1959.

—————— and ETTA E. KARP: *Reading Aids through the Grades: Three Hundred Developmental Reading Activities*, Teachers College Press, Columbia University, New York, 1956.

SPACHE, GEORGE D.: *Resources in Teaching Reading*, Reading Laboratory, University of Florida, Gainesville, 1955.

STRANG, RUTH: "Developing Oral Expression," *National Elementary Principal*, 45:36–41, November, 1965.

—————— and others: *Reading Diagnostic Record for High School and College Students*, Teachers College Press, Columbia University, New York, 1952.

SUGGESTED READINGS

ARTLEY, A. STERL: "The Place of Oral Reading in a Modern Reading Program," *A Report of the Thirteenth Annual Conference and Course on Reading*, University of Pittsburgh, Pittsburgh, June 17–28, 1957, pp. 105–107.

BROOKS, NELSON H.: *Language and Language Learning*, Harcourt, Brace & World, Inc., New York, 1960.

DELLA-PIANA, GABRIEL: "Analysis of Oral Reading Errors: Standardization, Norms, and Validity," *The Reading Teacher*, 15:254–257, January, 1962.

GRAY, WILLIAM S.: *On Their Own in Reading*, 2d ed., Scott, Foresman and Company, Chicago, 1960.

HERRICK, VIRGIL, and LELAND JACOBS: *Children and the Language Arts*, Prentice-Hall, Inc., Englewood Cliffs, N.J., 1955.

HILL, E.: "Diagnosis and Correction of Oral Reading Skills," in *Conference on Reading*, The University of Pittsburgh Press, Pittsburgh, 1960, pp. 151–154.

KERFOOT, JAMES F.: "An Instructional View of Reading Diagnosis," *Reading and Inquiry, International Reading Association Conference Proceedings*, vol. 10, 1965, pp. 215–219.

PRONOVOST, WILBERT L.: *The Teaching of Speaking and Listening in the Elementary School*, Longmans, Green & Co., Inc., New York, 1959.

ROBERTS, PAUL: *English Sentences*, Harcourt, Brace & World, Inc., New York, 1962.

ROBINSON, HELEN: *Oral Aspects of Reading, Proceedings of the Annual Conference on Reading*, The University of Chicago Press, Chicago, 1955.

RUESCH, JURGEN: *Therapeutic Communication*, W. W. Norton & Company, Inc., New York, 1961.

SPACHE, GEORGE D.: "Clinical Assessment of Reading Skills," *Reading and Inquiry, International Reading Association Conference Proceedings*, vol. 10, 1965, pp. 202–205.

Chapter Five

INTROSPECTIVE–RETROSPECTIVE REPORTS

Teachers and students are partners in the diagnostic process. Asking students to appraise their own reading shows the teacher's faith in the resources within each individual. Nobody knows better than the reader himself how he feels about reading and what makes reading easy or difficult for him. To be sure, some students may be reluctant to express themselves freely. Some may distort their true feelings. Some may lack the ability to analyze their reading problem. On the other hand, most students, when encouraged to write their educational autobiographies, subjective essays, or other kinds of self-evaluation, seldom fail to show considerable insight.

Retrospective reports may be made under different conditions and by different methods. They may be obtained while teaching, in panel discussions, through written reports, in diary records, and in personal interviews.

Retrospective-introspective verbalizations have possible value to the persons who make them, to teachers and counselors, and as a research technique. They show how the individual views his private world and give an understanding of mental processes that occur between the visual impression of the printed page and some mental or motor response to it. The students become more aware of the operations they are or have been using and the kind of thinking that results in accurate comprehension or in errors. Their perception of events to a large extent determines their behavior. The teacher learns which methods are used by good readers and poor readers and by individuals of different ages, abilities, and backgrounds. As a means of collecting data, these techniques have been used in a number of reading research studies (Strang, 1967).

RETROSPECTIVE REPORTS OBTAINED WHILE TEACHING

Retrospection should become an important part of the teaching-learning process. When a student pronounces an unfamiliar word correctly, or states the author's thought accurately, or makes a pertinent critical comment on a passage that he has read, the teacher may ask him how he did it. By describing his successful reading procedures, he is more likely to use them in reading other selections. In a class discussion with junior high school students, one teacher evoked many insights into their reading processes during a silent reading period. Members of the class profit by hearing about methods that good readers use.

THE READING AUTOBIOGRAPHY

The most common kind of retrospective report is the reading autobiography. What is a reading autobiography? What kinds of information can be obtained from it? How can it be used?

A reading autobiography is an oral or written developmental history of a student's reading experiences. Students with limited writing ability prefer the oral autobiography. Some of the most seriously retarded readers will welcome the opportunity to express their resentments, discouragements, and embarrassment about their poor reading. The personal attention of an adult who listens with interest and accepts what they say often stimulates them to try to find what is wrong with their reading and how they can improve.

The kind of information that is obtained from the reading autobiography will depend partly upon the directions that are given. These may take the form of a series of specific questions such as the following: [1]

	Yes	No	
1.	_____	_____	Did you learn to read before you came to school?
2.	_____	_____	Did any member of your family try to teach you to read?
3.	_____	_____	Did anyone often read aloud to you in your early preschool years?
4.	_____	_____	Do you remember the name of the first book you ever read?
5.	_____	_____	As a child, did you prefer books that were illustrated?

[1] Questionnaire developed by Mr. Paul Eagan and his tenth-grade class at Tucson (Ariz.) High School.

	Yes	No	
6.	___	___	Do you usually have something other than school work that you are currently reading?
7.	___	___	Do you read in bed?
8.	___	___	Do you reread a book you particularly enjoyed?
9.	___	___	Do you like to have the radio or record player on while you read?
10.	___	___	When you are reading a book in which you are particularly interested, do you often neglect other things?
11.	___	___	Do you ever read to younger children?
12.	___	___	Do you often find you have been reading without comprehending the meaning?
13.	___	___	Does your mother or father sometimes read aloud to the family?
14.	___	___	Does your family have group discussions of current events?
15.	___	___	Is more than one language spoken in your home?
16.	___	___	Do you read for pleasure during vacation time?
17.	___	___	Do you dislike English classes?
18.	___	___	Do you have a personal library of your own?
19.	___	___	Does your family subscribe to book clubs?
20.	___	___	Do you have and use a library card?
21.	___	___	Do you prefer reading the "digest" form of a novel in preference to the unabridged version?
22.	___	___	Do you read at the breakfast table?
23.	___	___	Do you agree with the girl who said, "Although I am in many clubs and engage in other activities, reading a good book is 'my first choice' "?
24.	___	___	When confined to bed with minor illnesses do you look forward to reading?
25.	___	___	Do you have a car available for your use?
26.	___	___	Do you ever read while riding in cars or buses?
27.	___	___	Do you read books or stories aloud with a friend?

28. How would you classify yourself as to reading speed (average reading speed for high school texts is around 250 wpm): _____ Average reader, _____ Slow reader, _____ fast reader?

29. Does reading make you sleepy? _____ Yes _____ No _____ Sometimes.

30. Do the members of your family recommend books and articles for each other? _____ Yes _____ No _____ Sometimes.

31. I go out approximately _____ evenings a week.

32. I spend _____ hours per week on extracurricular activities (clubs, sports, publications, etc.).

33. We have _____ television sets in our home.
    (number of)

34. I (do) (do not) watch television more than I read for pleasure.

35. Writing original compositions (has) (has not) helped my interest in reading.

36. I have usually obtained (better) (worse) grades in English than in mathematics.

37. Circle the parts of the newspaper that you usually read:
    A. Comics   C. Sports   E. Society
    B. News items   D. Editorials

38. In my spare time I do the following most frequently (number 1 to 4 in order of frequency):
    Watch television   Visit with friends
    Read   Other

39. Circle the types of books read aloud in your home:
    A. Juvenile literature   D. Current events
    B. Novels   E. None
    C. Short stories   F. Other (tell what kind)

40. In our home there are the following types of reading material:
    A. Hardback books consisting of (give number of)
       1. Approximately _____ novels, short stories, plays
       2. Approximately _____ essays and nonfiction other than science
       3. Approximately _____ scientific
       4. Approximately _____ others
    B. Paperback books _____
    C. Magazines as follows (list the names):
       _____   _____
       _____   _____

41. I make use of our
    A. Public library _____ times a month.
    B. School library _____ times a week.

42. When I read for my own pleasure I choose mostly (check):
    A. Novels   D. Science fiction
    B. Short stories   E. Essays
    C. Comic books   F. Other (name them)

43. Does the fact that you are expected to make a report on a book: ___ detract from your enjoyment of it, ___ deepen your understanding and enjoyment of it, ___ neither answer applies in all instances.

44. As far as your reading speed is concerned, do you: ___ read everything at about the same speed, ___ frequently "scan" certain types of reading material, or ___ change your speed with the kind of material and your purpose?

45. Do you prefer: ___ to read aloud, ___ to be read to, ___ to read to yourself?

46. When a "pleasure" book fails to interest you after twenty-five pages or so, do

you: ___ go ahead and finish it anyway, ___ stop reading it, ___ decide to read it at a later date?

47. Our family participated in reading aloud in the following ways:
    A. My ___ mother ___ father read to us at preschool age.
    B. My ___ mother ___ father have always read to us.
    C. My ___ mother ___ father never read to us.

48. How many schools have you attended since the first grade?

49. When I come across a word I don't know: I ___ look it up in the dictionary, ___ try to guess at its meaning from the context, ___ try to pronounce it by dividing it into syllables, ___ try to pronounce it by sounding it out, ___ skip over it. (Check more than one if they apply.)

50. Circle the following practices you follow when reading school work:
    A. Summarize material after you read it
    B. Raise questions before or when reading and then read to find the answers
    C. Underline key statements in your text during study
    D. Take notes for future reference: after reading a section ___, while reading ___

If these questions have called to your mind any comments you would like to make, please use the remaining space to do so. Any additions to this reading survey that you may be able to suggest would be greatly appreciated.

Although the checklist form of autobiography is easy to write and can be quickly tabulated, it does not give unique, personal insights or show relationships between separate items or indicate their relative importance. Unstructured questions that invite spontaneous creative response usually give more significant information.

To obtain a sequential and circumstantial written account of a student's reading development, one may ask questions that suggest the desired content, as in the following form:

Name _____ Age_____ Grade _____ Date _____

MY READING AUTOBIOGRAPHY

Here is a chance to write the history of your reading. Begin with your preschool experiences. Describe the very first reading you did. How did you learn to read? Tell about your reading in and out of school in the first grade, second grade, and so on through each year of elementary school. Tell about your reading right up to today. What do you read? What do you like to read? Why is reading hard or easy for you? Do you find reading in the junior high school harder than reading in the elementary school? Why?

Another approach is to give pupils a few questions to guide them in writing a free autobiography, such as:

Early experiences:
　When did you start to read?
　What did you read? (titles)
　Did you enjoy reading?
　What have been your reading interests through the years?
　Who or what has influenced your attitude toward reading?

Present experiences:
　What kind of reading do you enjoy now—books, magazines, newspapers, short stories, poetry?
　What do other members of your family like to read?
　What kind of reading do you dislike?
　When and where do you do most of your reading?
　What kind of reading material do you have in your home?
　When do you use the library?
　How do you read—fast or slow, eagerly or reluctantly, etc.?

Future experience:
　Are you dissatisfied with any of your reading habits, such as speed, or with your ability to understand and remember what you have read?
　If you have any trouble with reading, what kind of trouble is it, and what do you think can be done about it?

The students do not answer these questions specifically; they read them beforehand to get an idea of what should be included in a developmental history of their reading experiences and then write freely.

In a heterogeneous class, the teacher will obtain autobiographies that cover a wide range of content and writing ability. The following are samples of the reading autobiographies of students, ranging from slow learners to gifted students. The spelling and wording are unchanged.

A. In find my tow in read wend I was in the three grade and I didt know how to read wrold.

in school my mand traper is in English therr we have to read alouter. An I dont like to stande up to read at any time.

The only book I read is a motorcycle and a car book. I get the book one every month. And my tray to read much better because wend I get old eneft I wind like to become of State Tooper. And in that you have to have a high school deplomur. Our get in the motor cycle part of the army.

I sterp to have read troullz wend I was 13 year old and sent thin I have tropz.

B. The first time I can recall my reading anything was the book I was given in grade school. The book was of a boy and a horse. The every day life of the two were told. All through grade school I was given a book which was a half-term lower than the grade in which I was. My marks were not of the highest when I finished grade school.

   High school was not to grate a change for me because I was use to being with older people than myself. I had a deftinit gold when I entered high school which was to go thru high school with the highest makes I could get. I which to go to college and the only way that would be possible would be to get a scholarship for my gymnistics. If I did get the schollarship I would have to go to gym workout, therefor I would have to be able to do my classrork much faster than the other students.

C. Reading most people think your suppose to know or any way by the time you get out of grade school. As far back as I remember I have always had trouble reading but just realized it recently. This happened because I was never tested for it. I always had books around the house which I would start and put down. I would say it is boring, uninteresting or some excuse. My mother always would say "pick up a book." I would for five minutes and put it down again. My parents both read a great deal.

D. I shall try to give you a brief outline of my reading ability. As I told you yesterday I do very little reading. In the past few years my reading matter included magazines, comic books and newspapers. In the newspaper, I used to read the front page and the sport section. Since we have television in our house, I rely mostly on that to give me the world affairs of today. When there is an article about sports I like to read it especially if it is about baseball.

   I am not too interested in doing any reading for school. Most of the time I leave my required reading for the last minute.

   When I start to read I find that I am reading words and not getting the gist of the particular passage. The aid I am seeking is to help me to read with more understanding and care.

   I expect to go to college and I understand that reading is very important there, if I expect to do college work.

E. I guess I started to read some time during the 1st grade but before that both of my parents had read a great deal to me. I can remember having *To Think That It Happened On Mulberry Street* read to me and later reading other books by Dr. Seuse and so by the time I began to be taught to read in school the stories about "Jack & Jane" were more than a little dull.

   My father continued to read to both my brother and I until I was about 12 and even now occasionally will read us a passage of a good book.

   My reading interests from the time I was eight to about eleven consisted primarily of glancing through *Popular Mechanics, Popular Science,* and various flying magazines. At this time my interests turned towards science fiction & adventure. I think I went through all the Steven W. Meder & Howard Pease books in the Branch Library in my neighborhood & also several books by Robert Heihline. My reading became more narrow in the period between 12 & 14 and confined itself almost exclusively to science fiction. I read from cover to cover almost every issue of *Galaxy* & *Astounding Science Fiction* & many novels & short stories in that vein.

My interest recently have been mostly of a more classical nature because, for the first time, I am looking about my own house for reading material. For the purpose of giving you an idea of the nature of my most recent reading I'll list a few:

> *Stendhal* by Matthew Josephson
> *Martin Eden* by Jack London
> *Spoon River Anthology* by Edgar Lee Masters
> *Cross & the Arrow* by Albert Maltz
> *Inside Africa* by John Gunther
> *Insolent Chariots* by John Keats

I hadn't until recently used the Library to any extent but I was driven to it by the research necessary on my term theme & I find it not at all unpleasant. Since then I have spent a great deal of time studying & reading at the library because it is directly across the street from the high school.

I don't think there is any kind of reading that I dislike unless it is written in an elementary or overly technical fashion but I do tend to stay away from those subject which are unfamiliar to me.

During the school year my reading is done mostly just before I go to sleep or just after I wake but during the summer I just sit myself down with a book & read cover to cover unless it is of a technical nature and then it becomes to much to read in one sitting.

It seems to me that my reading is slow & it takes me forever & a day to get through only a few pages & when it comes to assigned reading, book reports, & the like it requires enormous amounts of my time although I enjoy most of what I read. This seems to be where my trouble lies I understand & enjoy most of what I read but I read far to slowly.

I don't know exactly what corrective measures I will undergo here but if they can speed up my reading without an appreciable drop in comprehension I would be more than satisfied.

What a vast difference in reading ability and in general maturity is represented in this small sampling of autobiographies! And what a wealth of diagnostic information they give about spelling and handwriting, vocabulary, organization of ideas, sentence structure, and overall richness of expression and depth of thought! Some accounts give admirable detail concerning the subject's early reading experiences, when and how he was taught, the range and variety of his reading, his home background, and his use of available resources. Other autobiographies reveal the writer's attitude, his special reading interests, and his difficulties. Sometimes they include his ideas about ways to overcome the difficulties that he has recognized.

Autobiography B, for example, was written by a seventeen-year-old boy whose Stanford-Binet IQ was 112 and whose scores on the survey test of the Diagnostic Reading Tests (Committee on Diagnostic Reading Tests, 1947–1958) were at the 2d percentile in rate and at the 18th percentile on total reading. On the Nelson-Denny Reading Test (1929–1960) his paragraph comprehension was at the 20th percentile and his vocabulary at the 40th percentile. He called his autobiography "The Story of My Reading"; it showed a long history of reading difficulty, recognized by the boy himself. His marks in elementary school reflected his reading inability and possibly other conditions which were affecting his achievement in other school work. His expressed desire to succeed in high school and to go to college helped the reading teacher to understand this boy's motivation and to take steps to help him realize his potentialities and achieve his goals.

In a number of autobiographies, a typical development picture emerges: a keen interest in reading in the first grades, which was lost for several years and then regained in the teens when the practical importance of reading became more evident.

Another common pattern is initial success in the primary grades followed by recognition of difficulty in the fourth and fifth grades.

Fortunately, some students make steady progress toward increasingly mature reading. Such progress was described by a gifted tenth-grade girl:

> When I first started to read I read very widely. I was kind of a bookworm in my younger days, and I accepted what I read completely as fact. But once I started to go into a subject—the life of Queen Elizabeth I, for instance—I read many books about her. After I had read five or six, I began to run up against contradictions. Then I began to think for myself a little more, and I think that is what makes a mature reader.

It is difficult but very important to learn more about bilingual children's perception of their reading problems. Although their ability to express their ideas in the second language is limited, they will give clues to their difficulties and how they overcome them. At seventeen one girl obtained a rating of grade 6.2 on vocabulary and 7.3 on comprehension on a standardized reading test. She had the desire to read and took initiative and responsibility for her own learning:

> When I first came to school I didn't know a word of English. In the first grade I learned to understand and speak a little. My parents didn't have time to read to me or to help me with my learning. When I got to the third grade I read quite well, but when I heard the other kids read faster, I would become panic. I love to read and I read anything that I am able to read. I still have trouble with new words. I watch closely how the teacher pronounces the new words, and I am learning.

Writing an educational autobiography may help the individual to get perspective on his reading, set goals for himself, and fill gaps in his reading development.

INTROSPECTIVE–RETROSPECTIVE STUDY OF THE READING PROCESS

Although students can explain their difficulties and some of the methods that have helped them to read better, it takes training to be able to describe the reading process itself, i.e., what really goes on in their minds between seeing the printed page and making some verbal or motor response to it. Too often they give their thoughts about what they have read rather than describing the thinking process that went on while they were reading. However, with practice they sometimes give glimpses of the process (1) in class discussions, (2) in their reading autobiographies, (3) in response to questions immediately following a reading exercise, and (4) in interviews.

In class discussions

At any time during the day the teacher may supplement his observation of students' responses to his instruction by asking an individual how he managed to pronounce an unfamiliar word, how he acquired the meaning of a difficult word (Elfert, 1960), or how he comprehended the author's thought so clearly.

The following are illustrations of the kind of insights that may be obtained in this way. In a first-grade class, the teacher obtained responses of this kind:

TEACHER: How did you know the new word *bring?*
PUPIL: I knew *sing* and put the *br* sound in place of *s.*
TEACHER: How did you know *singing?*
PUPIL: I knew *sing* and *ing* and I put them together.
TEACHER: How did you know that duck's name, *Ping?*
PUPIL: It begins like *pig* and then *ing.*
TEACHER: How did you know the word *seem?*
PUPIL: By the two *e*'s together.
TEACHER: How did you know the word *bark?*
PUPIL: Because I sounded the *b* and it was with *a* and *r* and ends in *k.*
TEACHER: Did anyone have a different way?
PUPIL: It looks like *park.*
TEACHER: What about *pail?*
PUPIL: It has two vowels together, so the *a* is long and the *i* is silent.
TEACHER: The title of the story—how did you know it was "Oswald"?

PUPIL: I saw it in the newspaper.

PUPIL: Yes, Oswald, he killed the President.

From these few retrospective reports the teacher, Mrs. Pamela Hoecker,[2] learned about the variety of ways in which her pupils were recognizing new words.

As part of the reading autobiography

The reading autobiography sometimes gives clues of a student's reading process and difficulties. In the following autobiography, a sixteen-year-old girl tried to explain her difficulty in reading history:

> To begin with, I don't like to read to myself. Probably because I'm not a good reader. It takes me quite a while to read and know what I just read. I am an especially poor reader if the subject doesn't interest me.
>
> Last year I didn't do well in World History because I found it very boring. It was very foolish of me to have decided from the beginning of the year that I couldn't do it. . . .
>
> If I really put my mind to a chapter I can learn it. The only thing wrong is that I read so slowly. If I want to learn what is in the chapter I have to read it carefully. Then after I've been reading for a while I get tired and start thinking of the other homework I've got or the dirty dishes that have to be washed. . . . If I can't give my undivided attention to the assignment I'm sunk.

Other able learners try to describe and analyze their reading processes, as in the following quotation:

> When I am up against some text material or something else that is concentrated and difficult to get immediately, I sometimes will go on reading without really coordinating my mind with the task; I will keep on reading the words without thinking about them at all. When I have come to the end of a page, I wouldn't be able to say what was on it. I have read it but it seems as though my eyes were working separately from my brain.

In response to questions immediately following a reading exercise

Immediately after reading a selection and answering the comprehension questions on it, the teacher may ask students certain questions about their reading process:

What did you do to get the main ideas?

What did you do to get the details?

What did you do when you met a word you did not know?

[2] First-grade teacher in District #1, Tucson, Ariz.

These and other questions have elicited responses such as the following from junior and senior high school students:

> If the selection is familiar to me and simple to understand, I read through it fast or skim over it.

> When I read a paragraph, I try to pick out the main points and establish them in my mind; after that I look for and try to remember important dates and details.

> When reading a news story, I read all details, for a headline just tells what happened; it doesn't give the details or tell why.

> When I do not know a word, I go back over the paragraph and try to find its meaning.

> I read carefully and slowly and try to remember the main points from each part.

> I read very fast, even a history book. I get quite a good deal out of it, even at a fast rate. I do not go over my reading. Sometimes, however, I go through the pages I have read and look at the headings, recall as much as I can about each heading.

> If there is a complicated section that I don't understand, I read it over until I get it.

> If the lesson is a hard one, I reread it, very quickly to see if I've got everything out of it.

> I read more slowly than most people, but very seldom do I read the book over again, unless it is history or geography. Then I only read it again if I have forgotten important facts and statistics.

Comments like these, made after the students have corrected their own answers to the comprehension questions, evoke a lively and profitable discussion of reading methods.

In interviews

To avoid influencing the individual's response, some interviewers prefer to use a completely unstructured approach, while others help him to explore his thinking process by specific questions. Piaget (Inhelder and Piaget, 1958) uses the latter method in his experiments. He may first ask a general question and then further explore the child's answer by asking specific questions that require the child to defend or modify or explain his point of view. A combination of the initial, unstructured question which invites the individual to describe what went on in his mind when he read, followed by specific questions such as "Why did you select that as the main idea?" seems most appropriate for exploration of the reading process. At the very end, the interviewer might use the Rorschach technique of "testing the limits" by asking directly, "Did you try to divide the word into syllables? Did you look for key words in the paragraph?"

Squire (1960) obtained high school students' responses to four short stories by asking them to respond freely and completely in describing the "feelings, ideas, opinions, or reactions" that occurred to them while reading or at the end of each story. Studies of this kind give understanding of the operations students are using and reveal differences in their abilities to analyze the language and to interpret the meaning of the passages they have read.

Occasionally in an interview a reading client will show unusual insight into his reading process, as in the following excerpts from the case study of a fifteen-year-old boy with a WISC IQ of 114. In response to the worker's question "Could you tell me about your reading and what you feel are your reading problems?" he began:

> Well . . . mainly in school you have all those rules about how to read. They say to take a line and read it, but I can't do that. I have to take it word, word, word, and sometimes even half a word, and I lose the meaning of what I am reading. . . .
>
> You see, I'm awfully slow in my reading. People say to speed up your reading by taking a whole sentence. I just can't do that 'cause I'll just read the words and not know what I'm reading. . . .
>
> When I read a book, I want to see what's coming next and I'm going too slow to find out. . . .
>
> I think my major problem is distraction. I will be reading along and put myself in the character's place and I ask "What would I have done?" Then I start dreaming and the next thing I know I'll be thinking about other things. . . .
>
> If I don't know a word, I usually figure it out by the rest of the sentence.
>
> WORKER: Then you use context clues, don't you?
>
> CLIENT: Yeah, and if I don't know the word completely, I'm lazy, I say, "Well, maybe I'll figure it out tomorrow."

When the client feels that the interviewer is listening intently and appreciates his attempts to describe his reading process, he is stimulated to analyze the process to the best of his ability.

INTROSPECTIVE STUDY WHILE READING

The most difficult type of introspection is made while reading a given selection. There is always the danger here that simultaneous introspection may interfere with the student's normal reading process, thus creating an artificial, distorted picture. However, some students have been able to describe their reading-thinking process, to tell what was going on in their minds as they read a selection. This takes practice, beginning with a single sentence and working up to a selection several pages long.

The following are several students' descriptions of the methods they had just used in reading a four-page selection on reptiles taken from their ninth-grade science textbook.

A superior reader wrote: "When I read, my eyes followed the lines and sometimes went a few lines ahead of what I was reading. I didn't look back. I didn't read every word but I didn't skip any lines. I read all the way through the article without stopping."

A very poor reader made this analysis. "Sometimes I missed a line. I looked at almost every word. My eyes moved faster than my mind could read. Sometimes my thoughts wandered. I usually read too fast. I didn't think about the ideas in the lesson I was reading. I didn't concentrate on my reading."

Such responses serve as content for class discussion. The students who read most quickly and well can give the others, in words they can readily understand, suggestions about the reading methods that they have found most effective.

SELF-APPRAISAL OF STUDY SKILLS

A set of questions to guide students in their self-appraisal of study skills has been found to differentiate between college students of diverse proficiency. Successful readers responded affirmatively to the following items more often than did retarded readers:

1. Do you skim material before reading it in detail?

2. Do you summarize the selection after you read it?

3. Do you raise questions when reading and then read to find the answers?

4. Do you note key statements in your text during study?

5. Do you review the previous assignment before proceeding to read the current one?

6. When you sit down to study, do you make an effort to read as rapidly and as carefully as you can?

7. Do you plan a flexible study schedule in advance and adhere to its main features?

8. Do you immediately reread sections of your assignment which are not clear?

9. Are you careful not to skip graphs, tables, and charts when you read your assignment?

10. Do you take notes of key ideas after you have read each section?

For slow-learning students, self-evaluation questions should be exceedingly simple, clearly stated, and very few in number. For example:

1. Why do you want to read better?

2. What advantage would it be for you to be a better reader?

Eleven boys aged nine to eleven with an IQ range of 80 to 95 were asked the above questions. Their ability to communicate was extremely limited; their retardation in reading and writing was extraordinary. They particularly disliked direct questions. Every one of these boys was withdrawn and uncommunicative. The teacher asked the questions in a casual way during a reading session. He would say, for example, "That was a fine job, Roy. You really have come quite a way in reading. Do you feel there is an advantage for you in becoming a better reader?" In some cases he added, "Why do you want to be a better reader?"

Three of the boys did not know the meaning of the word *advantage* until it was explained. With a few exceptions, these three boys spontaneously and, as a matter of fact, quite truthfully replied, "I don't know." However, even in this noncommittal reply they revealed some information by variations in their tones of voice. Some seemed to feel great discomfort and anxiety; some answered with a "don't bother me and leave me alone" tone; a few with an open, frank tone; one with a mocking undertone. Three boys were more explicit. One said, "Not to be stupid"; two said, "To get better jobs"; and one of the latter added this significant statement, "So nobody can cheat me."

Meager as these answers were, they revealed three dominant motivations for reading as these severely retarded readers perceived them: to maintain self-esteem, to be successful in a vocation, and not to be defenseless in a predatory society.

Another approach to slow-learning students, which incidentally is useful also in building their language patterns, is to ask a few simple questions about their reading environment, such as the following:

Question	One pupil's response
What I read	Funnybook
When I read	I dot know when
Where I read	Home
What books are in my house	All kinds off book
My mother reads	My mother reads the newspaper
My father reads	(Student wrote "all kinds" then crossed it out and wrote "My father reads the Bible.")
My brothers read	My brother reads the funnybooks
My sisters read	My sisters read storey book

This simple exercise gives a glimpse of the student's reading interests and the reading background of his home. It also shows difficulties in sentence structure and grammar.

SUBJECTIVE ESSAYS

A wider variety of information may be gained from subjective compositions. The following are topics that have elicited fascinating details about students' reading:

What Makes a Book Easy or Difficult to Read?

How Does Interest Affect My Reading?

How an Uninteresting Book Captured My Interest

How My Parents Helped or Hindered My Reading Development

How Books Have Influenced My Point of View, Attitudes, or Habits

How I Feel When I Read Aloud in Class

Children's perceptions largely determine their behavior. They are usually motivated by the acceptance and approval of the important persons in their lives—adults and peers. Their behavior is influenced by their perception of themselves and their perception of the way other people feel toward them. Davidson and Lang (1960, pp. 107–118) reported a positive correlation for fourth-, fifth-, and sixth-grade pupils between the children's perception of their teacher's feelings toward them and the children's perception of themselves. "The children who had a more favorable or more adequate self-concept, that is, those who achieved a higher self-perception score also perceived their teacher's feelings toward them more favorably" (p. 109). There was also a positive relation toward children's favorable perception of the teacher's feelings toward them and their academic achievement and classroom behavior. Introspective reports are a useful means of gaining understanding of perceptions that may be the key to serious reading problems.

In describing what makes a book easy to read, a high school student made this comment: "A book is easy if I am already acquainted with the subject and the terminology. Then I can fit my experience easily into the picture. If the book describes how to build or make things, it is easier to comprehend if steps in the process are illustrated and labeled."

In their essays on the manner in which early childhood experiences affected their reading, high school students often attributed their interest in reading to listening to children's classics and other books read aloud to them during the preschool years. One wrote: "Among other things, I remember most the times I would sit by my mother as she read Bible stories and other books such as *Heidi* to me."

Another high school student described his early experience in more detail:

> If I had to pick one person who influenced my reading most . . . I would pick my grandmother. She is the one who really started me reading. She used to sit and read to me by the hour when I was little. Now that I can read by myself, she just makes sure I have enough to read. She gives me about four or five books a year for my birthday or Christmas or some other occasion.
>
> I am quite an avid reader now and I think she is largely responsible for it (Strang and Eagan, 1961, p. 10).

Another boy gave this warning:

> In creating an interest in reading, I think it is important for adults to stay in the background. If they constantly badger the child by saying, "Why don't you read a book," they will build up an opposition to reading. On the other hand, they should set a goal for the child to strive toward (p. 11).

Other essays give insight into the role of the teacher in reading improvement:

> Because my teacher thought I was particularly good in reading I took a greater liking to it.

> The first person who stands out in my memories [as contributing to his reading development] would be my third grade teacher. . . . At this time I was having a little trouble pronouncing words. As I remember, she was the first teacher who was interested enough to stop and spend time on me. She explained how to pronounce words by syllables first and then put the syllables together (p. 11).

These few quotations give only a glimpse of the kinds of understanding that both teachers and students may gain from subjective essays.

STUDENTS' EVALUATION OF READING INSTRUCTION

Students can participate in improving reading instruction. No one should have a better basis for appraising a reading course than the students who have just taken it. Like the autobiography, evaluation forms may call for a wide range of responses—all the way from writing a completely unstructured appraisal to filling out a checklist.

One method of evaluation is to present the students with a list of the experiences they have had in the course and ask them to rate each according to its value in improving their reading. They should also tell why or in what way they think the experience was or was not helpful.

Each question on the following rating sheet calls for a statement of the reason for each rating:

Name_____Section_____Date_____

READING CLASS RATING SHEET

To each pupil: Please answer the following questions as completely and honestly as you can. By telling your teacher what you really think of this reading course, you will be helping him to improve the course for other boys and girls. Your answers will in no way influence your grade for the course; you need not even sign your name if you do not wish to. Thank you very much for your help and cooperation.

1. This course has helped me (underline one):
   (a) a great deal, *(b)* much, *(c)* some, *(d)* little, *(e)* not at all.
2. Please give your reasons for answering the first question the way you did. (You may use the other side of this sheet if necessary.)
3. Which activities helped you most? Explain.
4. Which activities helped you least? Explain.
5. I usually found the classes to be (underline one):
   (a) very interesting, *(b)* interesting, *(c)* of some interest, *(d)* of little interest, *(e)* of no interest. *Please tell why.*
6. Did this class in any way change your attitude toward reading? Please explain.
7. I am glad I took this course (check one): Yes ___, No ___. Why?
8. I believe a reading course next year for eighth-grade pupils would be helpful (check one): Yes ___, No ___. Why?
9. If an advanced course of this type were offered as an eighth-grade elective subject next year, I (would, might, wouldn't) elect to take it. (*Underline one word in parentheses.*)
10. Please write any other reactions to the course that you wish to add.

Obviously, the results of any subjective appraisal are valid only if the teacher obtains the interest and cooperation of the students.

DAILY SCHEDULE OR DIARY RECORD

The student may also contribute to the understanding of his reading by keeping a record of his daily activities for a week. For accuracy's sake he is asked to make entries all during the day, not to try to remember at the end of the day just what happened in the morning. If he is asked to include details about *what* he reads as well as *when* he reads, much may be learned about his reading habits and interests.

"Time is of the essence." It is our most common and valuable commodity. How do we spend it? "I'd like to read more, but I don't have the time." This is the excuse most frequently given by students who do little or no voluntary reading.

How can students become more aware of the way they use time? How can teachers gain information as to how much and what kind of reading their students are doing outside of school and what other activities are competing for their time?

The quickest and easiest way to obtain such information is to interest students in keeping a record of their daily activities for a school day and for a weekend. In presenting this idea, the teacher may use various appeals to ensure accuracy:

> Keeping this diary record is a way of helping you to save time for things you want to do.
>
> Other students have said, "It's fun to see how you spend your time, but it's sort of a nuisance to have to carry the record around with you all day."
>
> If you want to be scientific, you must be accurate in recording exactly what you do during the day.

As with all other kinds of personal documents, the daily schedule is worthless if the students are not interested and cooperative. No student should be forced to write a subjective-type record or composition if he objects to doing so. He can be given another kind of assignment.

The form for recording one's daily activities is simple. Plain lined paper may be used. The following directions and headings have been used successfully:

DAILY SCHEDULE

Directions: It is sort of fun to see how you spend your day. This is the way to keep a day's record or diary: Begin at 6:00 in the morning. Your first activity in the middle column will probably be "sleeping." When you get up, put the time on the second line under 6 A.M., and write in the middle column "got up, washed, and dressed." Then add the next thing you do and so on through the day until you go to bed at night. Carry this sheet around with you and write your activities as you engage in them during the day. Do not wait until the end of the day. Tell in detail what you do. For example, do not write just "read," but tell what you read. Do not say just "played," but tell what you played and with whom.

Time	*What I did in detail*	*No. of minutes in each activity*

Is this the way you usually spend a school day and a weekend? _____
If not, how is it different? _____

If the teacher wants to help students individually with their use of time, he asks them to sign their names on their schedules. If he wants to get an overview of the daily activities of his class or to use the records for research purposes, he may ask the students not to sign their names and thus avoid the inaccuracy that results from people's unconscious tendency to want to make a good impression.

It is amazing how much a teacher can learn about a class by spending an hour or two reading their daily schedules (Strang, 1953, pp. 336–357). He can learn how much or how little time students spend in reading, what they read, when they read, where they read, and what other activities are competing with their reading.

Some students include no reading at all. In other cases voluntary reading time is usurped by long assignments given by teachers who require a disproportionate amount of homework. Some students' days are overscheduled; they take private lessons in dancing, music, or French and engage in numerous social activities. With others, part-time employment occupies what might be leisure time. When children spend twenty-six hours a week viewing TV, they obviously have limited the time they could spend in reading. A very few seem to be reading excessively to the exclusion of outdoor activity and social experiences.

A class period may be profitably spent in discussing some of the students' schedules in a kind of "daily schedule clinic." The teacher reads a schedule aloud, anonymously of course, and the class members point out its good features, propose ways in which the individual might save time, and suggest the best times to fit in some voluntary reading. Such a discussion helps the student to make desirable and reasonable modifications of his original schedule. In individual conferences, the student may delve more deeply into the reasons why he is wasting time and reconsider his values and philosophy of life in relation to his use of time.

CONCLUDING STATEMENT

Each of these self-evaluation reports has possible therapeutic value for the person who writes it. The autobiography invites the writer to take an objective view of himself; it gives both student and teacher perspective on the writer's reading development. Compositions on various personal subjects give the individual a chance to express thoughts that may have been awaiting expression for a long time. The daily schedule shows the person how he is spending, or wasting, his time. When an interviewer invites an individual to describe his reading process and shows keen interest and appreciation of his attempts to do so, significant insights may be evoked.

Retrospective-introspective techniques give much needed understanding of the reading process to the students themselves as well as to counselors and reading teachers. These retrospective reports suggest reading instruction that teachers may give to students of different abilities and backgrounds.

SUGGESTED PROBLEMS: PRACTICE AND DEMONSTRATION

1. Write your own reading autobiography as a part of the study of your reading. What insights did you gain from it?

2. If you are teaching at present, obtain reading autobiographies from students in your class who are interested in writing or dictating them. As you read them, underline the especially significant statements and file them in each student's cumulative record folder.

3. Obtain one set of essays on any topic, such as those suggested in the section on Subjective Essays. Analyze and categorize these essays and summarize the students' ideas on each of the topics.

4. Obtain the interest and cooperation of a group of students in keeping a daily schedule for one school day and one weekend. Categorize the various

activities and calculate the number of minutes spent in each activity. Have students make bar graphs showing the average number of minutes spent per week in study; voluntary reading; looking at television; informal social activities with friends; conversation with members of family; listening to the radio; playing out of doors; part-time work or chores; group activities such as clubs, parties, trips, and excursions; sleep; and daily routines such as eating, washing, dressing. From these quantitative summaries draw conclusions about which activities are encroaching upon students' voluntary reading time. Make recommendations for a better-balanced schedule.

5. At one time in the history of psychology, extensive use was made of retrospection and introspection in research; later this method was somewhat discredited, but recently it has been used more extensively. Summarize the advantages and disadvantages of introspective and retrospective reports.

6. Work out at the beginning of your reading course, and later apply, a form for evaluating the instruction you give. Decide on the behavioral objectives and work out methods of obtaining evidence of whether these objectives have been attained.

REFERENCES

Committee on Diagnostic Reading Tests (Frances Oralind Triggs, chrm.): *Diagnostic Reading Tests*, Committee on Diagnostic Reading Tests, Inc., Mountain Home, N.C., 1947–1958.

CRONBACH, LEE J.: *Essentials of Psychological Testing*, 2d ed., Harper & Row, Publishers, Incorporated, New York, 1960.

DAVIDSON, HELEN H., and GERHARD LANG: "Children's Perceptions of Their Teacher's Feelings toward Them Related to Self-perception, School Achievement, and Behavior," *Journal of Experimental Education*, 24:107–118, December, 1960.

ELFERT, WILLIAM: "An Exploration of Sixth-grade Pupils' Acquisition of Word Meanings through Classroom Instruction," unpublished doctoral dissertation, Teachers College, Columbia University, New York, 1960.

INHELDER, BARBEL, and JEAN PIAGET: *The Growth of Logical Thinking from Childhood to Adolescence*, Basic Books, Inc., Publishers, New York, 1958.

NELSON, M. J., and E. C. DENNY: *Nelson-Denny Reading Test* (rev. by James I. Brown), for grades 9–12, College and Adults, Forms A and B; measures vocabulary, comprehension, and reading rate; Houghton Mifflin Company, Boston, 1929–1960.

SQUIRE, JAMES R.: *The Responses of Adolescents While Reading Four Short Stories*, Research Report no. 2, National Council of Teachers of English, Champaign, Ill., 1964.

STRANG, RUTH: *The Role of the Teacher in Personnel Work*, Teachers College Press, Columbia University, New York, 1953, pp. 336–357.

————: "Exploration of the Reading Process," *Reading Research Quarterly,* 2:33–45, Spring, 1967.

———— and PAUL J. EAGAN: "Teen-age Readers," *The PTA Magazine,* 55:10–12, June, 1961.

SUGGESTED READINGS

BONSALL, MARCELLA R.: "Introspections of Gifted Children," *California Journal of Educational Research,* 11:159–166, September, 1960.

BULLOCK, HARRISON: *Helping the Non-reading Pupil in Secondary School,* Teachers College Press, Columbia University, New York, 1956.

CAFONE, HAROLD: "Individual Differences in the Reading Process of Ninth Grade Retarded Readers," unpublished doctoral dissertation, Department of Education, University of Arizona, Tucson, June, 1966.

LETTON, MILDRED CELIA: "Individual Differences in Interpretive Responses in Reading Poetry at the Ninth Grade Level," unpublished doctoral dissertation, Department of Education, University of Chicago, Chicago, June, 1958.

OGDEN, CHARLES KAY, and I. A. RICHARDS: *The Meaning of Meaning,* Harcourt, Brace & World, Inc., New York, 1949.

PIEKARZ, JOSEPHINE A.: "Individual Differences in Interpretive Responses in Reading," unpublished doctoral dissertation, Department of Education, University of Chicago, Chicago, June, 1954.

RICHARDS, I. A.: *How to Read a Page,* Beacon Press, Boston, 1958.

ROGERS, CHARLOTTE DEE: "Individual Differences in Interpretive Responses to Reading the Short Story at the Eleventh Grade Level," unpublished doctoral dissertation, University of Arizona, Tucson, 1965.

RUSSELL, DAVID H.: "Contributions of Reading to Personal Development," *Teachers College Record,* 61:435–441, May, 1960.

SCHWYHART, KEITH: "Exploration of the Self-concept of Retarded Readers in Relation to Reading Achievement," unpublished doctoral dissertation, Department of Education, University of Arizona, Tucson, June, 1967.

STEMMLER, ANNE O.: "Reading of Highly Intelligent versus Highly Creative Secondary Students," unpublished doctoral dissertation, University of Chicago, Chicago, 1966.

STRANG, RUTH: "Reactions to Research on Reading," *The Educational Forum,* 26:187–192, January, 1962.

————: "The Reading Process and Its Ramifications," *Invitational Addresses, 1965,* International Reading Association, Newark, Del., 1965, pp. 49–73.

Chapter Six

ASCERTAINING INTERESTS

Interest is often the key that unlocks effort; it has a dynamic effect on the way students read. Consequently, a study of students' reading and other interests is an important part of any diagnostic procedure. Many methods of studying children's interests have been used, and many reports of the reading interests of children of different ages have been published.

INTEREST AS A DYNAMIC FORCE [1]

We have all observed the dynamic effect of interest on children's reading. A first-grade class's interest in a little white kitten who strayed into their classroom helped them to quickly recognize the words in their story about it. A class of mentally retarded children, who generally had a defeatist attitude toward reading, made progress in reading simplified versions of newspaper stories and articles which they themselves had selected as especially interesting. A group of older boys who had left school without learning to read went to work in earnest after they became aware of the importance of reading in getting and holding a job. They made remarks such as the following:

> I'm in a rut in my job because of my poor reading. There's no future in it and I'm afraid to take a good job that requires reading. I don't want to be a day laborer all my life. I'm twenty years old and if I don't learn to read now, I never will. It's now or never for me. I wouldn't dare to get married because I'd never feel secure in my job.

[1] Much of this section is quoted with permission from an article previously written by the author (Strang, 1957).

Another said:

> My boss wanted me to take a job in the office, but I knew I'd have to read letters and bills so I told him I was more valuable to him in the shipping room. He kept asking me and I kept stalling for about nine months; then he hired someone else.

An emotionally disturbed boy, who at first unconsciously was resisting all attempts to teach him to read, read with keen enjoyment a story the teacher had written especially for him. The story was written in his own idiom and expressed his feelings of hostility and anxiety. Because the boy had previously refused even to open a book, the teacher ingeniously wrote the story on cards, a sentence or two on each card.

Young people agree with psychologists on the efficacy of interest in learning. Direct quotations from the students support psychological theories of the dynamic effect of interest. In twelve different schools and communities, 250 youngsters from the sixth through the twelfth grades, with IQs of 82 to 150, were asked, "How does your interest in a book or assignment affect what you read, the way you read, and what you learn?" With very few exceptions they confirmed our impression of the dynamic force of interest. When asked, "What makes a book easy to read?" a large proportion of them said, "If it's interesting."

They described a pattern or sequence: If the book is interesting, they read it eagerly and with enjoyment. Their interest enlists their attention and impels them to read fast but effectively. Because they are concentrating harder than usual, they comprehend what they read. They remember what they have comprehended. The whole process is satisfying. This satisfying experience may lead them to read other books by the same author, look up more information on the same topic, and otherwise widen their interests. As one bright twelve-year-old boy said, "My interest in books and reading them broadens my knowledge of many things and increases my vocabulary. And the more interest, the more reading; the more reading, the more knowledge."

Students confronted with dull, drab, uninteresting reading material show the opposite pattern. They read reluctantly, their minds wander, they skip and skim so that they can "get it over with" more quickly. Consequently, they do not comprehend, organize, or remember much of what they read. Since this experience is so lacking in satisfaction, it does not lead to further reading or related worthwhile activities.

Interest and effort

Interest evokes effort. More than half a century ago, John Dewey clarified the concept of interest and effort. His view that interest and effort go hand in hand has been reinforced. If a book or article has meaning, use, and purpose for the individual, he will put forth effort to read it. The country boy who was considered a "remedial reading problem" in school was able to puzzle out the meaning of a difficult agricultural bulletin because he wanted to learn how to raise a prize pig. However, interest cannot completely compensate for lack of reading skills. The person whose reading ability falls below a certain critical point cannot get the meaning of a passage no matter how much interest he may have in the content.

Students express in various ways their ideas of the relation of interest to effort: "If you're not interested, you don't care whether you succeed or fail," and "If the assignment doesn't interest me, it may take me an hour when it would only take me twenty minutes if I were interested."

A thirteen-year-old girl in the ninth grade made this more comprehensive comment:

> The assignment affects what I read in this way: If it's on something that I'm interested in, I'm likely to read everything I can find on the subject. If I'm not interested, I'll read just as much as I have to. Also, if I'm interested in it, I'll concentrate so deeply that it would take an atom bomb to divert my attention.

Interest creates readiness, which is the precursor of effort. A seventh-grade boy expressed it in this quaint way:

> If I am interested in a subject I am much more susceptible to knowledge. I will read much better and easier. On the other hand, if I am not interested and the subject is boring, I may have some sort of a mental block. This is very foolish and I am trying to correct it. We sometimes have to work on things we don't like.

Interest is selective. It chooses one of the many things that lie within our field of perception at a given moment and directs our attention to it. Interest also lengthens the span and intensifies the degree of our attention.

Interest and personality development

Interest may be related to personal development in several ways. The student's basic interest in self-improvement may be reflected in his reading. His drive toward self-realization may be reinforced by biography and autobiography, by authentic historical novels, and by true-to-life accounts of people's strivings and frustrations, thoughts and actions in the modern world. If he identifies himself with characters who are vigorous, courageous, sincere, kind, helpful, successful, he will tend to develop these characteristics. On the other hand, if he habitually becomes absorbed in novels in which indolence is presented as better than effort, cowardice than courage, dishonesty than honesty, his character may change in these undesirable directions.

A dominant interest helps a young person to organize his experiences. A wholehearted interest in a book has an integrating effect on his personality. It is good for a young person to become absorbed in something bigger than himself and beyond himself, to identify himself with an admirable character, and to feel with another person, whether real or fictional.

Interest and wide reading

Interest in one book may also lead to further reading. A student selects a book because of some initial interest—a friend recommended it; he heard friends talking about the characters; the teacher read an excerpt that caught his interest; the title was appealing. A satisfying experience with this book may form the nucleus of a reading pattern; the student may go on to other books on the same topic, books with a similar appeal, or books by the same author.

Interest, comprehension, and memory

Interest aids comprehension and memory. Some psychological experiments have demonstrated that interesting content is comprehended and retained better than uninteresting content. Bernstein (1953) selected two stories which she made equivalent in readability as measured by the Flesch, Lorge, and Dale-Chall formulas. One story was full of action and suspense; it portrayed teen-age characters in situations of interest to teen-agers. The other selection, from a famous novel, was a long, wordy description of adult characters. The ninth-grade students who read both stories comprehended the first more quickly and more accurately. As would be expected, they rated it as more interesting than the other selection.

In another research, Wharton (1957) replaced the vague, general expressions in a college history text with more precise, picture-forming words; this, too, had a favorable effect on comprehension. Similarly, improvements in the organization and interest of a high school history text clearly facilitated comprehension (Peterson, 1954).

Many students firmly believe that interest underlies learning and remembering. When new material is related to the individual's past experience and to his expectations for the future, it is firmly anchored in his memory.

"If you are interest in sometink," wrote a seventh-grade youngster with an IQ of 72, "you will learn, but if you are not interest in what you reading you will not learn." An able learner in the tenth grade said, "If I'm really interested in a subject and am eager to learn it, I find myself learning as fast as I can read the knowledge off the page." A ninth-grade boy described his reaction to uninteresting books more concretely: "When I read a book that isn't interesting, I become very bored and start daydreaming or even sleeping. I begin to twiddle around with other things because I am not interested in what I'm reading. I learn very little unless the book is interesting and informative."

Students link enjoyment with efficient reading. A fourteen-year-old girl with an IQ of 126 emphasized her inability to remember books that she does not enjoy: "If I know I must read a particular book, I read it whether I enjoy it or not; although to tell you the truth, if I don't enjoy it, it goes in one ear and out the other . . . although I've read every word."

Certainly the dynamic force of interest should be more fully used, both in the development of reading ability and in personal development through reading.

CULTIVATION OF INTEREST

Few students seem to recognize the hard fact that one must sometimes read books one does not like. Most youngsters spoke with an air of finality about the importance of interest. Very few assumed any responsibility for building interest in an initially uninteresting subject. However, one put it this way: "Books or assignments are interesting only if you make them so."

When specifically asked, "How can you get interested in something you were not interested in at first?" a class of eighth-grade students offered many sound suggestions, such as the following:

First of all, you have to go at it with the attitude that it can be interesting. If you start out thinking it won't be interesting or fun, the chances are slight that you will end up liking it.

Second, you have to remember that a book may sound as if it wasn't going to be interesting but the more you find out about it, the more you will realize that it is really interesting. Before you say that it isn't interesting, you must know about it.

Third, try to find out the things about a subject that are interesting and concentrate mostly on these (Strang, 1962, p. 85).

INTEREST AND READING ABILITY

Few students mention reading inability as a cause of lack of interest; practically none see a relation between interest and general mental ability. The following quotations express a few of their ideas about these relationships:

A retarded reader said: "If you're used to books with little words and you're assigned a book that you can't make head or tail of, well, that affects your interest."

The hostility toward reading expressed by an eleventh-grade boy, who was reading at third-grade level, crowded out any consideration of interest: "The subject that I read makes no difference to me. Because I think reading is strictly for the birds. I hate anything to do with reading, such as books, teachers that make me read, etc."

Another poor reader pointed out that "If I read a book I must have a great interest in it because I don't like to read." The lower the reading ability, the higher must be the interest in the book. This statement highlights the need to provide highly interesting material for retarded readers.

Another explanation for lack of interest in a book or assignment mentioned by a fifteen-year-old girl in the tenth grade was distracting thoughts: "Sometimes I have things on my mind and that interferes a lot in my reading. If there is some way to get all that's in your mind out I know it would be a big help. But is there a way?"

Boredom is often a cause of lack of interest among gifted youngsters. One teen-age boy expressed a common feeling about repetitious material: "Doing too much of a certain thing, whether you liked it or not at first, will become tiring and boring."

WAYS OF ASCERTAINING READING INTERESTS

Observation

Of the many ways of studying students' reading interests, observation offers the alert teacher many opportunities in the course of his daily class contacts. The teacher notes which books a child chooses, the degree of concentration and enjoyment with which he reads them, his eagerness to talk about them, his desire to read more books of a like nature or books by the same author. When the teacher is reading a story aloud, he can easily sense the students' interest or lack of it by the quality of their attention, the degree of their eagerness to talk about it, and the insistence with which they ask for more.

Reviews written by students

More detailed information about reading interests may be gained from the reviews written by older students. If the reviews have the social purpose of acquainting others with interesting books, they are likely to be written carefully and thoughtfully.

Records of students' reading may take different forms, from a simple listing of books read to a comprehensive review such as one finds in news-papers and magazines. The type of review varies with the kind of book and the purpose for which it is read. The following is one of many forms that have been used in schools:

READING PROGRAM BOOK INFORMATION

Pupil _____ Grade _____ Age _____
Name of book _____
Author _____
Publisher _____
No. of pages _____ Year of publication _____
Pictures_____(none, few, many)
Other books I have read on the same subject or by the same author _____
_____

Description of the most important character _____
_____

One incident that occurred in this book (try to pick an interesting one) _____
_____

Five new words I learned in this book _____, _____, _____, _____,
_____
Interest rating I would give this book on a five-point scale and reason for the rating
_____
_____

An illustration I would like to draw for this book (optional)

In many schools students have become quite resistant to the formal book report. The practice of copying other students' reports or published reviews of the book seems to be quite prevalent. Students greatly prefer discussions to written reviews of books. They are often stimulated by the comments of their peers to read more widely.

Charts of reading interests

For a graphic method of showing the scope of a student's interest, one may use a published leaflet called My Reading Design. This record form has a page on which the student lists and numbers in order the books he has read. In the appropriate space on a pie graph, each segment of which represents a type of book, such as biography, art and music, science, horses, fairy tales, etc., the student writes the number of each book.

Choice of favorite stories

Students' actual choice of books is usually evidence of their reading interests. One eighth-grade teacher asked each student in a class of able learners, who had access to many magazines in their homes, to bring in one story or article that interested him very much and would interest his classmates. These youngsters brought in more nonfiction than fiction. Their selections represented a wide range of mature interests, including politics, science, music, and psychology.

As an alternative, students may be asked to summarize in their own words their favorite story, mention certain highlight features of it, and tell how they happened to read it. Using this technique, Gaier and Collier (1960, pp. 431–451) found that girls and boys aged nine or ten particularly liked stories about travel, tales of exciting, dangerous pursuit and escape, and stories about "social situations involving subterfuge and surprise, or humor and comical enjoyment." Their interest was heightened by memorable characters, illustrations, or style. Next to fiction, girls preferred fairy tales; boys preferred factual material. Girls preferred leading characters of their own age or only slightly older; boys preferred characters older than themselves. The favorite themes of girls were mystery, pleasant social relationships, and "small helpless children or animals who triumphed over stronger, older, usually male characters." Boys, on the other hand, chose stories whose characters showed remarkable physical or mental adequacy and settings remote in place and time. Animal stories were still favorites. These results are similar to those obtained in other studies of children's interests (Witty, 1961).

Although much information may be obtained by this technique, the results probably depend to some extent upon what books are available. For example, the interest in informative books might have been higher for both girls and boys if they had had access to some of the attractive new factual material.

Adolescents feel strongly about being permitted to choose the books they want to read. They resent having to read a prescribed list of books. Freedom of choice in voluntary reading is in accord with the general principle of self-selection; it encourages initiative and individuality. Growth in reading interests and tastes may be fostered by making appropriate books available and by introducing them to students in an appealing way.

At the same time, students should be learning to evaluate the quality of the books they read and their contribution to personal development. They should develop criteria of their own, not accept the often biased opinions of certain reviewers. If intelligent young people are taught to compare classics with cheap, incoherent, life-distorting novels and plays, they will be likely to reject the latter. In making their evaluations, students should have the support of several able literary critics such as Granville Hicks and Joseph Wood Krutch.

Rating titles or selections

Instead of asking the student about his favorite stories, one may offer him his choice of actual or fictitious annotated titles. An ingenious and unique study of reading interests was made by Thorndike and Henry (1940, pp. 751–763). In order to present each child with a uniform situation, uninfluenced by his previous experiences with books, the investigators prepared a large number of fictitious titles and annotations. For example:

Yes	No	?	*Lonesome Laddy Finds a Friend.* How a stray dog found a new master and showed his true love.
Yes	No	?	*Pilot Peters on Patrol.* The adventures of an airplane scout. What was the mystery plane that roared by in the dawn?

The child was asked to mark the titles which he would *really like to read*. Some children, particularly susceptible to social pressure, might feel they ought to mark *Famous Sermons by Famous Preachers, History of the Lutheran Church,* or *Brush Your Teeth,* even though they would never read such books. Slow-learning children, who are generally more susceptible to suggestion, actually chose more titles of this kind than did the fast-learning children. On this type of questionnaire, sex differences were much greater than differences in intelligence. There were "few individual titles that showed reliable differences between the bright and the dull children" (Thorndike and Henry, 1940, p. 762). However, comparison with the actual reading done by the same pupils showed marked differences between the slow and the fast groups in the number and quality of books read. The fast-learning group read twice as many books, covered a wider range of titles, and read books of better quality than the slow-learning children. Of the 282 items rated by the slow group, 100 were comics, whereas comics made up only 23 of the 560 items rated by the fast learners.

Instead of offering the student fictitious titles and annotations, one may ask him to rate actual selections. This technique was used effectively by Coleman and Jungblut (1961, pp. 221–228) in a study of the reading preferences of 750 children in grades 4 to 6. The students read and rated 81 selections, 225 to 400 words in length, on the following scale:

Could you read the selection? Yes ___ No ___
If you could read it, please put a cross (X) in the circle which tells best how you
feel about this selection.

- ○ Like very, very much
- ○ Like quite a lot
- ○ Like a little
- ○ Dislike a little
- ○ Dislike quite a lot
- ○ Dislike very, very much

Each selection was also rated by adults for its appeal to children of a
given age and its value with reference to educational goals. The investigators also appraised the difficulty of each selection by means of the Lorge
Readability Index. The children's interest-aversion ratings provided an important supplement to the readability index and the judgments of experienced adult educators.

Interest inventories

There are also numerous interest inventories of the checklist type. These
may list reading habits, types of books, characteristics of books, or actual
titles to be checked, usually under the headings of Like, Dislike, or Indifference.

One of the earliest and most comprehensive of the interest inventories
was developed by Witty and Kopel (see Witty, 1949, pp. 302–305). It
included many items on interests and activities other than reading; it also
elicited background information and called for short answers to specific
questions. More important than the information gained from checklists
and inventories are the student's awareness and self-appraisal of his reading
pattern.

In interpreting the responses on interest inventories, the instability of
an individual's reading interests must be recognized. Reading interests
change with age, with competing interests, with changes in the peer group,
with the influence of different teachers. We would not expect reading
interests reported at any one time to be permanent.

Although the interest inventory usually gives more detail about favorite
kinds of reading than merely asking a student what kind of books he
enjoys, it does not differentiate within broad areas of interest. For example,
an individual may say that he likes adventure stories, but within this
category there may be many kinds of adventure stories that he does not
like.

As with other types of self-report techniques, the student may conceal
his real interests in order to create a favorable impression. Since he knows

that wide reading of good books is approved, he may exaggerate the number or the quality of the books he reads.

An example of the short-answer type of questionnaire that covers several areas of reading interest is given below.

MY READING INTERESTS

1. Name_____Age_____Grade_____
2. Check the library or libraries below that you can use. Double check those you do use.
   Community library _____   School library   _____
   Church library   _____   Any other library _____
3. How many books have you borrowed from friends during the last month?
   _____
   Give titles of some _____
   _____
   _____
4. How many books have you loaned to friends during the last month? _____
   Give titles of some _____
   _____
   _____
5. Give the titles of some of the books in your home. _____
   _____
   _____
6. From what sources, other than those mentioned above, do you obtain books? Check below.
   1. Buy them _____   3. Rent them _____
   2. Gifts   _____   4. Exchanges _____
7. What are your hobbies and collections? _____
   _____
8. What do you intend to be? _____
   Are you going to college? _____ Where? _____
9. Name the five magazines you like best. _____
   _____
10. Name the three movies you last saw. _____
    _____
11. Name the three radio or TV programs you like best. _____
    _____
12. Name the state or country farthest away that you have visited. _____
    _____
13. What sections of the newspaper do you like best? Check below.
    1. Sports _____   4. News   _____
    2. Funnies _____   5. Editorials _____
    3. Stories _____   6. Other   _____
14. Which of the following have encouraged you to read? Check below.
    1. Parents   _____   6. Pals   _____
    2. Teacher _____   7. Club leader _____
    3. Librarian _____   8. Relatives   _____
    4. Hobby   _____   9. Club work   _____
    5. Friends   _____   10. Other   _____

Creative-type questionnaire and essay

A unique form of questionnaire elicited some fascinating specific information about reading interests: the preferred type of book, its appeal, its style of writing (Strang, 1946, pp. 447–482). An example of this form, as filled out by a girl in the eighth grade, is reproduced below; it will give an idea of the kind of insights that may be gained from this technique.

TO THE STUDENTS

Year in school _____ eighth _____ Boy _____ Girl ___ x ___
Name (You need not sign your name unless you want to.) ___ C.S.K. ___

  You have, right now, the best possible information about what high school students like to read. Will you share it with us by answering as thoughtfully and fully as possible the following questions:

1. What do young persons like you most want to read about? Adventure and mystery
2. What kind of a book or article would you choose to read above all others? Books about teen-age romances, etc.
3. Suppose you were going to write a book or article that persons of your age would all want to read, what would be its title? The Typical Teen-ager
4. Write a paragraph or two showing how you think this book should be written to appeal most to the boys and girls in your class.
  The book should be written in such a fashion that it would be both humorous and adventurous; appealing and interesting.
  Life of a teen-ager, not babyish stories, story of romance, adventure, mystery and pleasure.
5. Think of the books or articles you have read this year that you just could not stand. What was it in them that made you dislike them so much?
  In some books they skip from one subject to another. In mysteries they sometimes don't have any endings. Books that are mushy and foolish are also very unpopular. Stories that abuse animals I don't like.
6. Think of the books or articles you have liked most this year. What was it in them that made you like them so much?
  First of all they had a plot which made them interesting. I like dog stories, adventure, mystery, and almost anything in modern life that is written in typical teen-age level.
7. Which book or article that you have read during the last year interested you most keenly? Give the author, Margaret Vail, title Yours Is the Earth, magazine or publisher _____, and date _____ (if you remember it). Then write as much as you can about the book or article and why you liked it so much. (Use other side of page.)
  The book is an autobiography of part of her life in France.
  Margaret Vail married a French soldier. She was in Paris when her daughter was born. Then the war broke out.
  It is the thrilling tale of how she escaped France and got into Spain, climbing the mountains with her daughter, then four years old.
  The book had a plot. It was interesting and every page held me in suspense till the end. It was a war story, but not a gory, bloody tale.

From this type of questionnaire and from essays written on specific topics, one finds many common and many unique expressions of dislike for certain kinds of books and styles of writing:

"Hate anything like Dickens"

"Too much beating around the bush"

"Stories not true to life"

"Sob stories about teen-agers"

"Too much talk—just a bunch of people yakking"

Lack of action and suspense is frequently mentioned. Equally interesting are the reasons students express for liking a book:

"Grown-up but with words you can understand"

"Gives the feeling that you are there"

To sign or not to sign

The question of whether or not students should sign their names to these questionnaires often arises. The more personal the data, the more sensitive the individual is to the impression he is making. However, there is not the same problem with reading interest as with personality inventories. Usually students will answer questions about their reading interests thoughtfully and frankly whether they do or do not sign their names. If the information is to be used for individual guidance in reading, obviously it is necessary that the report be signed.

USING INFORMATION ABOUT INTERESTS

Information about students' interests may be used by teachers, librarians, and parents in guiding the reading of individuals, in introducing books, and in capitalizing on some common interest of a group. Observation of students' interests may be used immediately in guiding their choice of books. A third-grade child chooses a book from the class library to read in his free time. If the book is one that he can read independently, the teacher approves his choice. If it is too difficult for him, the teacher may say, "That's a good book to read later, Jimmy. Here's another book about cowboys you'd like to read right now." If a student is enthusiastic about a book he has just read, the teacher may suggest another book that treats a similar topic, has the same appeal, or is by the same author.

If a student shows no interest in reading any book, the teacher may try to uncover some other interest or activity to which reading might contribute. For example, a boy in a social studies class (Shepherd, 1961, pp. 140–142) did not choose any of the supplementary books on the early explorers which the teacher had brought into the classroom. Most of the other students, having made their choices, had started reading. The teacher asked John about his outside interests. When the teacher learned that John was absorbed in building a boat with his father, he said, "There's a book here I'm sure you would like. It's about the adventures of an early explorer who went around the Cape of Good Hope in a small boat." John took the book and later made an enthusiastic report on it to the class. By tying reading in with students' outside activities, the teacher utilizes the impetus of their interests.

In addition to daily observation, interest inventories filled out by all the members of a class guide the teacher in ordering new books or in getting books for the class from the library or bookmobile. Without this information the teacher might not be aware, for example, that his young adolescent boys are most interested in certain features of war, sports, and science and in stories about real people and that the girls are interested in mysteries and stories about teen-agers like themselves. If several students mention special interests such as medicine or current problems, the teacher may make available books that contribute to these interests.

Reports of reading interests may give clues to personality patterns and sources of emotional tension. For example, an adolescent may reveal his attitude toward life, his preoccupations and anxieties, or the quality of his human relationships by such comments as the following:

> I especially like stories of people who find out what their career is going to be. Stories of people such as Florence Nightingale and *The Life and Thought of Albert Schweitzer* get you to thinking and wondering about jobs in the field of medicine. Characters who work hard and show a great deal of courage make you want to be more like them. Some books make you want to work harder and do a better job at what you're doing. . . . Books that make you happy and make you laugh are very good to read when you feel downcast or afraid. These books can cheer you up and lift your spirits and make you less afraid (Strang, 1961, p. 391).

After reading a set of these papers, the teacher becomes more aware than ever of the unique personality of each member of his class.

Questionnaires, reviews, and compositions such as have been described in this chapter, when read anonymously to a class, serve as a basis for discussion. By hearing about one student's enjoyment of certain books, others may be stimulated to broaden their reading interests. Class discussion of what makes a book interesting and worthwhile may help students to build criteria for book selection.

Last, but not least, is the value of a study of their reading interests to the students themselves. It encourages them to appraise their choices of reading materials and to challenge the assumptions that underlie their interests or lack of interests.

CONCLUDING STATEMENT

Children are naturally interested. The more opportunities they have had to see and hear and associate with people, the wider are their interests. Children from disadvantaged homes who have not had the intellectual stimulation that more fortunate children have had often show lack of reading interests. They are the ones for whom teachers must supply, first of all, experiences that will arouse their undeveloped interests. Book clubs, discussions, role playing, and dramatization provide the social stimulation that will restore their capacity to become interested in the world which reading enables them to explore.

In general, junior and senior high school students feel strongly about the importance of having interesting reading material and interesting assignments. If the material is uninteresting, they will skim over it quickly, not caring what it says nor whether they finish reading it, getting little or nothing out of it, not noticing the important points, not remembering it, and consequently getting low marks in the subject. If they are interested they will enjoy reading, read carefully and eagerly, comprehend with less effort, note the important facts, get more out of their reading, remember it, search for more material on the same topic, and desire to learn more about related matters.

Being able to recommend the right book for the right child at the psychological moment is basic to success in teaching reading. The child's first experiences with books influence his attitude toward reading. The books recommended to an adolescent help determine whether he views reading as "strictly for the birds" or as "one of life's inexhaustible pleasures."

SUGGESTED PROBLEMS: PRACTICE AND DEMONSTRATION

1. Tell or read a story to a group of children and note the points at which they laugh, lose interest, become restless, want to ask questions, show keen interest. From a number of records of this kind summarize the style of writing, kind of story or article, difficulty, content, and other characteristics of stories that are most and least interesting for a certain age and grade group.

2. Give an interest questionnaire such as the creative-type questionnaire described in this chapter to an intermediate or secondary school class and summarize the understanding of students' interests gained from their responses.

3. In individual cases recommend books you think would be especially interesting and valuable for improvement in reading or for personal development.

4. Study students' comprehension of two passages differing in their interest appeal but otherwise comparable.

5. Read Dewey's *Interest and Effort* to obtain his main line of thought on this subject.

6. Plan a lesson in which a popular book that gives a distorted view of life is compared with a classic dealing with a similar situation.

7. Fill out a form such as "My Reading Interests" about your own reading interests.

REFERENCES

BERNSTEIN, MARGERY R.: "Relationship between Interest and Reading Comprehension," unpublished doctoral dissertation, Teachers College, Columbia University, New York, 1953.

COLEMAN, J. H., and ANN JUNGBLUT: "Children's Likes and Dislikes about What They Read," *Journal of Educational Research*, 44:221–228, February, 1961.

DEWEY, JOHN: *Interest and Effort*, Houghton Mifflin Company, Boston, 1913.

GAIER, EUGENE L., and MARY JEFFREY COLLIER: "The Latency-stage Story Preferences of American and Finnish Children," *Child Development*, 31:431–451, September, 1960.

"My Reading Design," *The News-Journal*, North Manchester, Ind. Forms A, B, C, and D for primary, intermediate, junior high, and high school, respectively.

PETERSON, ELEANOR M.: *Aspects of Readability in the Social Studies*, Teachers College Press, Columbia University, New York, 1954.

SHEPHERD, DAVID L.: *Effective Reading in the Social Studies*, Harper & Row, Publishers, Incorporated, New York, 1961.

STRANG, RUTH: "Reading Interests, 1946," *English Journal*, 25:447–482, November, 1946.

————: "Interest as a Dynamic Force in the Improvement of Reading," *Elementary English*, 34:170–176, March, 1957. Used with the permission of the National Council of Teachers of English.

————: "Evaluation of Development in and through Reading," in *Development in and through Reading*, Sixtieth Yearbook of the National Society for the Study of Education, The University of Chicago Press, Chicago, 1961, pp. 376–397.

————: "Prevention and Correction of Underachievement," in H. Alan Robinson (ed.), *The Underachiever in Reading, Report of the Twenty-fifth Annual Conference on Reading*, The University of Chicago Press, Chicago, 1962, pp. 79–86.

THORNDIKE, ROBERT L., and FLORENCE HENRY: "Differences in Reading Interests Related to Differences in Sex and Intelligence Level," *The Elementary School Journal*, 40:751–763, June, 1940.

WHARTON, WILLIAM P.: "Picture-forming Words and Readability of College History Texts," unpublished doctoral dissertation, Teachers College, Columbia University, New York, 1957.

WITTY, PAUL: *Reading in Modern Education*, Ginn and Company, Boston, 1949.

SUGGESTED READING

EMANS, R., and G. PATYK: "Why Do High School Students Read?" *Journal of Reading*, 10:300–304, February, 1967.

GETZELS, J. W.: "Problem of Interests: A Reconsideration," *Reading: Seventy-five Years of Progress*, The University of Chicago Press, Chicago, 1966, vol. 96, pp. 97–106.

JENKINS, W. A.: "Reading for Enjoyment and Personal Development," *Educational Leadership*, 24:404–406, February, 1967.

LARRICK, NANCY: *A Teacher's Guide to Children's Books*, Charles E. Merrill Books, Inc., Columbus, Ohio, 1960.

———— and JOHN A. STOOPS (eds.): *What Is Reading Doing to the Child?* Highlights from the Sixteenth Annual Reading Conference of Lehigh University, The Interstate Printers & Publishers, Danville, Ill., 1967.

MACKINTOSH, HELEN K.: "Children's Interests in Literature and the Reading Program," *The Reading Teacher*, 10:138–145, 1957.

NORVELL, GEORGE W.: *What Boys and Girls Like to Read*, Silver Burdett Company, Morristown, N.J., 1958.

ROBINSON, A. ALAN: "Developing Lifetime Readers," *Journal of Reading*, 11:261–267, January, 1968.

ROBINSON, HELEN M.: *Developing Permanent Interest in Reading*, Proceedings of the Annual Conference on Reading, The University of Chicago Press, Chicago, 1956.

————, SAMUEL WEINTRAUB, and HELEN K. SMITH: "Summary of Investigations Relating to Reading, July 1, 1966 to June 30, 1967," *Reading Research Quarterly*, vol. 3, no. 2, Winter, 1968, International Reading Association, Newark, Del.

SOARES, ANTHONY T., and RAY H. SIMPSON: "Interest in Recreational Reading of Junior High School Students," *Journal of Reading*, 11:14–21, October, 1967.

STRANG, RUTH: *Helping Your Child Improve His Reading*, E. P. Dutton & Co., Inc., New York, 1962.

————, ETHYLENE PHELPS, and DOROTHY WITHROW: *Gateways to Readable Books*, 4th ed., The H. W. Wilson Company, New York, 1967.

WITTY, PAUL, and ASSOCIATES: "Studies of Children's Interests: A Brief Summary," *Elementary English*, 37:469–475, November, 1960.

WOLLNER, MARY HAYDEN BOWEN: *Children's Voluntary Reading as an Expression of Individuality*, Teachers College Press, Columbia University, New York, 1949.

Chapter Seven

CONTRIBUTION OF TESTS

Tests add precision and completeness to the teacher's classroom observations. When the teacher uses tests, he attempts to control the stimuli to which the students respond. Since a test presumably presents a common stimulus to all students, comparisons of their differing responses are possible.

APPRAISAL BY TEACHER-MADE OR INFORMAL TESTS

The most informal way to screen a class for reading speed and comprehension is to ask the students to read silently a selection of four or five pages in their textbook. As each one finishes, he looks up and closes the book. This identifies the fast and the slow readers. When all have finished, the teacher asks questions based on the selection; the students write their answers. This test of their comprehension shows how well students understood and remembered the selection they have just read. Some will find it easy; others, too difficult.

A graded series of paragraphs similar to those described in Chapter 4 or to the individual reading inventory (see Chapter 10) may be given to an entire class. These serve as an informal silent reading test of ability to recognize paragraph thought and structure as an aid to efficient reading. The paragraphs are selected with the abilities and interests of the students in mind. Informal tests in each subject, described later in this chapter, are an especially valuable diagnostic, self-appraisal teaching instrument. Each informal measure contributes to the cumulative picture of a pupil's progress in reading.

Informal tests for different purposes

Many kinds of informal tests may be used for different purposes (Strang and others, 1967, chap. 4). To call attention to the importance of recognizing the author's intent, mood, and purpose, the teacher may use several short selections of such a nature that the reader who does not sense the writer's purpose will misinterpret them. For example, he may take seriously a poem or short essay written with a humorous intent. Or he may accept at face value easily detected misstatements of a writer whose aim is to persuade the reader to buy certain products. With selections of this kind, the reader should ask three questions: What does this paragraph say? What attitudes is the author trying to induce in the reader? How does he use words to serve his purpose?

To test ability to skim quickly for a certain bit of information, the teacher may use news stories or other short articles in which the reader is asked to find a single fact, such as the score of a football game or who won the race or a certain date in history. All the students begin reading when the signal is given and look up as soon as they have found the answer. Those who have succeeded most quickly then describe their methods to the others.

To test the students' ability to select the central thought of a paragraph, the teacher should at first use well-constructed, well-organized paragraphs. The test exercise may call for answers to multiple-choice questions, or a statement of the author's purpose, or the thought pattern or relationships: whole-part, cause-and-effect, sequential, comparison and contrast, co-ordinate-subordinate, or hierarchical relationships. The students may be asked to diagram these relationships, picture the structure of the paragraph, or draw his impression of the person and/or scene described.

To diagnose and improve students' ability to read different kinds of material for different purposes, Smith (1967) developed excellent testing-instructional-practice material based on extensive research: (1) tests of ability to identify the purposes for which certain selections should be read, (2) instruction in how to read for these different purposes, (3) selections in which reading for a particular purpose is appropriate, and (4) tests of comprehension of the selections.

To test for thoroughness of understanding of a factual article or an assignment in history or other subject, the teacher may ask for a summary, outline, or graphic matrix showing the relationships among the ideas.

Tests of ability to make deeper interpretations of various kinds of material would be based on selections from literature or from other content fields that require interpretation and critical thinking.

Informal tests in each subject

Every subject teacher needs to find out how well the students in a new class can read the books he expects them to use. He wants to know: What is their purpose or purposes in reading a given selection? What is being communicated to them—what have they learned and remembered from reading this section of the text or reference book? How well can they communicate orally or in writing the ideas gained? An informal "teaching test" in each subject will answer these questions.

These teaching tests have several advantages. They are similar to the content being taught and closely geared to instruction, whereas the items on standardized tests are too often remote from the content and skills being taught in a given classroom. The results of informal tests are easy for the teacher to apply in his daily instruction. The free or unstructured response shows how students approach a reading assignment, what they remember from it, and how well they communicate the ideas in it. These tests also promote student self-appraisal. By encouraging the student to take the initiative in analyzing his own reading process, they motivate learning. A series of similar tests, each followed by discussion of progress, analysis of errors, and suggestions for ways to improve, helps the student to read the subject more effectively. (For examples see Strang, McCullough, and Traxler, 1967, pp. 167–170; Strang and Bracken, 1957, pp. 222–233.) He then answers the questions without referring to the selection. Thus retention as well as comprehension is tested. Comprehension, retention, communication—this is what a teacher expects of a student after he has read an assignment.

The first question calls for a free or creative response. It may ask simply for a summary of the content: What did the author say? Or it may ask for a summary plus opinion: What did the author say, and what did he mean by this? Or it may combine summary, opinion, and consideration of the author's motive: What did the author say? What did he mean by this? Why did he say it? After obtaining answers to the first question only, the teacher will be amazed at the wide range of responses in a single class.

The free response may be supplemented by short-answer or multiple-choice questions. Some of these test the reader's ability to recognize the main ideas and supporting details; others, his ability to draw inferences and conclusions, to define key words, and to appreciate humor, character portrayal, or qualities of literary style. The test exercises can be varied to serve other purposes such as to answer questions on the passage or to extract ideas relevant to a particular topic.

Some students in a heterogeneous class will do poorly on this kind of informal test. The text for the grade is obviously too difficult for them. But they can be taught to get some ideas from it, and they usually want to have the same book as their classmates.

As students participate in the class discussion of one another's answers to the questions, they see more clearly why their free response rated only 1 or 2, whereas others deserved higher ratings on a 5- or 10-point scale. They become aware of the reasons why some definitions of words are more precise and clear than others. They learn about paragraph structure and how to identify quickly the purpose that a particular paragraph serves.

This informal reading test may be expanded into a comprehensive diagnostic self-appraisal teaching procedure. The instructional value of the informal diagnostic self-appraisal teaching procedure was more fully developed by Melnik (1960) using social studies content. The instruction

> starts by asking students to state their aims or goals in reading a social studies assignment. Most students of this age are vague about their reasons for reading and about the reading method that would be most appropriate. They are then asked to read a selection from a social studies book that is typical of the material the students will be expected to read in their classes. After reading the passage they answer two types of questions—creative responsive or open-end: What did the author say? and a number of multiple-choice questions that are designed to furnish evidence of the student's ability to get the literal meaning, to see relations, draw inferences, make generalizations, and understand the meaning of key words.
>
> As soon as the student has answered the questions, he has data before him for self-appraisal. He marks his own paper. He grades his free response on a five- or ten-point scale and analyzes the kinds of errors he has made in the multiple-choice questions (each choice represents a certain kind of error). Instruction immediately follows this self-appraisal, while the students are specifically motivated to learn how to get the right answers and to avoid the same errors next time.
>
> There is a next time; the whole procedure is repeated with another similar selection. After the second exercise is completed and analyzed, the students are able to note the progress they have made. A third application of the procedure makes further improvement in stating objectives and in comprehension possible (Strang, 1961, pp. 386–387).

Group reading inventories

The group reading inventory is used to obtain additional understanding of the reading proficiency of students in any class. The most important part of the inventory is the informal test already described. To this are added questions on study skills, location-of-information skills, and other skills needed in reading the particular subject. Ability to apply the ideas gained from the passage to current events or to personal problems may also be appraised in this informal group inventory.

Students mark their own papers to see for themselves their strengths and difficulties in reading. Junior high school students are especially interested in themselves as persons and like to know about their reading efficiency. When the student has corrected his inventory, he tabulates the results on the front page under each main heading. A check may indicate either skills in which the student needs instruction and practice or, if preferred, the skills he has mastered. If a student scores much below the average for his grade, he should be given an individual reading inventory (see Chapter 10).

Detailed directions for making group reading inventories for English, social studies, and science classes were worked out for teachers by Dr. David Shepherd when he was serving as reading consultant at the Norwalk (Connecticut) High School. The English Group Inventory is reproduced here with his permission. Permission for reprinting parts of the social studies inventories was obtained from Harper & Row, Publishers, Incorporated (Shepherd, 1960).

ENGLISH: Group Reading Inventory

Directions for making and administering a diagnostic survey test of reading skills using an English literature textbook:

1. Use between 35–40 questions.
2. Use questions designed to measure the following reading skills in the proportions shown below.
   (1) Using parts of a book. Include use of (three questions in all):
       a. Table of contents
       b. Index of titles
       c. Glossary   If such sections are included in the
       d. Biographical data   textbook
       e. Introductory paragraph to story
   (2) Vocabulary
       a. Meaning (seven to eight questions)
          1. General background of word meanings
             (a) select correct meanings from several dictionary meanings
             (b) antonyms, synonyms
          2. Contextual meanings
       b. Word recognition and attack (14–15 questions)
          1. Divide words into syllables
          2. Designate the accented syllable
          3. Note and give meaning of prefixes and suffixes
          4. Changing the part of speech of a word (i.e., noun to verb, adjective to adverb, etc.)

(3) Comprehension (11–12 questions)
   a. Noting the main idea
   b. Recalling pertinent supporting details
   c. Drawing conclusions, inferences
   d. Noting the sequence of ideas
(4) Reading rate—Have pupil note the time it takes for him to read the selection. Then figure his reading speed in words per minute. Example: Words in selection, 4,000; Time to read: 10 minutes; 4,000 ÷ 10 equals 400 words per minute. Time may be recorded by pupil's noting time by clock of starting and of stopping to get total number of minutes.
(5) Skimming to locate information (2–5 questions). Use a different selection that was not used for comprehension and speed purposes.
3. Choose a reading selection of not more than three or four pages.
4. In administering the inventory:
   (1) Explain to the pupils the purpose of the inventory and the reading skills the inventory is designed to measure. As the inventory is given, let the pupils know the skill being measured.
   (2) Read each question twice.
   (3) Questions on the use of the parts of the book are asked first. Pupils will use their books.
   (4) Introduce the reading selection, culling pupil background of experience on the topic and setting purpose for reading.
   (5) Selection read silently. Speed noted and figured.
   (6) Ask questions on vocabulary. Pupils will use books for questions measuring ability to determine meaning from context. They will not use books for other vocabulary questions. All other vocabulary questions need to be written on the blackboard or given on mimeographed sheet.
   (7) Ask questions on comprehension. Pupils will not use books—books are to be closed.
   (8) Skimming, new selection used. Pupils will use books to find answers to questions.
5. A pupil is considered to be deficient in any one specific skill if he answers more than one out of three questions incorrectly, or more than two incorrectly when there are more than three questions measuring a specific skill.
6. This inventory, being administered to a group, does not establish a grade level. Nonetheless, any pupil scoring above 90 per cent may be considered as reading material that is too easy for him, and any pupil scoring below 65 per cent as reading material that is too difficult for him. If the material is suitable, the scores should range between 70–90 per cent.

Form of Inventory (Sample)

Parts of book

1. On what page does the unit (section) entitled "Exploring One World" begin? (shows use of table of contents)
2. What section of your book would you use to find out something about the author of a story in the book? (determines knowledge of section on biographical data)
3. In what part of the book can you find the meaning of a word that you might not know? (determines knowledge of glossary)

Introduce story: explore pupils' background of experiences on the subject of the story and set up purpose questions. Pupils read selection silently. Time for reading speed determined.

Vocabulary meaning

4. What is meant by the word *crab* as it is used in the story? (top line, second column, page 178)

Contextual meaning

5. What is meant by the word *eliminated?* (third line, second column, page 181)

Synonyms and antonyms

6. What word means the opposite of *temporary?*
7. Use another word to describe the coach when he looked *amazed.*

General knowledge of meaning

8. Select the proper meaning of the word *entice.*
   a. To lure, persuade
   b. To force
   c. To ask
   d. To caution
9. Select the proper meaning of the word *initial.*
   a. The last or end
   b. The first or beginning
   c. The middle
   d. A letter of the alphabet
10. Select the proper meaning of the word *rectify.*
   a. To do wrong
   b. To make right
   c. To destroy
   d. A priest's home

Word recognition, syllabication

11. Divide the following words into syllables and show which syllable is accented.
12. and 13. Eliminated
14. and 15. Amazed
16. and 17. Undemocratic
18. and 19. Fraternities

Prefixes and suffixes

20. What does the prefix *un* mean as used in *undemocratic?*
21. What is meant by *pre* in the word *prescription?*

Parts of speech

22. Change the verb *astonish* to a noun.
23. Change the adjective *democratic* to a noun.
24. Change the noun *boy* to an adjective.
25. Change the adjective *slow* to an adverb.

Comprehension, main ideas

26. What is a _____? What happened when _____?
27. Such questions as indicated here that ask for
28. only the main points of the story.

Details

29. Questions to ask for specific bits of information
30. about the principal characters or ideas of the
31. material.

Drawing conclusions, inferences

32. Questions, the answers of which are not completely found in the textbook.
33. Questions beginning with "Why," making comparisons, predicting what
34. may happen usually measure the drawing conclusions skill. Example: Why did Bottle imagine he could perform such astounding athletic feats as setting the State high school record in jumping?

Sequence

35. (May be omitted.) Questions asking what
36. happened as a result of _____, what steps
37. did the police use to solve the mystery, etc.
38. Use a new reading selection. Questions
39. designed to have the pupil locate some
40. specific bits of information.

Directions for making a group reading inventory using the social studies textbook are similar to those for making the English inventory (Shepherd, 1960, pp. 20–22). The inventory includes similar questions on location-of-information skills; specific questions on the reading of maps, charts, and other visual aids; special vocabulary used in the social studies; questions on the main ideas, important details, inferences, conclusions, and generalizations appropriate to the subject.

The chart shown on page 131, with names of students to be listed along the left-hand side and types of reading difficulties enumerated across the top, summarizes the information for a class. When read horizontally, it describes the individual students; when read vertically, it shows which difficulties are common to the class. Thus the teacher learns what instruction is needed by the whole class and what special help is needed by individuals.

For students whose comprehension score is below 50 percent, Shepherd recommends administering the individual inventory described in Chapter 10. Appropriate instruction should follow the administration of the inventory; this, indeed, is its main purpose. When the inventory is repeated at the middle and at the end of the semester, both teachers and students get a sense of accomplishment as they see improvement in reading skills.

Name	Use of parts of book	Vocabulary	Meaning	Contextual meanings	Synonyms and antonyms	General knowledge	Word recognition	Syllabication	Accent	Prefixes and suffixes	Part of speech	Comprehension	Main ideas	Supporting details	Drawing conclusions	Sequence of ideas	Skimming	Speed in wpm	Comments
John Jones	√			√	√	√									√			194	(Check wherever
Robert Brown	√	√	√	√	√	√	√	√	√	√					√	√		150	pupil is deficient)

Name of class _____   Section _____   Teacher _____

Summary Chart

Such a group reading inventory bridges the gap between the hurriedly made teacher test and the standardized test. It gives the teacher a concrete model for further testing-teaching-evaluating based on the text or reference books used by his particular class.

The "cloze" technique

This procedure has been used as a measure of readability, of grammatical complexity of sentences (Bormuth, 1964), of reading comprehension, of ability to use context clues and to understand syntax position of words in sentences (Cromer and Weiner, 1966), and as a teaching device (Schneyer, 1965).

The name suggests the gestalt psychology concept of "closure." Students are instructed to insert the missing words that have been systematically omitted in a passage, usually every fifth or tenth word. To study the effect of omission of certain grammatical categories (nouns, verbs, modifiers, prepositions, conjunctions, and noun determiners), each of these syntactical units may be systematically deleted. Noun deletions seem to offer more clues to comprehension than do modifiers. The diagnostic value of the technique is increased by asking the student to state his reason for inserting certain words.

There are two methods of scoring: (1) according to the precise word used by the author or (2) according to an appropriate word, though not the exact word used in the original passage (Schneyer, 1965; Bloomer, 1962).

There is a positive relationship between results on the cloze technique and reading achievement (Bormuth, 1967). Poor readers and those unfamiliar with the structure of language and with book language would have difficulty in supplying the missing words in cloze exercises. In some instances the correlations between cloze technique results and reading achievement have been higher than those with intelligence test scores.

APPRAISAL BY STANDARDIZED TESTS

If a teacher has clearly in mind specific reading skills and appreciations which his pupils need to acquire, and if he has analyzed each of these into a learning sequence, he can obtain essential diagnostic information as he teaches. If he gives informal tests from time to time, he will quickly obtain a basis for instruction and practice needed by the whole class, by certain groups, and by individuals. Does he also need to use standardized reading tests? If so, what purposes do they serve?

The standardized test is the most widely used instrument for appraising students' reading proficiency, measuring their reading progress, and evaluating reading programs. There are many well-constructed standardized reading tests from which to choose. Complete lists of reading tests, together with descriptions and evaluations of those that are frequently used, are available in several sources: Bond and Tinker, 1967, pages 529–537; Buros, 1965; *Review of Educational Research*, 1968; Strang and others, 1967, chapter 5 and pages 206–211. (See also the Appendix.)

Abilities measured, and not measured, by reading tests

In the past, most standardized tests have measured a narrow range of reading abilities (Hunt, 1955). The abilities most often measured are vocabulary and comprehension; less frequently, rate of comprehension, oral reading, and study skills. When the scores on rate and comprehension are interdependent, the comprehension scores of the student who reads thoroughly may be lowered. Another student may make a high rate score at the expense of accurate comprehension. On time-limit tests, the fast reader has an advantage over the slower, more thoughtful reader. The student handicapped by lack of basic vocabulary and word recognition skills cannot achieve the higher levels of comprehension he might be capable of.

There are many important aspects of reading that standardized reading tests do not adequately measure at present, such as ability to (1) adapt rate and method of reading to one's purpose and to the kind of material being read, (2) use context clues effectively, (3) organize ideas while reading, (4) recognize the author's purpose, and (5) read critically and with appreciation. From standardized tests alone the teacher cannot distinguish between the slow learners and those who have potential mental ability to read better. Moreover, tests do not shed light on the student's reading process: how he arrived at his answers or what difficulties he encountered in the reading tasks. Tests are concerned with product rather than with process. Two students may get the same score on a test, but one may arrive at his comprehension of the passage by a much more mature thought process than the other. Some of these limitations would be minimized if teachers would analyze and discuss students' answers with them.

We might also ask: What *do* reading tests actually measure? Reading ability, intelligence, educational opportunity, industry, or family background? Or various linguistic abilities? Or the individual's values, purpose, or self-concept? The results for a particular student will vary with his familiarity with the subject, with the similarity of the test selections to the reading he has been doing, with his understanding and interpretation of the directions, and with the kind of reading instruction he has had. All these factors enter into reading achievement in different degrees, for reading is a dynamic interaction of psychological forces. Anything as complex as the reading process cannot be fully measured by standardized tests.

Types of tests

Survey tests, in addition to assessing the student's general level of reading development, are often used to show the range of reading ability in a given class and to place students in more homogeneous reading groups. They can be administered to a whole class as well as to individuals.

By studying the subtest scores, analyzing the errors, and encouraging students to discuss their responses, the teacher may extract some diagnostic information from even the survey type of test. Other tests include more diagnostic features. They may yield three to five subtest scores and thus indicate group and individual weaknesses and strengths.

Tests of reading speed are probably the least reliable for several reasons. Each individual has different rates of comprehension, depending upon his purpose and the difficulty of the content. Speed cannot be separated from comprehension. Moreover, results of speed tests are especially dependent upon the instructions given and upon the way the individual interprets the instructions.

It is quite common for students given instruction in speed reading to increase in rate but lose in comprehension. They also frequently show a loss in rate some weeks after instruction has ended. Initially rapid readers may make the greatest gains and maintain them better than initially slow readers. In remedial work with slow readers, additional diagnosis of the causes of their slow rate should be made. They should be given practice in speed of comprehension and especially in adjusting their rate to their purpose and to the difficulty of the reading material.

Diagnostic tests give a more detailed picture of a student's strengths and specific weaknesses. If a student does poorly on the survey test, difficulties blocking his progress may be detected by a diagnostic battery. By making a profile showing the student's relative strengths and weaknesses, the teacher can see at a glance the skills in which instruction and practice are needed.

Some tests provide more adequate diagnostic clues than do others. But if a test attempts to cover too many aspects of reading ability, its subtests are likely to be too short to be reliable.

Individuals differ with respect to their preferred modes of learning. Some learn more easily through auditory, others through visual, channels. Some tend to observe wholes; others, to focus their attention on details. Many seem to learn equally well by all methods. An elementary *learning methods test* has been developed to guide teachers in selecting the best methods to use with individual students. This unique Learning Methods Test devised by Mills (1954–1955) consists of four trial lessons in word recognition, each taught by a different method. Comparable words are presented in each lesson, and the student's actual learning is tested both at the time of the lesson and one day later. This test gives clues to the method by which an individual student may learn best.

Choice of reading tests

Since reading tests measure a variety of reading skills often differently labeled, and sometimes the same skill under different names, the first questions to ask in choosing a reading test are the following:

> What is my purpose in giving the test? What are my objectives— what specific reading abilities do I want my students to achieve?
>
> Which of these objectives *can* be measured adequately?
>
> Which of these objectives does *this* test measure adequately?
>
> For which of the objectives must I use some nontest procedure?

For example, the vocabulary part of the Metropolitan Reading Test, Intermediate Level, Form R, directly measures the association of word forms with their correct meaning and, as a prerequisite, accurate discrimination of word forms. The paragraph reading section measures the abilities to grasp the meaning of paragraphs and to cope with such factors as unusual word order, complexity of sentence structure, and abstract ideas.

When making a diagnosis, the reading teacher or psychologist chooses a variety of tests that do not overlap. If the tests or subtests are highly correlated, they contribute little to an understanding of the individual's specific reading skills and difficulties.

Items in the analysis of a reading test

The following form is a useful guide in careful test selection.

General facts: Title, author, publisher, designated function.
Reading abilities measured: Are they significant and suitable?
Validity: Does the test measure what it purports to measure?
Reliability: Is the test accurate and consistent?
Diagnostic value: Does it indicate the students' special difficulties and give clues to why they are having these difficulties?
Norms: What types of norms are available? Are they representative of the total population or of certain groups?
Pupil performance: What does the pupil do?
Construction of test: How were the exercises selected?
Manual: Are the directions complete and easily intelligible? Are norms included, uses of the test described, and other data given about test and teaching aids?
Costs:
Mechanical considerations: Is it legible, etc.?

For brief analyses of a few representative reading tests, see the Appendix.

Diagnostic information from standardized reading tests

The amount of useful diagnostic insight that is actually extracted from standardized tests covers a range from practically none to a great deal. A single total score gives a basis for comparison with students of the same chronological age or grade. But emphasis on norms runs counter to the point of view that every child should be helped to develop *his* potentialities, rather than be expected to reach a grade standard or national norm.

Subtests, although too short to be reliable, do suggest inequalities among reading abilities such as vocabulary knowledge and paragraph comprehension.

An analysis of the student's correct responses and errors on each reading item yields additional information, depending upon the variety of responses called for in the test. Some test items call merely for knowledge of the common meaning of words. Others test the ability to select the particular meaning that fits the context, to answer specific factual questions, to find the main ideas of the passage, to sense the author's mood and purpose, to recognize literary devices, to make generalizations, to draw inferences and conclusions, or to interpret character and motives. Analysis of the responses to specific questions has been worked out in detail in the reading section of the Sequential Tests of Educational Progress—Teachers' Guide, Cooperative Test Division, Educational Testing Service, Princeton, N.J., 1959, pp. 20, 21. The Educational Testing Service Committee states that STEP Reading Test 1A measures five major reading-for-comprehension skills:

1. Ability to reproduce ideas
2. Ability to translate ideas and make inferences
3. Ability to analyze motivation
4. Ability to analyze presentation
5. Ability to criticize

The tables on pages 137–138 represent one method of identifying which of the five skills listed above are tested by each question in Part One and Part Two of the test. By noting the incorrect responses in the blank columns, the student may more clearly identify those skill areas on which he requires further practice. A similar analysis may be made of any test that consists of exercises that measure different skills.

From further analysis of a student's errors the teacher may recognize certain difficulties. For example, in a vocabulary test in which each mislead of the multiple-choice questions represents a different kind of error, he may note that a student frequently confuses two words that are similar in form or details. From this observation he may assume a tendency to give overpotency to the shape of a word or to certain prominent details in it. If the student gives a correct dictionary definition of a word but not the meaning that is called for by the context, the teacher may infer that the student is not sufficiently concerned with the meaning of what he reads. If he mentions only isolated details in a free-response question, he probably needs instruction and practice in organizing the author's thought. If he does much better on the factual multiple-choice questions than on those calling for inferences or interpretation, the teacher may assume that the reader has not been taught or has not learned the higher-level reading skills or that he is not mentally equipped to do the kind of reasoning that they require. There are, of course, any number of possible reasons for any type of error.

To check inferences based on an analysis of errors, the teacher needs another method: introspection. The examiner or teacher sits down with the student and invites him to try to explain how he made his errors and how he arrived at his correct responses. In this way both the examiner and the student will gain further insight into the reading process.

A depth analysis of a reading test has much educational value: It makes

ANALYSIS OF SKILLS TESTED IN STEP READING TEST

PART ONE

No. of exercise	Skills measured				
	a	*b*	*c*	*d*	*e*
1		x			
2		x	x		
3		x	x		
4				x	
5		x			
6	x				
7			x		
8			x		
9		x	x		
10			x		
11	x				
12		x			
13			x		
14		x			
15				x	
16		x			
17		x			
18		x	x		
19	x				
20			x	x	
21	x				
22			x		
23	x				
24			x	x	
25		x			
26	x	x			
27	x				
28	x				
29				x	
30		x			
31			x	x	
32					
33		x			
34				x	
35				x	
Total	8	14	12	8	

PART TWO

No. of exercise	Skills measured				
	a	b	c	d	e
1	X				
2		X			
3			X		
4				X	
5		X			X
6		X	X		
7		X			
8			X		
9					X
10			X		
11				X	
12		X			
13	X	X			
14			X		
15					X
16				X	
17				X	
18		X			
19				X	X
20				X	
21		X			
22			X		
23			X		
24					X
25		X			
26	X				
27			X		
28		X			
29		X			
30		X			
31		X			
32			X		
33				X	
34		X			
35					X
Total	3	14	9	7	6
Total I	8	14	12	8	0
Total II	3	14	9	7	6
Total I and II	11	28	21	15	6
Percentage	14	34	26	19	7

the student aware of his reading methods, motivates him to do better, and increases his receptivity to instruction on the specific skills in which he sees the need for improvement. What the teacher does with the diagnostic information thus obtained is, of course, of prime importance.

Uses of standardized tests

The reading test scores of a school or school district are often summarized and publicized. The results may call attention to the need for improvement in reading, but they may also lead to unjust comparisons between classes and schools if conditions influencing reading achievement are not taken into account. Far more important is their use in improving instruction, in diagnosis rather than prediction. "Measurement should be used to improve status . . . rather than to determine status" (Hamburger, 1965, p. 75).

STUDYING READING ABILITY OF A CLASS By ranking all the students in order according to their standardized reading test scores, the teacher will see the range of reading ability represented in the class as measured by a particular reading test. He will realize, however, that another test might produce somewhat different estimates of reading level. He may use this information to group students tentatively according to their present reading performance so that he may provide suitable reading material for each group. However, Bond and Tinker (1967, p. 178) make clear that to select reading material and to provide remedial instruction as indicated by the test would often overestimate the level on which instruction should begin.

By recording not only the total reading score but also the subtest scores, the teacher will see variations in the reading abilities of individual students and of the group. Some students having the same total score may be low in vocabulary and high in paragraph comprehension, or vice versa. The group as a whole may need special instruction in one of the skills measured.

STUDYING READING ACHIEVEMENT IN RELATION TO INTELLIGENCE TEST SCORES
By also recording the student's mental ability converted into grade scores and the grade scores on other achievement tests, especially arithmetic, the teacher will gain some idea of the student's reading achievement as related to his scholastic aptitude (see Chapter 11).

A series of tests of achievement and intelligence such as the Sequential Tests of Educational Progress (STEP) and the School and College Ability Tests (SCAT) (Alpert and others, 1956–1957; Early and others, 1956–1957), which have been standardized on the same population and whose scores have been converted into standard scores and percentile bands, may throw some light on a student's reading potential. For example, if he is in the highest quarter on SCAT and in a lower quarter on STEP, we may have some indication that he has the mental potential to read better. But we must also take into consideration the facts that SCAT requires reading ability and that there is more than a chance difference between the two scores only if the student's percentile bands for the two tests do not overlap.

STUDYING READING ACHIEVEMENT OF INDIVIDUALS   In working with an individual, the teacher cannot rely on group averages; the individual may be one of the extreme deviates. The teacher is more concerned with the student's strengths and weaknesses, and with inequalities among his performances on various reading tasks, than with differences between his score and that of his classmates.

A further understanding may be gained by the flexible use of standardized tests in individual cases. In 1937 Vernon said that the clinical psychologist

> doubts the efficacy of standardizing the objective conditions of testing, since it may fail to standardize the "subjective situation," i.e., the meaning of the situation to the person tested; and it is this meaning which will determine the test response. . . . In our direct dealings with one another, qualitative distinctions appear to predominate, and single vectors of mind are seldom considered in isolation from the complex structure of the personality. . . . Only when such measures [of purely cognitive variables] are considered synthetically with other information about the personality can they tell him anything about the individual which will be of assistance in diagnosis and treatment (p. 101).

Testing often contributes to an individualized profile or description of the student. The profile may show graphically the level and variations in achievement in different aspects of reading, such as those measured by the Silent Reading Diagnostic Tests (1955). One student may be consistently a little above average on each of the subtests except following directions. Another may have high total reading expectancy but be low in speed, ability to predict outcomes, and word meaning in context. A third student may be consistently far below the average and make the lowest score possible on certain subtests (Bond and Tinker, 1967, p. 188).

The individualized profile may merge into a case study which interprets, relates, and integrates information from many sources (see Chapter 14). In addition to the results of informal and standardized tests, the case study includes information on physical and personality factors and an appraisal of home and school conditions that may be influencing the individual's reading achievement. Personal data from all these sources are interpreted and synthesized in the case study.

Tests may serve as a springboard for promoting self-evaluation and independence. By going over their own test exercises, students gain an understanding of their competencies and their difficulties. This understanding should lead to a clearer view of specific goals for improvement. Many students can raise their sights. Too often the reading task set serves as a ceiling, not a challenge. If students are free to set their own goals, they may surpass their previous performance and do more than teachers expect of them. They no longer aim simply to "get by." Instead of merely meeting the teacher's standards when he is present to enforce them, they will work on their own initiative.

Once they have determined to correct certain errors and to reinforce their correct responses, they are receptive to instruction. Parallel with and following instruction and practice, they keep their own records. Freedom of choice, accompanied by a sense of responsibility for their acts, accords with their desire to be independent.

Using tests to help students make a self-appraisal is a far cry from the common administrative use of tests. Though both uses share the common aim of promoting better reading, self-appraisal makes a more direct and effective approach because it evokes greater student motivation and is associated with the individual's basic tendency toward self-actualization.

EVALUATING READING PROGRAMS AND TESTING HYPOTHESES Standardized tests have also been used almost exclusively to evaluate reading programs and methods of instruction. Hundreds of studies of this kind have been made, without sufficient recognition of the inadequacy of available tests to measure all the important outcomes of reading instruction. In comparison or control group studies, the failure to control all the variables that influence students' learning makes the results of the experiments inconclusive.

In research, reading tests have been used extensively to test hypotheses. Although standardized test results provide a more objective and dependable basis than general impressions for accepting or rejecting a particular hypothesis, they often afford only a partial measure of the outcomes.

Summary of criticisms of the interpretation and use of standardized tests

Tests are often given without a clearly defined purpose. Too little attention is given to the background of the students and the conditions under which the test is given. For example, McDonald (1960) obtained experimental evidence that reading comprehension is impaired by periodic interruptions during testing. This detrimental effect was especially evident in students rated as highly anxious. Other personality factors which influence test performance are stress and tension, need for achievement, impulsiveness, introversion-extroversion, tendencies to acquiesce and to give socially approved responses. Rankin (1963) found that the greater the degree of extroversion, the smaller the reliability and validity appeared to be.

Much valuable diagnostic information is never extracted from the tests. The information obtained is often not used directly to help students improve their reading.

In retesting, the practice effect frequently is ignored; the gains are attributed to general improvement in reading.

Interpretation of test scores may be misleading if the population tested is different from that on which the test was standardized.

Tests have been overused as well as misused. It is significant that physicians have criticized the overuse of routine medical laboratory tests for several reasons: It is costly and wasteful and may cause needless anxiety on the part of patients. Physicians feel that too great a reliance on fallible tests and reports is misleading, and that reliance on routine procedures may promote a stereotyped rather than a thoughtful, analytical approach to clinical problems. Educators might well consider whether the same criticism might not apply to the overuse of tests used in diagnosing reading ability.

The limitations of standardized tests themselves may not be recognized. To be aware of them will help to prevent errors in diagnostic formulation:

> Some tests overestimate students' reading ability (Leibert, 1965); thus the grade level estimated by the test may be higher than the grade level of books the students can actually read.

> "Comparable" forms of the same test, assumed to be parallel, often are not.

> The influence of the speed emphasis may distort the total scores of some tests.

> The validity of a test may vary with the student's age level and reading level.

> Guessing may raise scores on some tests more than on others.

> For some groups the test ceiling is too low; it will not measure the most able students.

> Standardized tests may be an unsatisfactory measure of the progress of individual students, especially when their progress is slight. Because of the error of measurement, a fairly low score on the initial test might conceivably represent greater achievement than a higher final score.

Despite these limitations in standardized reading tests, many teachers feel more secure in using them than in using informal reading inventories, and their scores may indeed show a considerable discrepancy. When McCracken (1962) compared the grade-level ratings of a group of sixth-grade children on the Iowa Test of Basic Skills, Form I, with ratings obtained on an informal reading inventory, he found an average difference of 2.3 years between the Iowa reading-comprehension grade levels and the instructional-reading levels as indicated by the informal reading inventory. Although the correlation was .78, the difference in estimates in some individual cases was from three to five years. The Iowa test rated most of the children higher in both comprehension and vocabulary than did the informal inventory. Thus a book on the grade level indicated by the standardized test might actually be on the child's frustration level.

CONCLUDING STATEMENT

There are indications that teachers' observations of children's day-by-day performance in reading different kinds of material give the best possible basis for diagnostic teaching. Observation may be supplemented by informal tests and inventories based on reading that students are doing in the classroom. Group standardized tests make possible comparisons with other students, if that is necessary or desirable, and provide more precise measurement of certain reading abilities.

If a test does not help a teacher, directly or indirectly, to teach better, there is not much point in administering it. Much effort and money are wasted in giving tests that are not needed and by failing to use the results of tests that are given. The Cooperative Test Division of the Educational Testing Service is influential in helping teachers to make better use of tests.

In making any decision or comparison, it is very important (1) to consider the error of measurement in a test score and (2) to use all other sources of information about the student's characteristics, background, and experience in conjunction with the test scores. No test score is infallible. A child making a grade score of 3 on a reading test may not be able to read a third-grade book. A difference between two scores, such as between a reading and an intelligence test score, may be canceled out by the errors of measurement of the two tests. An observed difference is not always a real difference.

The cautious, flexible, purposeful, apppropriate use of informal and standardized tests, insightfully interpreted, will yield much valuable diagnostic information.

SUGGESTED PROBLEMS: PRACTICE AND DEMONSTRATION

1. Take a college-level reading test such as the STEP, score it, analyze your responses, summarize the results, and make recommendations for improving your own reading.

2. Summarize research on the relation between intelligence test scores and reading ability. A number of doctoral studies on this topic have been reported in *Dissertation Abstracts*, published yearly by the University of Michigan, Ann Arbor (see especially vols. 19–23). Microfilm copies of all dissertations reported may be obtained from University Microfilms, Ann Arbor.

3. Make, administer, score, and use with a class an informal group inventory in a given subject.

4. Using the directions given in this chapter, make an analysis of a recent reading test.

5. Describe a class or school situation, state the objective for reading improvement, and select a test that would best meet all the criteria given in this chapter.

6. Score, analyze, record, and use the results of the reading test selected and given to an elementary or high school class.

7. Discuss with several individual students their responses on a group test.

REFERENCES

ALPERT, HARVEY, and others: *Sequential Tests of Educational Progress: Reading*, Cooperative Test Division, Educational Testing Service, Princeton, N.J., 1956–1957. For grades 13–14, Level 1; for grades 10–12, Level 2; for grades 7–9, Level 3; for grades 4–6, Level 4; Forms A and B yield one overall score.

BLOOMER, RICHARD H.: "The Cloze Procedure as a Remedial Reading Exercise," *Journal of Developmental Reading*, 5:173–181, Spring, 1962.

BOND, GUY L., and MILES A. TINKER: *Reading Difficulties, Their Diagnosis and Correction*, 2d ed., Appleton-Century-Crofts, Inc., New York, 1967.

BORMUTH, JOHN R.: "Mean Word Depth as a Predictor of Comprehension Difficulty," *California Journal of Educational Research*, 15:226–231, November, 1964.

———: "Comparable Cloze and Multiple-choice Comprehension Test Scores," *Journal of Reading*, 10:291–299, February, 1967.

BUROS, OSCAR K. (ed.): *The Sixth Mental Measurements Yearbook*, The Gryphon Press, Highland Park, N.J., 1965.

Committee on Diagnostic Reading Tests: grades kindergarten–4, 4–6, 7–13, vocabulary, comprehension, rate, word attack; Committee on Diagnostic Reading Tests, Mountain Home, N.C., 1947–1960.

CROMER, WARD, and MERTON WIENER: "Idiosyncratic Response Patterns among Good and Poor Readers," *Journal of Consulting Psychology*, 30:1–10, February, 1966.

EARLY, MARGARET J., and others: *Sequential Tests of Educational Progress: Listening*, Cooperative Test Division, Educational Testing Service, Princeton, N.J., 1956–1957. For grades 13–14, Level 1; for grades 10–12, Level 2; for grades 7–9, Level 3; for grades 4–6, Level 4; Forms A and B yield one overall score.

HAMBURGER, MARTIN: "Measurement Issues in the Counseling of the Culturally Disadvantaged," in *Proceedings of the 1964 Invitational Conference on Testing Problems*, Educational Testing Service, Princeton, N.J., 1965, pp. 71–81.

HUNT, J. T.: "Selecting a High School Reading Test," *High School Journal*, 39:49–52, October, 1955.

KARLIN, ROBERT, and HAYDEN JOLLY: "The Use of Alternate Forms of Standardized Tests," *The Reading Teacher*, 19:187–191, 196, December, 1965.

KENDER, JOSEPH P.: "How Useful Are Informal Reading Tests?" *Journal of Reading*, 11:337–342, February, 1968.

LEIBERT, ROBERT E.: "An Investigation of the Differences in Reading Performance on Two Tests of Reading," unpublished doctoral dissertation, Syracuse University, Syracuse, N.Y., June, 1965.

MAYER, ROBERT W.: "A Study of the STEP Reading, SCAT and WISC Tests, and School Grades," *The Reading Teacher*, 12:117–142, December, 1958.

MC CRACKEN, ROBERT A.: "Standardized Reading Tests and Informal Reading Inventories," *Education*, 82:366–369, February, 1962.

MC DONALD, ARTHUR S.: "Factors Affecting Reading Test Performance," in *Research and Evaluation in College Reading*, Ninth Yearbook, National Reading Conference, 1960, pp. 28–35.

MELNIK, AMELIA: "The Improvement of Reading through Self-appraisal: A Procedure for Teaching Reading in Junior High School Social Studies," unpublished doctoral dissertation, Teachers College, Columbia University, New York, 1960.

MILLS, ROBERT E.: *Learning Methods Test*, Mills Center, Inc., Fort Lauderdale, Fla., 1954–1955.

PARSLEY, K. M., JR., and MARVIN POWELL: "Relationships between the Lee-Clark Reading Readiness Test and the 1937 Revisions of the Stanford-Binet Intelligence Test, Form L," *Journal of Educational Research*, 54:304–307, 1961.

RANKIN, EARL F., JR.: "Reading Test Reliability and Validity as Functions of Introversion-Extroversion," *Journal of Developmental Reading*, 6:106–117, Winter, 1963.

Review of Educational Research, 38:1–110, February, 1968.

SCHNEYER, J. WESLEY: "Use of the Cloze Procedure for Improving Reading Comprehension," *The Reading Teacher*, 19:174–179, December, 1965.

School and College Ability Tests, Educational Testing Service, Princeton, N.J., 1952. Levels 1–5 cover grades 4–14; four forms of Level 1 and two forms each for other levels yield a verbal score, a quantitative score, and a total score.

SHEPHERD, DAVID: *Effective Reading in the Social Studies* and *Effective Reading in Science*, Harper & Row, Publishers, Incorporated, New York, 1960.

SMITH, HELEN K.: "The Responses of Good and Poor Readers When Asked to Read for Different Purposes," *Reading Research Quarterly*, 3:53–83, Fall, 1967.

STEP Manual for Interpreting Scores: Reading, Cooperative Test Division, Educational Testing Service, Princeton, N.J., 1959.

STRANG, RUTH: "Evaluation of Development in and through Reading," in *Development in and through Reading*, Sixtieth Yearbook of the National Society for the Study of Education, The University of Chicago Press, Chicago, 1961, chap. 21.

—— and DOROTHY KENDALL BRACKEN: *Making Better Readers*, D. C. Heath and Company, Boston, 1957.

——, CONSTANCE M. MC CULLOUGH, and ARTHUR E. TRAXLER: *The Improvement of Reading*, McGraw-Hill Book Company, New York, 1967.

TRAXLER, ARTHUR E.: "Standardized Tests: What They Are, How They Are Used—and Misused," *NEA Journal*, 48:18–20, November, 1959.

VERNON, P. E.: "The Stanford-Binet Test as a Psychometric Method," *Character and Personality*, 6:99–113, December, 1937.

SUGGESTED READINGS

ANASTASI, ANNE (ed.): *Testing Problems in Perspective: Twenty-fifth Anniversary Volume of Topical Readings from the Invitational Conference on Testing Problems*, American Council on Education, Washington, D.C., 1966.

BOAG, A. K., and M. NEILD: "Influence of the Time Factor on the Scores of the Triggs Diagnostic Reading Test as Reflected in the Performance of Secondary School Pupils Grouped according to Ability," *Journal of Educational Research*, 55:181–183, December, 1961.

CLYMER, THEODORE A.: "A Study of the Validity of the California Test of Mental Maturity, Elementary Language Section," in *The Eighteenth Yearbook of the National Council of Measurement Used in Education*, Ames, Iowa, 1961, 125–128.

CONANT, MARGARET M.: *The Construction of a Diagnostic Reading Test*, Teachers College Press, Columbia University, New York, 1942.

DELECATO, C. H.: *The Diagnosis and Treatment of Speech and Reading Problems*, Charles C Thomas, Publisher, Springfield, Ill., 1963.

DEUTSCH, MARTIN, and others: "Guidelines for Testing Minority Group Children," *Journal of Social Issues*, 20:129–145, April, 1964.

EBEL, ROBERT L.: "The Social Consequences of Educational Testing," *Proceedings of the 1963 Invitational Conference on Testing Problems*, Educational Testing Service, Princeton, N.J., 1964, pp. 130–143.

"Educational and Psychological Testing," *Review of Educational Research*, 38:1–110, February, 1968.

FISKE, DONALD W.: "The Subject Reacts to Tests," *American Psychologist*, 22:287–296, April, 1967.

GOSLIN, DAVID A.: "The Social Impact of Testing," *Personnel and Guidance Journal*, 45:676–682, March, 1967.

HAFNER, LAWRENCE E.: "Cloze Procedure," *Journal of Reading*, 9:415–421, May, 1966.

KING, MARTHA (ed.): *Critical Reading*, J. B. Lippincott Company, Philadelphia, 1967.

KOLSON, C. J., and G. KALUGER: *Clinical Aspects of Remedial Reading*, Charles C Thomas, Publisher, Springfield, Ill., 1963.

LAMB, GEORGE S.: "Teacher Verbal Cues and Pupil Performance on a Group Reading Test," *Journal of Educational Psychology*, 58:332–336, December, 1967.

LEE, L. C.: "Evaluation of Standardized Tests Used in Diagnosis," *Conference on Reading*, The University of Pittsburgh Press, Pittsburgh, 1960, pp. 39–53.

LORETAN, JOSEPH O.: "Alternatives to Intelligence Testing," *Proceedings of the 1965 Invitational Conference on Testing Problems*, Educational Testing Service, Princeton, N.J., 1966, pp. 19–30.

MACKINNON, A. R.: *How Do Children Learn to Read? An Experimental Investigation of Children's Early Growth in Awareness of the Meanings of Printed Symbols*, The Copp Clark Publishing Co., Ltd., Toronto, Canada, 1959.

MEHRENS, WILLIAM A., and ROBERT L. EBEL: *Principles of Educational and Psychological Measurement*, Rand McNally & Company, Chicago, 1967.

RANKIN, E. F., JR.: "The Cloze Procedure. A Survey of Research," in E. L. Thurston and L. E. Hafner (eds.), *The Philosophical and Sociological Bases of Reading*, Yearbook of the National Reading Conference, vol. 14, pp. 133–150, 1965.

ROSWELL, FLORENCE G.: "Improved Diagnostic Procedures in Reading at the Junior High School Level," in *Reading and Inquiry, International Reading Association Conference Proceedings*, vol. 10, 1965, pp. 180–181.

SWENSON, ESTHER J.: "A Study of the Relationships among Various Types of Reading Scores on General and Science Materials," *Journal of Educational Research*, 36:81–90, October, 1942.

TINKER, MILES A., and CONSTANCE M. MC CULLOUGH: *Teaching Elementary Reading*, 2d ed., Appleton-Century-Crofts, Inc., New York, 1962.

WESTOVER, FREDERICK L.: "A Comparison of Listening and Reading as a Means of Testing," *Journal of Educational Research*, 52:23–26, September, 1958.

SUGGESTED READINGS

BARON, D., and H. W. BERNARD: *Evaluation Techniques for Classroom Teachers*, McGraw-Hill Book Company, New York, 1953.

HOLMES, DAVID S.: "Search for 'Closure' in a Visually Perceived Pattern," *Psychological Bulletin*, 70:296–312, November, 1968.

Making the Classroom Test, Evaluation and Advisory Service, ser. 4, Educational Testing Service, Princeton, N.J., 1959.

ODELL, C. W.: *How to Improve Classroom Testing*, William C. Brown and Company, Dubuque, Iowa, 1953.

Selecting an Achievement Test, Evaluation and Advisory Service, ser. 3, Educational Testing Service, Princeton, N.J., 1958.

WOOD, DOROTHY ADKINS: *Test Construction: Development and Interpretation of Achievement Tests*, Charles E. Merrill Books, Inc., Columbus, Ohio, 1960.

INDIVIDUAL
METHODS

Chapter Eight

INTRODUCTION

Although all the methods discussed in Part One may be used with individual cases, most of the procedures to be described in Part Two must be applied individually. Some of these are relatively objective and standardized, such as visual and auditory screening tests, oral reading tests, the individual reading inventory, and the standardized individual diagnostic reading tests. On a higher level of psychological complexity are the individual intelligence tests and projective techniques which must be administered and interpreted by competent psychologists or clinicians. Apparently quite simple but actually requiring specialized clinical skill are the diagnostic interview, play therapy, and other kinds of therapy which may uncover the subtle factors that underlie severe reading disability. Since the reading process is so extremely complex, we need a diversity of methods for gaining understanding of it.

THE DYNAMIC VIEW

The dynamic view seeks to ascertain the conditions that have caused or are now causing a given reading problem. It also seeks to detect "trigger reactions" that may release an individual's desire to improve his reading. The clinician may think of some serious reading problems as symptoms of an underlying personality disturbance or disorganization. He tries to create external conditions that may modify some of the psychological factors. He tries to discover the client's latent capacities for satisfaction in work, play, and creative activities. Success in learning to read often has a therapeutic influence. The teacher, though not a therapist, may, through skillful instruction, have a therapeutic effect.

CONDITIONS AND CHARACTERISTICS THAT MAY LEAD TO READING DIFFICULTY

Because of the complexity of the reading process, the reading clinician needs a background knowledge of the wide variety of conditions that may prevent an individual from attaining his reading potential. Some of these conditions, described fully in references at the end of this chapter and in other chapters, will be briefly mentioned here.

Physical and neurological conditions

Physical conditions such as visual and auditory impairments may aggravate or precipitate reading difficulty. Malnutrition, glandular disturbances, and prolonged illness interfere with the child's overall development and thus inevitably hinder his reading achievement. Illnesses or accidents that change the child's concept of himself often have disturbing secondary effects on his reading development. Maturational lag and disturbed patterns of mental and physical growth may especially affect a child's beginning reading progress and make it difficult for him to catch up with his classmates. However, other children with reading difficulty seem to be in excellent physical condition. Some of these try to compensate for their poor reading by achievement in athletics.

Among the possible organic causes of reading retardation are brain damage, confused laterality, and neurological disorganization (Eames, 1960). Some brain-damaged children are bright but so overactive and easily distracted that they have difficulty in focusing their attention on specific reading tasks. They also have difficulty in the synthesis or integration of spelling patterns, words, and sentences (Farnham-Diggory, 1967). The relation of mixed laterality to reading, once a controversial issue (Vernon, 1957), has recently been shown to be of slight diagnostic significance (Capobianco, 1966; Belmont and Birch, 1965; Stephens, Cunningham, and Stigler, 1967). Neurological disorganization is considered by some to be a primary cause of severe reading difficulty but is extremely difficult to diagnose.

Perceptual-motor abilities

Perpetual-motor skills play an important role in the beginning stages of learning to read, perhaps a more important role than emotional disturbance or mental ability. Many research studies have shown a positive correlation between difficulties in visual perception and achievement in reading. In general, average and superior readers tend to perform better than retarded readers on tests of perceptual differentiation, tests of closure, and measures of lag in perceptual-motor maturation (Koppitz, 1964; Chang and Chang, 1967; McLeod, 1967). M. D. Vernon (1966) published abstracts of fifty-five studies of perception of shapes and words by children and adults.

Visual perception is built on sensorimotor experiences. Not only visual acuity, but also hand-eye coordination, left-right body orientation, and other visual-spatial abilities are involved. Reading requires the ability to hold in mind the word, phrase, or sentence as a whole, and also to attend to the individual parts in sequence (Goins, 1958). Visual sequencing is closely related to success in word perception.

Perception is an intermediate process between sensation and thought. Associations with previous experience give meaning to the incoming sensory impressions. Perceptual training, in turn, contributes to concept formation. A retarded reader may not be able to deal with abstraction because he does not have the necessary background of experience. This perceptual-concept continuum is an important factor in reading development.

Proficiency in perceptual abilities changes with age. Errors in perception of shapes and pictures tend to decrease with age from five to eight years; nonsystematic patterning, to decrease in favor of complex patterning (Elkind and Weiss, 1967). Seventh-grade children with reading disabilities were found to be significantly inferior to the control group in ability to reproduce visually presented letter sequences and auditorily presented words (McLeod, 1967).

Early recognition and correction of perceptual-motor deficits are strongly recommended. Tests of visual and auditory perception should be included as part of the diagnostic procedure for kindergarten and first-grade children (Mertens, 1968). Beyond the age of eleven years, successful readers seem either to be less dependent upon the perceptual field or to have corrected or compensated for their deficiencies. By that age the verbal IQ has become more closely related to reading level than are perceptual and manipulative skills (Belmont and Birch, 1965).

The need for practice in some of these perceptual skills, figure and background discrimination, for example, was indicated by a ten-year follow-up study of retarded readers (Silver and Hagin, 1964). Significant gains can be made by kindergarten children as a result of training in visual discrimination. Cohen (1966–1967) reported significant gains by first graders resulting from ten weeks of training with the Frostig program, but no corresponding gains in reading. Using original practice exercises for developing underlying perceptual abilities, perceptual speed, visual memory, auditory memory, sound blending, visual closure, auditory closure, and concept formation, Burkholder (1968) obtained gains in reading as well as in these underlying abilities of second-grade children. Such exercises are most effective when they progress from pictures and geometric forms to letters and words and from the concrete to the abstract. They are also more effective when practice is accompanied by instruction.

Auditory perception and the ability to discriminate and say words presented auditorily have also been shown to be essential to success in beginning reading (Birch and Belmont, 1964; Dykstra, 1966). Wepman (1960) described three levels of sequential development of auditory perception: acuity, understanding, and discrimination and retention. He found significant differences in mean reading scores between a group of first- and second-grade pupils who were adequate in auditory discrimination and articulation and a group who were inadequate. His correlation between scores on the Kuhlman-Anderson Intelligence Test and auditory discrimination scores was .32.

Of special importance is the ability to integrate auditory and visual stimuli (Birch and Belmont, 1964; Magginitie, 1967). After a period of rapid growth between kindergarten and second grade, which reaches a peak by fifth grade, the correlation between reading and auditory-visual integration decreases with age. However, retarded readers seem to be faced with special difficulties in integration, which could occur if either sensory avenue were impaired. The diagnostic procedure, therefore, should include (1) tests of auditory and visual efficiency, (2) tests of auditory and visual perception, discrimination, and memory, (3) a test of auditory-visual integration, and (4) a test of ability to categorize.

Inadequate education

Educational deprivation of various kinds—which may be due to prolonged absence from school, ineffective instruction, or dislike of the teacher—may seriously affect children's reading progress in the primary grades. Even in the upper grades, serious consequences may ensue when basic instruction in reading for all students and special instruction and practice needed by retarded readers are neglected. The total curriculum and methods of instruction may have a pervasive effect on a child's reading development.

Environmental conditions

Out-of-school environmental conditions may create or intensify reading difficulties (Rhodes, 1967). Unfavorable conditions in home and neighborhood background, such as an anti-intellectual attitude, associated with failure in reading are being increasingly recognized. Family constellations and birth order do not seem to be of great importance (Cicirelli, 1967).

Diagnosis should include an analysis of the situation and the interaction of the child with his environment. Following such a diagnosis, an effort would be made to change the situation instead of the child.

More significantly related to reading achievement are family relationships. Achieving boys seem to identify with their fathers; girls with mothers who are affectionate toward them. It seems reasonable that parents of superior readers would encourage their children's independence, communication, and initiative and not restrict them unduly (McGinnis, 1965). Parental differences of opinion regarding child-rearing practices were found to influence the reading achievement of sixth-grade boys (Kramer and Fleming, 1966).

Another study of certain home-family-community factors related to fifth- and sixth-grade children's achievement in reading in an elementary school. Van Zandt (1963) showed that children in the highest quarter of achievement (1) scored much higher in all subtests of the WISC than the lowest quarter, (2) had more realistic educational and vocational aspirations, and (3) were fortunate in having more favorable home and family conditions. Although deprivation of cultural opportunities and intellectual stimulation may be found on all socioeconomic levels, most studies have shown a relationship between low socioeconomic status and backwardness in reading (Hill and Giammatteo, 1963; Lovell and Woolsey, 1964; Sutton, 1964). One exception to this generalization is Durkin's report (1966) that more than half the parents of early readers were foreign-born and came from the "blue collar" class. Diagnostic information should always be interpreted in the light of environmental conditions that may be interfering with or facilitating students' reading progress in any socioeconomic group.

There seems to be no clear research evidence that mobility of the family is associated with the children's failure in reading (Bollenbacher, 1962; Evans, 1966). In fact, Snipes (1966) reported higher reading achievement among sixth graders who moved most. Morris, Pestaner, and Nelson (1967) found significantly greater variations in achievement for mobile than for nonmobile pupils in the low, but not in the high, socioeconomic levels. In individual cases of retarded readers who have moved frequently, other factors may be more influential than mobility.

One factor that is most clearly related to success in reading is the educational level of the parents (Malmquist, 1960). The mother's education seems to be particularly significant. Research warrants the practice of obtaining information on the education of parents in diagnostic studies.

On the lower economic levels, experiments in providing special guidance, instruction, and cultural advantages for the disadvantaged social groups are being conducted in many large cities.

Linguistic abilities

Linguistic factors contribute greatly to reading proficiency. Listening comprehension (auding) and reading comprehension have about eighteen factors in common (Duker, 1966). The coefficients of correlation between these two language arts are positive and significant, from .45 to .70 with a mean of .58. Individuals who are high in auding tend to be high in reading comprehension. In general the auditory avenue is preferred by the less able student and for less difficult content; the visual, by the more able student and for the more difficult material. Persons interested in structural linguistics emphasize the importance of a good foundation in spoken language for success in beginning reading. To get the author's thought, the mature reader depends on his word knowledge, word recognition skills, and sense of sentence and paragraph structure.

Mental abilities

Lack of mental abilities to remember, to see relationships, and to solve problems of word meaning obviously blocks progress in reading, since reading is a reasoning process (see Chapter 11).

Personality problems

Innumerable emotional difficulties may hinder progress in reading. Secondary emotional difficulties may stem from initial failure in reading, from feelings of inferiority engendered by parental or peer attitudes toward the slow learner, or from physical disabilities. Not all emotionally disturbed children are poor readers, however, nor are all poor readers emotionally disturbed.

Even children who have average or above-average intelligence, who are not suffering from any organic limitations that can be detected, and who seem to come from economically secure homes where reading is encouraged may still lack sufficient drive to succeed in reading. They may be "lacking in spontaneity, enthusiasm and general outgoingness" (Vorhaus, 1946, p. 129). These deficiencies may originate in an unfortunate pattern of interpersonal relations. According to one theory, the child is unconsciously resisting parents' overmanipulation of him and demands that he conform to their expectations, expectations that neglect his basic need to call his soul his own.

Therapy in these cases is directed toward helping the child gain "a better understanding of the growing-up process, which will make it possible for him to substitute adjusted ways of fitting into his role for the repressive and destructive actions which had led to frustration and failure" (Vorhaus, 1946, p. 131). Another child may resent his parents' preference for a more able brother or sister, or he may feel guilty about the trouble and expense he is causing his parents. Talking out these feelings with a sympathetic, understanding person may relieve the tension and anxiety that are interfering with the child's progress in reading.

Many kinds of anxiety and fear seem to be associated with reading difficulties (Frost, 1965). Some of these may originate in infancy or early childhood if the baby is seriously deprived of his mother's affection and personal contact with his mother or mother substitute. The resultant anxiety and apathy, if extreme, seem to persist and to be quite resistant to therapy. It may be that some of our adolescent retarded readers who seem to be willing but unable to put forth the effort to improve their reading have suffered emotional deprivation. Dealing with such cases requires a process of reeducation or reconditioning which involves overcoming fear and apathy by substituting feelings of security and adequacy. The reading teacher may relieve some of the individual's fears and conflicts incidentally as they work together on his reading problem.

The procedure of "behavior modification" has been applied successfully with emotionally disturbed children (Hewett, 1967). It consists of assigning carefully graded tasks analyzed into a sequence of steps that the child can take successfully. His success is rewarded in ways that attach satisfaction to each genuine accomplishment, however small. The technique of behavioral modification may be applied to the child's attention span, to orderly responses in the classroom, or to a specific reading skill.

After reviewing the research on physical and environmental factors that might be significantly related to reading disability, McDonald (1961) emphasized the multicausal aspect. According to this view, reading is a function of the whole personality and is one aspect of the individual's growth. The self-concept is of central importance. Physical, intellectual, social, and personal development must all be considered in the diagnosis and treatment of reading disability.

PARTICULARLY BAFFLING CASES

Cases of severe reading disability—variously called *dyslexia, strethosymbolia, word blindness*—often seem to stem from some neurological deficit. To ignore this possibility and attempt prematurely to teach reading to these children usually causes intense frustration with resulting passivity or aggression that interferes with later learning. On the other hand, even when part of the brain is impaired, new pathways may be substituted for the injured portions (De Hirsch, 1963).

Equally baffling are cases who apparently have adequate ability and favorable home conditions but still do not learn to read. One of these extreme cases is an adolescent boy from a well-to-do family. He has attended school up to the twelfth grade, has learned mathematics and science, but cannot read at all.

His parents have taken him to numerous clinics. He has had neurological, psychiatric, and psychological examinations and years of psychotherapy and remedial reading instruction. The parents, ever hopeful, wanted to take him to a new reading center. This possibility was discussed with the psychologist who last worked with the boy. Several courses of action were considered:

1. Refer the boy to the new reading center. This possibility was rejected because another futile referral would merely increase the boy's sense of hopelessness. (However, if a recently recognized deficit has not been included in the previous remedial treatment, this neglect may be discussed with the boy and his decision obtained to work on it.)

2. Ignore the reading problem for the present and use other avenues of learning with which he has been successful. This approach might remove some of the pressure from him, relieve his anxiety, help him to succeed in the things he can do, and build up his self-confidence. It is well established that although a certain degree of tension is a necessary condition for learning, intense anxiety disrupts learning. There are gradients of anxiety that should be recognized (Sullivan, 1953, pp. 151–154). Later, when his fear of reading has decreased, he may be accessible to instruction.

3. If, for some obscure reason, he seems to be incapable of learning to read, as a small fraction of 1 percent apparently are, this disability should be recognized. He should be taught by means of pictures, diagrams, films, discussions, recordings, and other instructional media and methods through which he *can* learn. The curricula in high school and college should be adjusted to him. He should be permitted to sit in class and listen but should not be expected to read. He should have a congenial buddy who will read him the captions of pictures and diagrams. He should also have a reader and records such as are available to the blind. All his teachers should be given an understanding of the case and be asked to cooperate in this highly specialized program.

These recommendations were based on the assumption that the previous diagnosis was competent and would have uncovered any remediable physical, psychological, or educational factors that were blocking potential reading achievement. It should be emphasized again that such extreme cases of reading disability are very rare.

METHODS OF WORK WITH INDIVIDUALS

Any diagnostic procedure has possible influence on the individual—therapeutic or detrimental. For example, taking a standardized test may either bolster an individual's self-esteem or increase his feelings of inferiority or inadequacy. Composing a reading autobiography may give one student helpful perspective on his reading development but may leave another with an increased sense of hopelessness. Projective techniques may arouse vague feelings of anxiety. In most interviews, "relationship therapy" plays a part in varying degrees; improvement often results from the one-to-one relationship.

Personal interview

The focus of the treatment interview is on helping the individual with his reading problems. But, although diagnosis is subordinate to this main purpose, many insights into the nature and causes of the reading difficulty may be obtained during the interview. Conversely, in connection with every technique described, even when the focus is on diagnosis or appraisal, the interviewer may find opportunity to reinforce positive attitudes, to help the individual gain new insights, and even to impart instruction. Aid given at the moment of discovering an error or a need is of maximum effectiveness.

Interviews are held with reading cases for many purposes; some are primarily tutorial, others are exclusively therapeutic. If the student has had poor instruction in reading and is now eager to make up this deficiency, skillful instruction and ample practice in the reading skills he needs will have a therapeutic effect and will give him the stimulation of success. However, if the individual has inner conflicts that are making it impossible for him to concentrate on reading, then counseling procedures are necessary before he is receptive to reading instruction.

The interview with reading cases usually combines diagnosis, counseling, and instruction. After hearing the individual read a paragraph orally, the interviewer may give him instruction in how he might have read it more effectively. While discussing the student's daily schedule, the interviewer may encourage him to suggest ways of using his time more efficiently. If conversation with the student suggests a disturbed father-son relationship, the interviewer may suggest that he read a story such as "My Father

Doesn't Like Me" (Scott, 1966, pp. 208–230), which may help the child or adolescent clarify this relationship and cope with the problem more effectively.

Appraisal and diagnosis are integral parts of the complex process of understanding an individual and of helping him understand himself and use that understanding to improve his reading.

Working with parents

Recognizing the role of the parent in helping the student take a new attitude toward his reading problem, reading clinicians are more and more involving parents in the reeducation process. For example, Studholme (1961) held a series of meetings with the mothers of six boys who had failed to improve after a year or more of remedial reading. These mothers were so eager to talk about their boys' reading problems that they practically took over most of the sessions. They seemed to profit most from being able to express their feelings of despair, hostility, and guilt; from knowing that other mothers have similar problems and feelings; and from hearing one another's concrete suggestions and those given by the discussion leader. They met over a period of several months. During that time the investigator noted marked changes in their expressed attitudes and reported behavior toward their children. Sympathy for the child began to replace resentment; there was less nagging and more appreciation of the child's progress. In discussions with groups and in interviews with individual parents, teachers and clinicians may gain much insight into parental attitudes and behavior toward their retarded children (Strang, 1962, chap. 1).

Usually the child is not present when the clinician interviews his parents or when professionally trained observers are present. However, some promising departures from this procedure have been made (Dreikurs, 1951). For over twenty-five years at the Chicago Community Child Guidance Centers, children have been counseled and diagnosed in family groups and in the presence of professionally trained persons. Even a few minutes' experience with this procedure in a strange situation seems to produce a deeper and more constructive impression on the child than does the usual individual counseling. The child expresses himself more accurately than in situations for which he has ready-made responses. He seems to be at ease and to feel free to talk with friendliness and frankness. One explanation of this positive response is that the child enjoys being the center of attention and is impressed by a novel setting in which adults are listening to him with interest, sympathy, and a desire to help. The parents are impressed with the child's insights into the nature of his problems and his understanding of adults. The discussion that takes place is enlightening to the adults. Obviously a procedure of this kind can be employed successfully only by a highly skilled, experienced person.

CONCLUDING STATEMENT

Any technique that is administered individually has many advantages. First and most important is the personal relationship with someone who is sincere, feels with the individual, is concerned about his welfare, and has a positive regard for him. Such a relationship may produce improvement in reading regardless of the methods of instruction used. A second advantage lies in avoiding waste of time: The student has the teacher's undivided attention; he does not sit idle while other students are being taught. The third advantage is the opportunity presented by the individual technique for adapting the procedure in accordance with the student's response. The worker can follow up clues that the client gives, ask for clarification or elaboration of some of his comments, and reinforce his positive insights. For these and other reasons, group methods should be supplemented by individual procedures so far as time permits.

SUGGESTED PROBLEMS: PRACTICE AND DEMONSTRATION

1. Compile a complete bibliography of case studies of reading difficulties by making a thorough canvass of sources of case studies in recent books, pamphlets, and articles.

2. If possible, view over closed-circuit television a comprehensive diagnostic procedure with two cases of markedly different ages and reading problems.

3. Read several complete case studies; interpret and synthesize the facts as you read. Also, list the diagnostic instruments used which seemed most appropriate for the particular case. What seemed to be the conditions giving rise to the individual's present reading development? What were the favorable factors in the individual and in his environment? What deficiencies or errors need the teacher's attention? Compare the causes of reading failure in these cases with the causes summarized in this chapter.

4. For information about each of the conditions that might lead to reading difficulties, read the pertinent references listed at the end of the chapter; for example, see Cruickshank on methods of work with brain-injured or hyperactive children, Vernon on confused laterality, or Robinson on the reasons pupils fail in reading.

REFERENCES

BELMONT, LILLIAN, and HERBERT G. BIRCH: "Lateral Dominance, Lateral Awareness and Reading Disability," *Child Development*, 36:57–71, March, 1965.

BIRCH, HERBERT G., and LILLIAN BELMONT: "Auditory-Visual Integration in Normal and Retarded Readers," *American Journal of Orthopsychiatry*, 34:852–861, October, 1964.

BOLLENBACHER, JEAN: "A Study of the Effect of Mobility on Reading Achievement," *The Reading Teacher*, 15:356–360+, March, 1962.

BURKHOLDER, RACHEL: "The Improvement in Reading Ability through the Development of Specific Underlying or Associated Mental Abilities," unpublished doctoral dissertation, University of Arizona, Tucson, 1968.

CAPOBIANCO, R. J.: "Ocular-Manual Laterality and Reading in Adolescent Mental Retardates," *American Journal of Mental Deficiency*, 70:781–785, March, 1966.

CHANG, THOMAS M. C., and VIVIAN CHANG: "Relation of Visual-Motor Skills and Reading Achievement in Primary Grade Pupils of Superior Ability," *Perceptual and Motor Skills*, 24:51–53, February, 1967.

CICIRELLI, V. G.: "Sibling Constellation, Creativity, IQ, and Academic Achievement," *Child Development*, 38:481–490, October, 1967.

COHEN, RUTH I.: "Remedial Training of First Grade Children with Visual Perceptual Retardation," *Educational Horizons*, 45:60–63, Winter, 1966–1967.

COLEMAN, J. C., and M. A. SANDHU: "A Descriptive-Relational Study of 364 Children Referred to a University Clinic for Learning Disorders," *Psychological Reports*, 20:1091–1105, June, 1967.

DE HIRSCH, KATRINA: "Concepts Related to Normal Reading Processes and Their Application to Reading Pathology," *Journal of Genetic Psychology*, 102:277–285, June, 1963.

DREIKURS, RUDOLF: "Family Group Therapy in the Chicago Community Child Guidance Centers," *Mental Hygiene*, 35:291–301, April, 1951.

DUKER, SAM: *Listening: Readings*, The Scarecrow Press, New York, 1966.

DURKIN, DOLORES: "The Achievement of Pre-school Readers: Two Longitudinal Studies," *Reading Research Quarterly*, 1:5–36, Summer, 1966.

DYKSTRA, ROBERT: "Auditory Discrimination Abilities and Beginning Reading Achievement," *Reading Research Quarterly*, 1:5–34, Summer, 1966.

EAMES, H.S "Some Neural and Glandular Bases of Learning," *Boston University Journal of Education*, 142:3–36, April, 1960.

ELKIND, D., and JUTTA WEISS: "Studies in Perceptual Development III: Perceptual Exploration," *Child Development*, 38:553–561, November, 1967.

EVANS, JOHN W., JR.: "The Effect of Pupil Mobility upon Academic Achievement," *National Elementary Principal*, 45:18–22, April, 1966.

FARNHAM-DIGGORY, SYLVIA: "Symbol and Synthesis in Experimental 'Reading,'" *Child Development*, 38:221–231, August, 1967.

FROST, B. P.: "Intelligence, Manifest Anxiety, and Scholastic Achievement," *Alberta Journal of Educational Research*, 11:167–175, January, 1965.

GOINS, JEAN T.: *Visual Perceptual Abilities and Early Reading Progress*, Supplementary Educational Monograph no. 87, The University of Chicago Press, Chicago, 1958.

HEWETT, FRANK M.: "Educational Engineering with Emotionally Disturbed Children," *Exceptional Children*, 33:459–467, March, 1967.

HILL, EDWIN H., and MICHAEL C. GIAMMATTEO: "Socio-economic Status and Its Relation to School Achievement in the Elementary School," *Elementary English*, 40:265–270, March, 1963.

KOPPITZ, E. J.: *The Bender-Gestalt Test for Young Children*, Grune and Stratton, Inc., New York, 1964.

KRAMER, D. P., and ELYSE S. FLEMING: "Interparental Differences of Opinion and Children's Academic Achievement," *Journal of Educational Research*, 60:136–138, November, 1966.

LOVELL, K., and M. E. WOOLSEY: "Reading Disability, Nonverbal Reasoning, and Social Class," *British Journal of Educational Research*, 6:226–227, June, 1964.

MAGGINITIE, WALTER H.: "Auditory Perception in Reading," *Education*, 87:532–538, May, 1967.

MALMQUIST, EVE: *Factors Related to Reading Disabilities in the First Grade of Elementary School*, Almquist & Wiksell, Stockholm, 1960, pp. 1–428.

MC DONALD, ARTHUR S.: "What Current Research Says about Poor Readers in High School and College," *Journal of Developmental Reading*, 4:184–196, Spring, 1961.

MC GINNIS, DOROTHY J.: "A Comparative Study of the Attitude of Parents of Superior and Inferior Readers toward Certain Child Rearing Practices," *The Philosophical and Sociological Bases of Reading*, E. L. Thurstone and L. E. Hafner (eds.), Yearbook of the National Reading Conference, 14:99–105, 1965.

MC LEOD, J.: "Some Psycholinguistic Correlates of Reading Disability in Young Children," *Reading Research Quarterly*, 2:5–31, Spring, 1967.

MERTENS, MARJORIE: "A Visual Perception Test for the Prediction and Diagnosis of Reading Ability," unpublished doctoral dissertation, University of Arizona, Tucson, 1968.

MORRIS, J. L., MARIANA PESTANER, and A. NELSON: "Mobility and Achievement," *Journal of Experimental Education*, 35:74–80, Summer, 1967.

RHODES, WILLIAM C.: "The Disturbing Child: A Problem of Ecological Management," *Exceptional Children*, 33:449–455, March, 1967.

SCOTT, WILLIAM R.: "My Father Doesn't Like Me," in *Teen-age Tales*, book 2, D. C. Heath and Company, Boston, 1966, pp. 208–230.

SILVER, ARCHIE A., and ROSA A. HAGIN: "Specific Reading Disability: Follow-up Studies," *American Journal of Orthopsychiatry*, 34:95–102, January, 1964.

SNIPES, W. T.: "The Effect of Moving on Reading Achievement," *The Reading Teacher*, 20:242–246, December, 1966.

STEPHENS, W. E., E. S. CUNNINGHAM, and B. J. STIGLER: "Reading Readiness and Eye-Hand Preference Patterns in First Grade Children," *Exceptional Children*, 33:481–488, March, 1967.

STRANG, RUTH: "A Dynamic Theory of the Reading Process," *Merrill Palmer Quarterly of Behavior and Development*, 7:239–245, October, 1961.

————: *Helping Your Child Improve His Reading*, E. P. Dutton & Co., Inc., New York, 1962.

STUART, I. R.: "Perceptual Style and Reading Ability: Implications for an Instructional Approach," *Perceptual and Motor Skills*, 24:135–138, February, 1967.

STUDHOLME, JANICE: "Changes in Attitudes of Mothers of Retarded Readers during Group Guidance Sessions," unpublished doctoral dissertation, Teachers College, Columbia University, New York, 1961.

SULLIVAN, HARRY S.: *The Interpersonal Theory of Psychiatry*, W. W. Norton and Company, Inc., New York, 1953.

SUTTON, M. H.: "Readiness for Reading at the Kindergarten Level," *The Reading Teacher*, 17:234–240, January, 1964.

VAN ZANDT, WAYNE: "A Study of Some Home-Family-Community Factors Related to Children's Achievement in Reading in an Elementary School," unpublished doctoral dissertation, Wayne State University, Detroit, 1963.

VERNON, M. D.: *Backwardness in Reading*, Cambridge University Press, New York, 1957.

———— (comp.): *Visual Perception and Its Relation to Reading: An Annotated Bibliography*, International Reading Association, Newark, Del., 1966.

VORHAUS, PAULINE G.: "Non-reading as an Expression of Resistance," in *Claremont College Reading Conference*, Eleventh Yearbook, Claremont, Calif., 1946, pp. 129–131.

WEPMAN, J. M.: "Auditory Discrimination, Speech, and Reading," *Elementary School Journal*, 60:325–333, March, 1960.

SUGGESTED READINGS

ALEXANDER, DUANE, and JOHN MONEY: "Reading Ability and the Problem of Direction Sense," *The Reading Teacher*, 20:404–409, February, 1967.

BALOW, I. H.: "Lateral Dominance Characteristics and Reading Achievement in the First Grade, *The Journal of Psychology*, 55:323–328, April, 1963.

BARSCH, RAY H.: A *Perceptual-Motor Curriculum*, vol. 1, *Achieving Perceptual-Motor Efficiency*, Special Child Publications, Seattle, Wash., 1967.

BELMONT, LILLIAN, and H. G. BIRCH: "The Intellectual Profile of Retarded Readers," *Perceptual and Motor Skills*, 22:787–816, June, 1966.

COHN, R.: "The Neurological Study of Children with Learning Disabilities," *Exceptional Children*, 31:179–185, December, 1964.

CRUICKSHANK, WILLIAM: A *Teaching Method for Brain-injured and Hyperactive Children*, Syracuse University Press, Syracuse, N.Y., 1961.

DELACATO, CARL H.: *The Treatment and Prevention of Reading Problems,* Charles C Thomas, Publisher, Springfield, Ill., 1959.

DEUTSCH, CYNTHIA P.: "Auditory Discrimination and Learning: Social Factors," *Merrill Palmer Quarterly of Behavior and Development,* 10:277–296, July, 1964.

DEUTSCH, MARTIN: "The Role of Social Class in Language Development and Cognition," *American Journal of Orthopsychiatry,* 35:78–88, January, 1965.

EPHRON, BEULAH: *Emotional Difficulties in Reading,* The Julian Press, Inc., New York, 1953.

FERNALD, GRACE M.: *Remedial Techniques in Basic School Subjects,* McGraw-Hill Book Company, New York, 1943.

GIBSON, ELEANOR J., J. J. GIBSON, ANNE D. PICK, and H. OSSER: "A Developmental Study of the Discrimination of Letter-like Forms," *Journal of Comparative and Physiological Psychology,* 55:897–906, June, 1962.

HARRIS, ALBERT J.: *How to Increase Reading Ability,* 4th ed., David McKay Company, Inc., New York, 1961.

HILL, WALTER R.: "Factors Associated with Comprehension Deficiency of College Readers," *Journal of Developmental Reading,* 3:84–93, Winter, 1960.

KASS, CORINNE C.: "Psycholinguistic Disabilities of Children with Reading Problems," *Exceptional Children,* 32:533–539, April, 1966.

KEPHART, N. C.: "Perceptual-Motor Problems of Children," in *Proceedings of the Conference on Exploration into the Problems of the Perceptually Handicapped Child,* Fund for Perceptually Handicapped Children, Inc., Evanston, Ill., 1963, pp. 27–30.

LAMPARD, DOROTHY M.: "Early Diagnosis of Reading Disability," *Reading and Inquiry, Proceedings of the Annual Convention,* vol. 10, International Reading Association, Newark, Del., 1965, pp. 191–193.

RADAKER, L. D.: "Imagery and Academic Performance," *The Elementary School Journal,* 63:91–95, November, 1962.

REITAN, RALPH M.: "Relationships between Neurological and Psychological Variables and Their Implications for Reading Instruction Meeting Individual Differences in Reading," in *Proceedings of the Conference on Reading* held at the University of Chicago, vol. 26, The University of Chicago Press, Chicago, 1964, pp. 100–110.

ROBINSON, HELEN M.: *Why Pupils Fail in Reading,* The University of Chicago Press, Chicago, 1946.

————: *Clinical Studies in Reading I and II,* Supplementary Educational Monograph nos. 68 and 77, The University of Chicago Press, Chicago, 1949 and 1953.

SILVAROLI, N. J., and W. H. WHEELOCK: "An Investigation of Auditory Discrimination Training for Beginning Readers," *The Reading Teacher,* 20:247–251, December, 1966.

SMITH, DONALD E. P., and PATRICIA M. CARRIGAN: *The Nature of Reading Disability,* Harcourt, Brace & World, Inc., New York, 1959.

STRANG, RUTH, and others: *The Improvement of Reading*, 3d ed., McGraw-Hill Book Company, New York, 1961.

THOMPSON, BERTHA B.: "A Longitudinal Study of Auditory Discrimination," *Journal of Educational Research*, 56:376–378, March, 1963.

TRAXLER, ARTHUR: *Research in Reading during Another Four Years*, Educational Research Bureau, New York, 1960.

VERNON, MAGDALEN D.: "Ten More Important Sources of Information on Visual Perception in Relation to Reading," *The Reading Teacher*, 20:134–135, November, 1966.

WILLIAMS, JOANNA P., and H. LEVIN: "Word Perception: Psychological Bases," *Education*, 87:515–518, April, 1967.

WOOLF, MAURICE D., and JEANNE A. WOOLF: *Remedial Reading: Teaching and Treatment*, McGraw-Hill Book Company, New York, 1957.

Chapter Nine

PHYSICAL FACTORS IN READING DIAGNOSIS

Visual and auditory defects, malnutrition, glandular and other chemical disturbances, and illness may be primary or contributing causes of reading difficulty. Even if a physical defect—an eye defect, for example—is not severe enough to cause obvious interference with a child's reading, it may involve enough discomfort to make him reluctant to read. To learn to read and to read with comfort, the child needs adequate vision. Physical factors should be checked for all children, not only retarded readers, in order that teachers may provide the optimum conditions for their education.

VISUAL FACTORS

The reading process starts with seeing—seeing dynamically, that is, co-ordinating the two eyes carefully and precisely along the lines of print. Unless there is a clear-cut retinal image, there will be confusion in perceiving letters of similar configuration. Words become blurred. Meaning becomes obscured. Perceiving and conceptualizing, basic to understanding and reflecting, are blocked.

Seeing printed words is a learned process. The ability to accommodate for close vision is developed, at least to some degree, in early infancy. Some patterned vision—a tendency to maintain a central fixation of pattern rather than using peripheral vision—is present even in the infant. During the first six months there is a marked increase of precision in focusing the eyes. Both maturation and learning contribute to visual efficiency.

Visual efficiency involves the making of many adjustments. The child beginning to learn to read must learn to change his focus from distant scenes to the page of the book in his hand. He has to maintain this focus to prevent the print from blurring. At the same time he must use the six

167

little muscles of each eye to turn the eye inward just enough to keep from seeing the print double. He must do all this while his eyes are moving from left to right across the page. To these physical adjustments he must add the ability to get meaning by relating the sensory impression to his previous experience.

Many children make all these adjustments. Others learn to suppress the vision in one eye when they have difficulty in fusing the images of both eyes. Some children learn to ignore distant vision and focus more and more on near distances, as one must do in reading. These children thus become myopic, but they are often good readers. The children who cannot adjust to the difficulties and discomforts of close seeing find the visual task so difficult that they give up trying to read.

Vision also has psychosomatic elements (Kelley, 1961, p. 349). For example, substantial temporary improvements in myopic conditions have been obtained by the skillful use of suggestion, which can produce actual changes in the refractive state of the eye. In interpreting the results of visual testing, the examiner should recognize psychological factors and fatigue as well as observed physical efficiency.

Relation of vision to reading difficulties

On this topic Robinson (1958, pp. 107–111) wrote a key article. She and other investigators (Rosen, 1965; Spache and Tillman, 1962; Huelsman, 1959) consider the following visual factors to be most closely related to the reading process:

1. *Binocular coordination in visual performance*—seeing with both eyes at the same time and being able to fuse the two images in the brain (Gruber, 1962). Fortunately this accommodative-convergence relationship is almost entirely a learned one and can be improved by training (Robinson, 1953, p. 127). Astigmatism, aniseikonia, and muscular imbalance may interfere with convergence and thus result in poor fusion.

2. *Far-sight or hyperopia* causes more difficulty in reading than near-sightedness. Eames (1959, pp. 2–35) in a study of 3,500 children, half of whom were reading failures, found farsightedness in 43 percent of the reading failures as compared with 12 percent in the unselected children. However, myopia should not be ignored; it is a handicap in seeing the board and in other activities that require distance vision.

Children who show these defects on a screening test should be referred to a competent eye specialist. At the University of Chicago Clinic, Robinson (1953) found that more than half of the reading cases had a history of visual problems; every third or fourth retarded reader needed referral.

In view of the difficulty in interpreting visual screening tests and the possibility of missing some cases that could be helped by corrections, referral for any eye condition that might be related to reading is recommended for all severely retarded readers.

The relationship between reading proficiency and visual difficulty has not been clearly established, although in individual cases investigators have found that visual defects are one cause of reading difficulty. The relationship may vary with different individuals. It has been reported that functional visual difficulty has a more definite relationship to reading achievement in younger than in older children; the latter may have learned over the years to compensate for their visual defects. A combination case study and developmental approach would yield more definitive conclusions. Even if an individual has learned to read effectively despite a visual handicap, he has done so at considerable cost. With the defect corrected and the necessary reading instruction provided, he could read with more efficiency and physical comfort and with less nervous tension and strain. The age of seven seems to be a critical period, requiring special supervision.

Since visual defects are important as part of the overall conditions that affect reading performance, every effort should be made to detect visual difficulties (Figurel, 1961). As a first step, the teacher's daily observation plays an important role. He can observe (1) the appearance of the eyes—watering of the eyes, frequent sties, redness; (2) behavior—bodily posture, position in which the book is held, signs of tension; and (3) complaints of headaches, nausea, blurring, seeing double. To assist teachers in becoming familiar with these symptoms of visual difficulties, Dr. Lois B. Bing and a committee on Visual Problems of Children and Youth of the American Optometric Association (St. Louis, Missouri) have prepared a set of materials comprising slides and a manual under the title "Children's Vision and School Success."

Older students may be asked to fill out a form such as the following:

Name_____Date_____

1. Do you have any difficulty in seeing clearly at a distance? At reading distance?
2. Do you have headaches from reading?
3. Do you often find it difficult to concentrate and sustain effort while reading or studying?
4. Do you sometimes see double (not blurred) when looking in the distance or reading?
5. Do you have a stiff neck or backache after you read or study for an extended time?
6. How long can you continue to read or study comfortably and effectively at one time?

The student's answers to these questions give clues to whether he needs a vision screening test, which would in turn show whether he needs a more thorough eye examination.

Visual screening tests

To detect the various visual difficulties that may affect an individual's reading, many tests are needed. Among these are tests of:

> Visual acuity at far and near distance, ability to follow a moving object with each eye separately and with both eyes together

> Ocular coordination at far and at near points, which is necessary for the formation of a single clear image

> Other aspects of fusion

> Movement of eyes too far inward or outward (known as phorias)

> Ability to hold single monocular vision (known as ductions)

> Uneven dominance of the two eyes (aniseidominance)

> Unequal size and shape of images projected on the retina by the two eyes (aniseikonia)

> Stereopsis or depth perception

> Binocular skill indicated by speed of reading and number of errors when reading with one eye and with two

> Facility of accommodation, changing focus from far to near and back again

> Eye span—the number of letters or words one can see in one exposure

Other tests that may be more closely related to reading have not yet been developed. However, combinations of existing tests may show a relation of visual difficulties to reading ability when single tests do not. Accordingly, patterns or clusters of test results should be studied in relation to reading. Screening tests, though sometimes in error, are the most practical first step in the detection of visual deficiences in children.

Comparative studies have been made of the results obtained with different screening instruments:

1. The illuminated Snellen Chart, supplemented by tests of far-sightedness, muscular imbalance, and depth perception. This combination of procedures can be administered in about three to five minutes by a teacher or nurse who has been given instruction in their use. The equipment is not expensive. A detailed description of this procedure is given by Sweeting (1959, pp. 715–722).

2. The School Vision Tester, originally the Ortho-Rater, now adapted for school use by Bausch and Lomb, Rochester, New York. This efficient visual screening machine measures at far point and at reading distance vertical and lateral phoria, acuity of right and left eyes separately and together, and depth perception.

3. The Massachusetts Vision Test, Welch-Allen, Auburn, New York, now included in the American Optical Company's AO Vision Screening Test. This test measures right and left eye acuity and vertical and lateral muscle balance.

4. The Keystone Visual Survey Tests, Keystone View Company, Meadville, Pennsylvania. This device tests at both far point and reading distance. It is used along with these important tests: (a) the long form of the vision test, (b) Spache Binocular Reading Test, (c) Gray Standardized Oral Reading Check Test.

5. T/O School Vision Tester, Titmus Optical Company, Department of Applied Visual Science, Petersburg, Virginia. This test takes five minutes to administer and two minutes to score. It is especially designed for occupational guidance.

The Chicago Reading Clinic supplemented the Bausch and Lomb School Vision Tester with the Wirt Stereotest (Three Dimension Company, 4132 West Belmont Avenue, Chicago 60641) as a near-depth measure and the Spache Binocular Reading Test (Keystone View Company, Meadville, Pennsylvania). This combination is quite dependable. When the screening program does not include tests of binocular vision at the reading distance, many children handicapped in reading by visual difficulty are not discovered.

These screening tests can be administered successfully by nurses and reading teachers who have been given training in their use. More experience is needed in testing kindergarten and first-grade than older children.

In an extensive survey (Crane and others, 1952), results of seven screening tests were compared with examinations by ophthalmologists. Of the 609 sixth-grade children examined by the ophthalmologists, 31 percent were identified as having visual defects. The screening tests—Ortho-Rater, Sight Screener Test, and Telebinocular Test—administered by nurses and technicians referred correctly about three-fourths of the children identified by the ophthalmologists. However, these tests incorrectly referred about 30 percent who did not need to be refracted. The percentage of incorrect referrals for first grade was still larger.

In general, referral standards depend upon the purpose of the testing. For retarded readers, one should use the procedure that refers the highest number correctly. Despite the expense involved in overreferral, it is better to refer some who do not need correction than to miss some who will be handicapped by an uncorrected visual defect.

To study the problem of overreferral, workers in the field have suggested that the practitioners in a community meet together to determine (1) the tests to be included in the screening program, (2) the criteria or standards for referral, and (3) the items to be included in a complete clinical eye examination.

Following the vision screening tests, the first step is referral to a broadly trained eye specialist who will cooperate with parents and teachers. A further step may be orthoptic or visual training which can relieve fusion difficulties caused by faulty muscle functioning. It is the responsibility of the reading specialist to check on the corrections made to see whether the student's discomfort in reading has been reduced.

Reading materials prepared for those of limited vision should be made available as needed (Matson and Larson, 1951). Students with visual handicaps may obtain mechanical aids, "talking books," certain types of training, and other items of assistance from the National Society for the Prevention of Blindness and the American Foundation for the Blind, New York City. Extra training in visual discrimination will help to compensate for some irremediable visual defects.

MACHINES FOR DIAGNOSIS AND TREATMENT OF VISUAL FACTORS

In addition to the vision screening and hearing testing machines and machines to photograph eye movements, there are tachistoscopic instruments and pressure devices. Reading teachers and specialists are often confronted by the problem of whether to deplete a limited budget by buying machines or to spend the money on reading material. Administrators often ask advice on this question. We shall briefly consider the purpose for which each of these instruments is used and its value in connection with the diagnosis of reading efficiency.

Tachistoscopic methods

A tachistoscope in its simplest form is a slide projector with a shutter. The shutter exposes pictures, numbers, words, phrases, or sentences for as short a time as 1/100 second. With practice, individuals can recognize many single characters and even sentences in this amazingly short exposure.

Researchers and educators do not agree on the teaching value of this device. What is the evidence? The early reports on the results of tachisto-scopic training of various adult groups stimulated much interest. Four elementary school systems attributed large gains in the early grades to tachistoscopic training. Goins (1958), on the other hand, in a carefully controlled experiment with first-grade children, found that "no positive effect was produced by the tachistoscopic training on the reading skill of the group as a whole" (p. 98). She added that her findings do not rule out the possible value of such training for selected older pupils who are having specific difficulties related to visual efficiency.

The age of the pupils and the nature of the material used would affect the value of training in the recognition of visual forms. Leestma (1957, p. 94) studied 261 pupils who ranged in age from seven to seventeen and represented grades 2, 4, 6, 8, 10, and 12. He reported significant growth over the age range studied for all four kinds of material: digits, unrelated letters, unrelated words, and related words. Rate of growth was most rapid during the early years studied. Beyond ages nine or eleven the rate of growth slowed down. The amount of growth was directly related to the meaningfulness of the material and to the developmental level of the perceiver.

Various instruments have been designed for giving training in quick word perception. A simple device for individual use is the Educational Develop-ment Laboratories' Flash-X. This instrument makes possible individual or team practice in quick recognition of words and phrases, either at home or in the classroom. Watching the exposure window carefully, the student flicks the tab, and the shutter opens for 1/25 second. To check the accuracy of his perception and recognition of the word, the student flicks another tab which gives a longer exposure of the word. With a turn of the card, the next exposure is ready. In addition to reinforcing the recognition of basic words, Flash-X training purports to build perceptual speed and accuracy. Each student may practice at his own pace for any length of time desired.

Other machines, such as the Keystone Flashmeter (Keystone View Com-pany, Meadville, Pennsylvania), use slides. The Keystone Reading Pacer is used only with book materials. The Learning-through-Seeing filmstrips may also be used to provide tachistoscopic training. According to the company's description (Educational Development Laboratories, McGraw-Hill Book Company, Huntington, New York),

> the Tach-X tachistoscope is a challenging and effective way to develop the ability to *see*.
>
> All eyes watch the screen. At the touch of a button, a series of numbers or words, pops into view and then is gone. For a split second, perhaps only 1/100, the students reach out visually, learning to see rapidly.

Two Instruments for Tachistoscopic Training

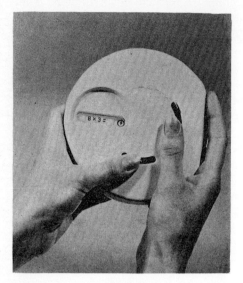

Flash-X

Tach-X

Pictures from Educational Development Laboratories, Inc., McGraw-Hill Book Company, Huntington, N.Y. Illustrations and descriptions of similar instruments may be obtained from The Keystone View Company, Meadville, Pa.

Rather than exposing separate words and phrases for a fraction of a second, the reading film, such as the original Harvard Reading Films (Harvard University), uses connected sentences for training purposes. Since the film more closely resembles ordinary reading, its transfer value should be greater than that of the flashmeter. It also has the advantage of giving the student practice in getting the author's thought at the first reading. The contents of the Harvard films are appropriate for college freshmen; comprehension is adequately tested by excellent multiple-choice questions. The Iowa Reading Films (Iowa State University) are more appropriate for high school students. Another machine of this kind is the Controlled Reader, which features a library of 330 filmstrips. It is described by its producers as follows. The Controlled Reader aims

> to develop simultaneously the interpretive and the functional aspects of reading.
>
> The students follow the story on the screen as it unfolds in a left-to-right fashion. The rate (0 to 1,000 words per minute) has been set so as to challenge them, and, because there is no chance to look back, they learn to organize their thoughts rapidly and remember well.

Many teachers who have used the tachistoscope in their classrooms have reported increased motivation and interest, better ability to concentrate, and greater willingness to put forth effort. As the student learns to recognize more words at a single quick exposure, he feels proud of his achievement. He has demonstrated to himself that he can read more efficiently than he thought possible.

The effectiveness of tachistoscopic training depends somewhat upon the manner in which it is introduced and used in the classroom. There may be some prestige value in mentioning to the students that it is used in business and in the armed forces. The goal of learning to recognize words and phrases in 1/100 second is specific, and success in doing so is impressive. The habit of alertness that the instrument requires may carry over to other reading and study tasks. Tachistoscopic devices can be used in some situations to develop and extend the reading ability of students in grades above the first. But it is also recommended that such training be given on the basis of individual diagnosis, in not more than ten- to twenty-minute periods, and that it be tied in with a broad reading program.

Study of eye movements

It is well known that the eyes do not move smoothly along a line of print, but rather in a jerky sort of way in a series of stops and starts—fixations followed by swift movements. Sometimes they move backward, that is, make regressions over the line. Eye-movement records have given clues

Instruments for Eye-movement Measurement and Training

Controlled Reader

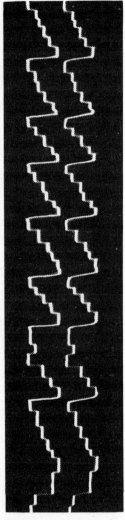

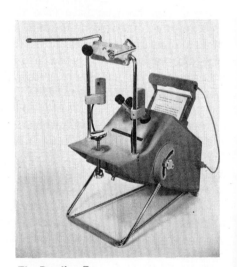

The Reading Eye

Eye-movement Record

Pictures from Educational Development Laboratories, Inc., McGraw-Hill Book Company, Huntington, N.Y.

about the nature of the reading process. However, according to Tinker this type of research has probably made its major contribution (1958, pp. 215–231).

CONCLUSIONS FROM STUDIES   The results of research on eye movements have shown that:

1. The unit of word recognition is the word or group of words.
2. Rhythmic patterns are found in only a few good readers.
3. More difficult material is read with more fixations, other things being equal.
4. Eye movements also vary with the degree of the reader's familiarity with the material and the purpose for which he is reading it. Mature readers change their pace according to their purpose and the nature of the material; poor readers tend to be inflexible.
5. Eye movements reflect rather than produce reading efficiency.
6. Eye movements become more efficient with age; the most rapid growth is during the first four grades; there is very little change during the high school and college years. Progress seems to be related to the practice and instruction afforded by approved methods of teaching reading.
7. "The improvement obtained [by techniques that 'pace the eyes'] with or without elaborate apparatus is no greater than that resulting from well-motivated reading practice alone." [1]

Another conclusion to be drawn from Tinker's review of studies of eye movements relates to speed of reading. There is a physiological limit to actual eye span and the rapidity of reaction time. One investigator set this limit at 1,451 words per minute. The psycho-physiological limit, which allows for comprehension time, is probably not more than 800 or even 500 words per minute. How, then, should we interpret the claims frequently made in popular articles that one can read 1,500 or more words a minute? The misunderstanding arises from a confusion between speed of steady reading, to which there is a definite physiological limit, and skimming speed. The latter has no limit and is determined much more by the reader's skill in finding what he is looking for than by physical factors.

PHOTOGRAPHS OF EYE MOVEMENTS   The instrument used to study eye movements is a camera which photographs the pauses that the eyes make on each line of print as the person reads. One commercial form of the eye-movement camera is called The Reading Eye. The makers of this instrument (Educational Development Laboratories, Huntington, New York) describe the process of eye-movement photography as follows:

[1] Miles A. Tinker, "Eye Movements in Reading," reprinted from the May, 1959, issue of *Education*, p. 225, by special permission of The Bobbs-Merrill Company, Inc., Indianapolis, Ind.

As an individual reads a test selection appropriate for his level of reading achievement, small beads of light are reflected from his eyes and photographed on to moving film. After a comprehension check, the filmed record is analyzed and the reader's performance is compared with national norms in terms of fixations, regressions, span of recognition, duration of fixation, rate with comprehension, and relative efficiency.

The eye-movement camera may detect gross difficulties in convergence and accommodation during reading (Waldstreicher, 1966); but in general the eye-movement record is unreliable in assessing binocular coordination, muscle imbalance, and fusional ability (Gruber, 1962). It is not a substitute for an examination by a competent specialist.

The interpretation of eye-movement records is difficult. The subjects vary in their familiarity with the test material, in the purpose for which they are reading it, in the quality of their comprehension, and in other subjective factors. For example, one group of college freshmen made much poorer records than previous classes because some of the students who had previously taken the test warned the newcomers that they would have to answer specific comprehension questions. In another case a poor reader made a surprisingly good eye-movement record on difficult material. Later, the examiner found that he had merely moved his eyes rhythmically across the lines without making any effort to comprehend. He made enough clever guesses on the easy comprehension test to get an acceptable score. Regressive movements are not necessarily detrimental to reading proficiency; the more able students may regress so that they may comprehend relationships more accurately.

INFORMAL METHOD   The eye-movement camera, or a more elaborate electrical method, is used for research purposes and in some reading clinics. There is also an informal method that may be used by the teacher, the so-called "peep-hole" method that has been described by Tinker as follows:

Upon a 9 × 12 inch cardboard attach two paragraphs of 6 to 10 lines of reading material of appropriate difficulty, one paragraph just above the center of the card and the other just below the center. In the middle of the cardboard cut a small hole, ¼ to ⅜ inches in diameter. Hold the cardboard at the proper reading distance directly in front of a pupil and place your eye immediately behind the opening. You now have the most advantageous viewpoint from which to see the successive movements and fixation pauses of one of the pupil's eyes as he reads the material on the cardboard. The movements are seen most easily when you fixate your attention upon the dividing line between the colored zone and the white of the pupil's eye. The fact that the pupil sees only the reading material before him reduces the distraction that would occur if you were to attempt direct observation (as looking over the top of a book) without concealing your face behind the card.

This method may be used to determine the number of fixation pauses per line of print, to detect the presence of regressions, and confusions shown by detailed examination of a word or phrase. Even after practice, this method is not entirely accurate since some eye movements will be missed. Nevertheless, the technique is quite satisfactory in the classroom where the teacher wishes to detect signs of very good and very poor reading in comparison with the average, or wishes to find out what the eye movements of a particular pupil are like.

To insure a fair degree of accuracy, practice in counting the eye movements of another teacher for a few paragraphs should be undertaken before working with the children. Since there is a fixation pause at the end of each move, the number of pauses per line is easily obtained. Count the number of eye movements for the whole paragraph and divide by the number of lines. Do not attempt to note regressions and words that cause confusion while counting the interfixation movements. Look for these other things when a second or a third selection is read.[2]

This informal method of studying eye movements has one advantage over the machine methods. When the individual makes an unusually long pause, a regression, or a detailed examination of a word or phrase, the teacher can ask him what happened at that point. Perhaps the word was unfamiliar and he was trying to puzzle it out; perhaps his eyes had moved too far ahead of his mind, and he had to go back to get the meaning. From this kind of introspective information the teacher may gain insight into the reading process, or, more specifically, into the factors that may be causing faulty or inefficient eye movements.

TRAINING EYE MOVEMENTS Since eye-movement patterns often merely reflect the degree of difficulty that the reader is having with the reading material and "the clarity of perception and comprehension taking place in the mind of the reader," [3] it is better to improve his vocabulary and comprehension skills than to focus on eye movements directly. We need not only to teach students how to read rapidly, but also to teach them when rapid reading is appropriate. We should also help them to acquire the skills that are needed for different kinds of comprehension.

[2] Miles A. Tinker, "Eye Movements in Reading," reprinted from the May, 1959, issue of *Education*, p. 576, by special permission of The Bobbs-Merrill Company, Inc., Indianapolis, Ind.

[3] Miles A. Tinker, "Eye Movements in Reading," reprinted from the May, 1959, issue of *Education*, p. 578, by special permission of The Bobbs-Merrill Company, Inc., Indianapolis, Ind.

Although eye-movement patterns are good diagnostic signs of reading disability, specific training of eye movements is ordinarily not necessary to bring about improvement in reading. More efficient eye movements automatically appear as the reading is improved by other approved methods.[4]

Other mechanical devices

Despite lack of experimental evidence that machines are capable of training eye movements more effectively than well-motivated instruction and practice in basic reading skills, a number of machines have been devised for this purpose. The tachistoscopic devices have already been mentioned. Other machines merely provide a mechanical stimulus to read faster.

These pressure methods may take the simple form of timing the student while he reads a selection. An informal method is to set a time limit, thirty minutes for example, and record the number of lines or words he reads in the given time. Pressure may also be exerted by a machine that has a lever or some other device by which one can set the pace for an individual reader. There are a number of these machines on the market, such as:

> The Rateometer, Audio-Visual Research, Chicago, Illinois.
>
> SRA Reading Accelerator, Science Research Associates, Chicago, Illinois.
>
> The Franklin Reading Pacer, Franklin Research, Berkeley, California.
>
> Shadowscope Reading Pacer, Psychotechnics, Inc., Chicago, Illinois.

Any pressure method merely urges the person to read faster; it gives little or no attention to his ability to vary his rate and method of reading different kinds of material for different purposes.

MOTOR AND EYE–HAND COORDINATION

Manual dexterity, body orientation and coordination, and ocular-motor patterns set the stage for perception and other aspects of reading development. Recently so much emphasis has been placed on the relation of motor coordination to reading achievement that several schools, concerned

---

[4] Miles A. Tinker, "Eye Movements in Reading," reprinted from the May, 1959, issue of *Education*, p. 579, by special permission of The Bobbs-Merrill Company, Inc., Indianapolis, Ind.

with retarded readers, have employed a special physical education teacher to work with awkward, poorly coordinated children.

Indications of a child's eye-hand coordination may be obtained by observing him in different situations: bouncing or throwing a ball, erasing the chalkboard, driving a nail, cutting paper with scissors, copying a design, tying his shoes, picking up a small object from the floor, replacing a cap on a pen, touching the end of his nose first with one eye shut then with the other eye shut. Several tests such as the Leavell Hand-Eye Dominance Test (Leavell, 1959), give this kind of information with more precision. The Perceptual Achievement Form Test, Lions Research Foundation, Winter Haven, Florida, can be given in a group to detect difficulties in form discrimination and reproduction. The Procedure Manual—Perceptual Training Forms, Winter Haven Lions Research Foundation, Winter Haven, Florida, 1960, gives practice first in drawing simple geometric forms within a template which directs the child's movements, then in copying, and finally in reproducing the forms from memory. Motor and eye-hand coordination is normally developed by many play activities in which preschool children usually engage. A device for providing practice in using eye and hand together was developed by Leavell (1959). The child draws around a number of pictures, always from left to right.

Poor hand control may interfere with the child's writing. He grips his pencil too lightly, exerts more pressure than necessary, or has difficulty in forming letters.

In reading, the child shows difficulty in eye-hand coordination by his inability to keep his place in reading, to find the place again in the pattern of printed words, and to maintain the motor adjustment as long as is necessary to comprehend word, phrase, or sentence. His tendency to skip lines may arise from inability to direct the eyes accurately to the beginning of the next line.

NEUROLOGICAL CONDITIONS

Among the most deeply underlying causes of reading failure are the neurological. Attempting to teach reading to children whose neurological deficits make learning impossible is worse than useless; it often causes intense frustration, resulting in withdrawal or aggression with respect to reading.

Mixed dominance (see also Chapter 8)

The effect of mixed dominance or incomplete lateralization on reading achievement is still a controversial issue. Recently a strict correspondence between handedness and "brainedness" has been disproved. The cerebral hemisphere opposite to the preferred hand is not always dominant for language functions. The left cerebral hemisphere usually subserves language functions in both right- and left-handed persons. But if damage to one cerebral hemisphere occurs in childhood, a transfer may occur to the other hemisphere (Reitan, 1964, p. 100).

Left-handedness, left-eye dominance, mixed hand or eye dominance, crossed dominance, directional confusion, confusion in identifying right and left sides of the body have all been reported as related to reading disability. One of the two aspects most frequently associated with reading difficulty is lateral preference or inconsistency in hand and eye preferences. Tests of mixed dominance cover a range from casual observation to elaborate exercises for eyes, hands, and feet. Harris's test (1957) for handedness is one of the most widely used. Each item on the test is demonstrated and the child is then asked to show how he throws a ball, hammers a nail, cuts with a knife, etc.

A number of researches have reported no significant relationships between lateral preferences or inconsistency and reading difficulties in the general school population. (See Chapter 8 and Beck, 1960; McConville, 1960; Balow and Balow, 1964; Belmont and Birch, 1965; Coleman and Deutsch, 1964; Capobianco, 1966.)

Medical men are likely to attribute reversals and similar difficulties in word recognition to organic causes. Psychologists and educators more often give a psychological explanation. Educators take the view that, in many cases, laterality is learned. Many children in the general school population with confused lateral dominance do not have reading difficulties. In clinic samples the association of disturbed cerebral dominance with reading difficulty is higher. If education is the important factor, then parents and teachers can encourage the child to use the preferred hand in daily activities and can emphasize the left-right direction in reading and writing. Delacato (1959), who takes an extreme neurological view, advocates such measures as games that involve only the dominant eye and hand, choral speaking, but not singing, and controlling the child's posture while he is sleeping.

After a thorough review of research on laterality as related to reading, Vernon concluded:

> It is of course possible that incomplete lateralization is a sign of a general lack of maturation in the development of cortical functions, which also affects reading. . . . But clearly such cases form a small minority of all the cases of reading disability. . . . The investigations which have been cited give no clear evidence as to the existence of any innate organic

condition which causes reading disability, except perhaps in a minority of cases; though certain innate factors may predispose the child towards difficulty in learning to read (1957, pp. 109–115).

Brain damage

There are cases of identifiable brain injury in which explicit and detailed diagnosis by a neuropsychological battery is useful in identifying basic difficulties in visual form perception and in dealing with words as symbols (Rabinovitch, 1962). A distinction should be made between clearly identified and unidentified brain injuries. The latter has erroneously been called "minimal brain damage." If it cannot be identified, there is no justification for labeling it "minimal brain damage." Such a label has too frequently been given to parents and teachers as explaining severe reading disability which, in fact, may have other multiple causes.

Even when brain damage is definitely identified, remediation is generally based on the behavioral symptoms, not on the neurological findings. The treatment is psychological. Prevention of distractions is helpful because these cases have difficulty in concentration and in distinguishing "figure from ground." The Fernald kinesthetic or tracing method is useful because it establishes visual and auditory sequences. Associating the new learning with patterns already established and intact helps build new neural pathways. General psychological principles of motivation and relationship therapy are of basic importance in treating these cases of severe reading disability.

AUDITORY AND SPEECH DIFFICULTIES

Hearing loss may result in defective auditory perception and discrimination, which in turn may prevent clear enunciation and lead to difficulty in word recognition. However, many children are able to hear sounds perfectly but cannot distinguish different sounds in words, as, for example, the sounds of *care* and *car* or *boat* and *coat*. They apparently do not hear the sounds of letters and letter combinations clearly enough to remember them accurately enough to pronounce the printed words that they see. These children have normal hearing but are deficient in auditory discrimination.

Although research on the relationship between auditory functions and reading is conflicting, there is evidence enough to include tests of auditory acuity, discrimination, and memory in the diagnosis of reading problems. Hearing loss and fluctuations in auditory acuity may impede reading progress because they make it difficult for children to learn sound-letter associations.

There is a positive correlation between reading ability and speech development. The relation of defective speech to reading disability, however, is not so clearly established, even during preschool years. Sampson (1962) reported that reading achievement was not incompatible with maladjustment in speech; he described an effective program of speech therapy with eight-year-old children. Defects in speech tend to occur in children who are also low in intelligence and from disadvantaged homes.

In view of the importance of auditory acuity and auditory discrimination, both should be tested. To test auditory acuity in an entire class simultaneously the Western Electric Company's Model 4C audiometer may be used except for young children, who cannot make the necessary response of writing numbers. The Verbal Auditory Screen for Children (VASC) is also being used as a screening device. Volunteers with medical guidance can administer this test successfully. Information about early screening for both hearing and vision can be obtained from the Preschool Medical Survey, Minnesota Medical Association, 375 Jackson Street, St. Paul, Minnesota, 55101.

If these quick and more accurate methods of appraising auditory efficiency are not available, the teacher may use informal screening devices. In a quiet room he may hold a loudly ticking watch about 48 inches from the child's ear and then withdraw the watch slowly and record the distance at which the child fails to hear the ticking. Or he may use the whisper test with several children who stand 5 feet away with their backs to the examiner. The teacher gives a direction and notices the children who hesitate or fail to follow the directions. Other signs of possible hearing difficulty are inattention, misunderstanding of directions, frequent requests to repeat directions, a ringing or buzzing in the head, a blank expression, or posture indicating strain.

Children with auditory defects tend to learn better by visual than by auditory or phonic methods.

Deficiencies in auditory discrimination may be detected by asking the child to distinguish between words that sound alike and those that sound different. More definite tests of auditory discrimination require the child to name the beginning, middle, or final letter or letters of words that the examiner clearly pronounces. The Wepman Auditory Discrimination Test (1958, 1960) measures ability to recognize different phonemes of the spoken language, even when the sounds are highly similar. Many children from homes where English is spoken correctly will have learned to distinguish likenesses and differences in many words. Even these children may not be able to distinguish slight differences in sound such as the differences between *wear* and *where*. The initial digraph *wh*, according to competent linguists, may quite properly not be aspirated. When it is aspirated, the digraph is pronounced *hw* and is classified as one of the phonetic irregularities.

To improve auditory discrimination, the teacher may use teaching materials such as those in the *Peabody Language Development Kits*, American Guidance Service, Inc., Minneapolis. To give a child with impaired hearing practice in discriminating various phonetic elements and word combinations, Haspiel and Bloomer developed the Maximum Auditory Perception Word List in 1961.

The speaking vocabulary is more closely related to success in reading in elementary school than in high school or college. However, faulty pronunciation and inadequate speaking vocabulary may account for some of the errors in comprehension made by seriously retarded high school and college readers. Pronunciation, articulation, enunciation, pitch, and stress are all involved in the interpretation of language. Incorrect formation of speech sounds is more likely to be related to reading achievement than is stuttering. Moreover, any speech or auditory difficulty, insofar as it makes the individual feel less adequate as a person, may also make him less adequate in the reading situation.

BIOCHEMICAL AND PSYCHOBIOLOGICAL FACTORS

More and more frequently, certain medicines are being advocated for use in the treatment of reading problems. Insofar as reading is an intellectual task dependent upon the functioning of the nervous system, any drug that affects neural activity may be expected to be either detrimental or beneficial to reading.

Important discoveries in the chemistry of learning have been made through psychobiological experiments (Krech, 1968). Two kinds of memory, immediate and long-term, have been described physiologically. Immediate memory involves a short-lived electron chemical process which triggers a second process in the brain which is also chemical in nature. This second process involves the production of new proteins and induces enzymatic activity in the brain cell. It is crucial for long-term memory. If the production of new protein enzymes is interfered with, no memory of a former experience remains.

Certain injections of central nervous system stimulants such as strychnine and Metrazol increase the probability of successful long-term learning 40 percent. The effect of Metrazol varies with the individual and the size of dosage. Dull mice improved up to 10 milligrams; bright mice up to 5 milligrams. Dull mice, when treated with 10 milligrams, did slightly better than the untreated superior mice; but "there is a limit to the intellectual power of even a hopped-up Southern California Super Mouse" (Krech, 1968, p. 49). Beyond these optimum amounts, increase in dosage caused a deterioration in learning.

The effect of a substance called *deanol* on sixty pairs of retarded readers in junior and senior high school was studied by Staiger (1961). He found no significant differences in reading performance between the experimental group who were given the drug and the control group. In all but one instance, however, the differences favored the experimental group. The drug had some effect on perceptual speed and accuracy, but on the more complex aspects of comprehension its effect was negligible. Certainly no medication of this kind should be given by teachers or reading specialists.

Further evidence of the relation of biological factors to learning comes from the nutrition laboratory (Scrimshaw, 1968). An inadequate diet, especially in proteins, during the first years when the brain is growing most rapidly results in smaller brain size and damage to the central nervous system. The effect of this impairment on children's learning can only be inferred.

Using this knowledge of the physiological and chemical factors involved in learning, experimenters (Krech, 1968) have demonstrated the effect of an educationally stimulating environment on the actual increase in the cortex of the brain, in brain cells vital in the nutrition of the neurons, in the size of neurons and their nuclei, and in the blood vessels supplying the brain. These changes in the brain were shown to be related to the problem-solving ability of the animals.

Although direct application cannot be made from the results of animal experiments to children's learning, this basic biological-psychological research is significant and suggestive when interpreted scientifically.

CONCLUDING STATEMENT

The close relation between mind and body makes work with reading cases more than an intellectual task. Any one of a number of physical and physiological factors may affect a child's reading development directly or indirectly. To prevent a detrimental effect, a physical examination including the features mentioned in this chapter should be given to every child at critical stages in his development.

SUGGESTED PROBLEMS: PRACTICE AND DEMONSTRATION

1. Fill out for yourself the questionnaire on indications of visual difficulties given in this chapter. Use whatever screening instrument is available to make a record of your visual efficiency. Compare the results of the visual screening test with the questionnaire and with an ophthalmological examination, if the screening test shows that one is needed.

2. Send for information on vision testing available from the National Committee for the Prevention of Blindness, the National Foundation for the Blind, or other similar associations.

3. At a teachers' meeting, arrange to show American Optometric Association slides describing visual difficulties of children.

4. Following directions in this chapter, make the peep-hole device to observe an individual's eye movements while he is reading, and ask him to explain the causes of excessive fixations or regressions in his movements.

5. Summarize the facts about eye movements. What are your conclusions?

REFERENCES

BALOW, I. H., and B. BALOW: "Lateral Dominance and Reading Achievement in the Second Grade," *American Educational Research Journal*, 1:139–143, May, 1964.

BECK, HARRY S.: "The Relationship of Symbol Reversals to Monocular and Binocular Vision," *Peabody Journal of Education*, 38:137–142, November, 1960.

BELMONT, LILLIAN, and H. G. BIRCH: "Lateral Dominance, Lateral Awareness, and Reading Disability," *Child Development*, 36:57–71, March, 1965.

CAPOBIANCO, R. J.: "Ocular-Manual Laterality and Reading in Adolescent Mental Retardates," *American Journal of Mental Deficiency*, 70:781–785, March, 1966.

COLEMAN, R. I., and CYNTHIA P. DEUTSCH: "Lateral Dominance and Right-Left Discrimination: A Comparison of Normal and Retarded Readers," *Perceptual and Motor Skills*, 19:43–50, August, 1964.

CRANE, MARIAN M., and others: *Study of Procedures Used for Screening Elementary School Children for Visual Defects*, National Society for the Prevention of Blindness, New York, 1952.

DELACATO, CARL H.: *The Treatment and Prevention of Reading Problems*, Charles C Thomas, Publisher, Springfield, Ill., 1959.

EAMES, THOMAS H.: "Visual Handicaps to Reading," *Boston University Journal of Education*, 141:2–35, February, 1959.

FIGUREL, J. ALLEN (ed.): *Changing Concepts of Reading Instruction, Inter-*

national Reading Association Conference Proceedings, vol. 6, Scholastic Magazines, Inc., New York, 1961, pp. 89–97.

GOINS, JEAN TURNER: *Visual Perceptual Abilities and Early Reading Progress*, Supplementary Educational Monographs no. 87, The University of Chicago Press, Chicago, 1958, p. 98.

GRUBER, ELLIS: "Reading Ability, Binocular Coordination and the Ophthalmograph," *Archives of Ophthalmology*, 67:280–288, March, 1962.

HARRIS, ALBERT J.: "Lateral Dominance, Directional Confusion, and Reading Disability," *Journal of Psychology*, 44:283–294, October, 1957.

Harris Tests of Lateral Dominance, rev. for ages 6 and up, The Psychological Corporation, New York, 1958.

HUELSMAN, C. B.: "Some Recent Research on Visual Problems in Reading," *American Journal of Optometry and Archives of American Academy of Optometry*, monograph 240, 1959, pp. 1–7.

KELLEY, CHARLES R.: "Psychological Factors in Myopia," *American Psychologist*, 16:349, July, 1961.

KRECH, DAVID: "The Chemistry of Learning," *Saturday Review*, Jan. 20, 1968, pp. 48–50, 68.

LEAVELL, ULLIN W.: "Ability of Retarded Readers to Recognize Symbols in Association with Lateral Dominance," *Peabody Journal of Education*, 37:7–14, July, 1959.

LEESTMA, ROBERT C.: "Age Changes in Tachistoscopic Span," *Dissertation Abstracts*, 17:94, 1957.

MATSON, CHARLOTTE, and LOLA LARSON: *Books for Tired Eyes*, American Library Association, Chicago, 1951.

MC CONVILLE, CAROLYN B.: "Handedness and Psychomotor Skills," *Journal of Developmental Reading*, 4:47–52, Autumn, 1960.

PARK, G. E.: "Medical Aspects of Reading Failures in Intelligent Children," *The Sight Saving Review*, 29:213–218, Winter, 1959.

RABINOVITCH, RALPH D.: Recording made for a conference of the Arizona Intermediate Counsel of the SRA, 1962.

REITAN, RALPH M.: "Relationships between Neurological and Psychological Variables and Their Implications for Reading Instruction," in *Meeting Individual Differences in Reading, Proceedings of the Annual Conference on Reading*, no. 26, H. Alan Robinson (comp. and ed.), The University of Chicago Press, Chicago, 1964.

ROBINSON, HELEN: *Diagnosis and Treatment of Poor Readers with Vision Problems*, Supplementary Educational Monograph no. 77, The University of Chicago Press, Chicago, 1953, pp. 9–28.

————: "Vision and Reading Difficulties: The Findings of Research on Visual Difficulties and Reading," in *Reading for Effective Living, International Reading Association Conference Proceedings*, Scholastic Magazines, Inc., New York, 1958, pp. 107–111.

ROSEN, CARL L.: "Visual Deficiencies and Reading Disability," in A. J. Kingston (ed.), Research for the Classroom, *Journal of Reading*, 9:57–61, October, 1965.

SAMPSON, O. C.: "Reading Skill at Eight Years in Relation to Speech and Other Factors," *The British Journal of Educational Psychology*, 32:12–17, February, 1962.

SCRIMSHAW, NEVIN S.: "Infant Malnutrition and Adult Learning," *Saturday Review*, Mar. 16, 1968, pp. 64–66, 84.

SPACHE, G. D.: "What Teachers Should Know about Vision and Reading," *Optometric Weekly*, 57:27–31, Oct. 20, 1966.

—— and C. E. TILLMAN: "A Comparison of the Visual Profiles of Retarded and Non-retarded Readers," *Journal of Developmental Reading*, 5:101–108, Winter, 1962.

STAIGER, RALPH C.: "Medicine for Reading Improvement," *Journal of Developmental Reading*, 5:48–51, Autumn, 1961.

SWEETING, ORVILLE J.: "An Improved Vision Screening Program for the New Haven Schools: A Case History," *Journal of the American Optometric Association*, 30:715–722, May, 1959.

TINKER, MILES A.: "Recent Studies of Eye Movements in Reading," *Psychological Bulletin*, 55:215–231, July, 1958.

——: "Eye Movements in Reading," *Education*, 79:575–579, May, 1959.

——: "How Children and Adults Perceive Words in Reading," *Invitational Addresses, 1965*, International Reading Association, Newark, Del., 1965, pp. 75–91.

VAN DE RIET, V., and H. VAN DE RIET: "Visual Motor Coordination in Underachieving and 'Normal' School Boys," *Perceptual and Motor Skills*, 19:731–734, December, 1964.

VERNON, M. D.: *Backwardness in Reading: A Study of Its Nature and Origin*, Cambridge University Press, New York, 1957, pp. 109–115.

WALDSTREICHER, J. S.: "Eye-movement Photography an Effective Diagnostic Aid," *The Optical Journal and Review of Optometry*, 103:23–27, December, 1966.

Wepman Auditory Discrimination Test, Joseph M. Wepman, Chicago, copyright 1958.

WEPMAN, JOSEPH: "Auditory Discrimination, Speech, and Reading," *Elementary School Journal*, 60:325–333, March, 1960.

SUGGESTED READINGS

BING, LOIS B.: "A Critical Analysis of the Literature on Certain Visual Functions Which Seem to Be Related to Reading Achievement," *Journal of the American Optometric Association*, 22:454–463, March, 1951.

BOND, GUY L., and MILES A. TINKER: *Reading Difficulties, Their Diagnosis and Correction*, Appleton-Century-Crofts, Inc., New York, 1957, part 3.

BUSWELL, GUY: *How Adults Read*, The University of Chicago Press, Chicago, 1937.

CAPOBIANCO, R. F.: "Diagnostic Methods Used with Learning Disability Cases," *Exceptional Children*, 31:187–193, December, 1964.

CARRIGAN, PATRICIA N.: "Broader Implications of a Chemical Theory of Reading Disability," *Journal of Developmental Reading*, 5:15–26, Autumn, 1961.

EWALT, H. WARD: "Visual Performance and Its Relation to Reading Achievement," *Journal of the American Optometric Association*, 33:825–829, June, 1962.

KNOX, G. E.: "Classroom Symptoms of Visual Difficulty," in *Clinical Studies in Reading: II*, Supplementary Educational Monograph no. 77, The University of Chicago Press, Chicago, 1953, pp. 97–101.

LEESTMA, ROBERT C.: *Audio-visual Materials for Teaching Reading*, Slater's Book Store, Ann Arbor, Mich., 1954.

MC CORD, H.: "Note on the Use of the Psychogalvanometer as an Aid in the Diagnosis of Certain Persons with Reading Difficulties," *Journal of Developmental Reading*, 5:137–138, Winter, 1962.

PERRY, WILLIAM G., JR., and CHARLES P. WHITLOCK: "The Right to Read Rapidly," *Atlantic Monthly*, 159:88–96, November, 1952.

RABINOVITCH, RALPH D., and WINIFRED INGRAM: "Neuropsychiatric Considerations in Reading Retardation," *The Reading Teacher*, 15:433–438, May, 1962.

SPACHE, GEORGE D.: "Auditory and Visual Materials," in *Development in and through Reading*, Sixtieth Yearbook of the National Society for the Study of Education. The University of Chicago Press, Chicago, 1961, part I, pp. 206–225.

———: "Classroom Reading and the Visually Handicapped Child," in *Changing Concepts of Reading Instruction*, International Reading Association Conference Proceedings, vol. 6, Scholastic Magazines, Inc., New York, 1961, pp. 93–97.

——— and LOIS B. BING: *Children's Vision and School Success*, American Optometric Association, St. Louis, 1962.

——— and CHESTER E. TILLMAN: "A Comparison of the Visual Profiles of Retarded and Non-retarded Readers," *Journal of Developmental Reading*, 5:101–109, Winter, 1962.

STRAUSS, ALFRED A., and NEWELL C. KEPHART: *Psychopathology and Education of the Brain-injured Child*, vol. II, Progress in Theory and Clinic, Grune & Stratton, Inc., New York, 1955.

TAYLOR, EDITH: *Psychological Appraisal of Children with Cerebral Defects*, Harvard University Press, Cambridge, Mass., 1959.

TINKER, MILES A., and DONALD G. PATTERSON: "The Effect of Typographical Variations upon Eye Movement in Reading," *Journal of Educational Research*, 49:171–184, November, 1955.

Chapter Ten

READING TESTS ADMINISTERED INDIVIDUALLY

The techniques of observation and of informal and standardized group tests which form one end of a diagnostic continuum have been described in Chapters 3 and 7. The other end, which includes a variety of individual inventories and tests, will be presented in this chapter.

Expertly constructed single tests and batteries of tests are available for studying specific abilities underlying reading achievement, such as visual and auditory perception, discrimination, memory and integration; visual-motor coordination; spatial orientation; directionality; and closure. More pervasive underlying abilities such as memory; attention; concentration, and the ability to see relationships, analyze, generalize, and synthesize are measured by tests of psycholinguistic abilities and individual intelligence tests. Dexterity in the administration and interpretation of these tests requires special training and psychological background.

Informal individual reading inventories are a bridge between the group tests and the more technical standardized individual tests. When a student flounders on an informal group test, the next step is to find out what his specific difficulties are. It is fascinating to study interindividual differences by noting how children of different abilities and backgrounds respond. But it is still more significant from the standpoint of diagnosis to see patterns of various abilities within a child, i.e., intraindividual differences.

While administering a test individually, the teacher can observe the student closely. His chance remarks, his facial expressions, bodily positions, and expressive movements often give clues to his attitudes toward himself and toward reading. His casual conversation may give insight into his early reading experiences and interests and his present family relationships. He will often tell how he thinks teachers have helped or hindered his progress in reading and what makes reading easy or difficult for him. His reading of paragraphs on different levels of difficulty gives information about his approach to reading, his methods of word recognition, and the quality of his comprehension. In addition to these specific values, the individual inventory helps to establish a constructive student-teacher relationship. It may also enable the student to see his reading difficulties objectively.

THE INDIVIDUAL READING INVENTORY (IRI)

The individual reading inventory combines the diagnostic values of oral reading and observation. It is administered to individuals while the rest of the class are working independently. As described here, the individual reading inventory is informal and flexible. The teacher may modify it in numerous ways to explore with the student his reading performance and process. The IRI is specifically useful in the appraisal of proficiency in basic vocabulary, word recognition, and comprehension of paragraphs of different levels of difficulty. Every reading teacher should be prepared to use it.

Construction of an IRI

The individual reading inventory consists of a series of graded paragraphs which the student reads aloud; he then answers questions about their content. The paragraphs may be selected from various sources: from a graded basal reading series the student has not read, from *My Weekly Reader*, or from any other kind of graded reading material. The teacher may also write paragraphs especially for this purpose and check them for reading difficulty.

As in other testing situations involving achievement and capacity, it is desirable to elicit the optimum response from the individual. Since reading requires effort, and since effort can be motivated by interest, the material chosen obviously should be as interesting as possible. Otherwise, lack of achievement is confused with lack of effort. Paragraphs from primary basal readers often are too childish in content for the bright child or the older retarded reader; he may resent being given such "baby stuff" and may not even try to read it.

The comprehension questions for an IRI should be of four kinds at least: questions of fact, questions requiring a grasp of the main thought, questions of inferences or conclusion, and questions of word meanings.

The following is an example of an individual reading inventory such as any teacher might make, selecting paragraphs of special interest to his students and asking questions appropriate to their level of understanding.

INDIVIDUAL READING INVENTORY (Teacher's Record Form)

Some seeds travel
in the water.
Some seeds travel
in the air.
Some seeds travel
on animals.
Some seeds travel
on people's clothes.[1]

First Grade: "How Seeds Travel"
Questions:
1. What are these sentences about? (2 points)

2. How do some seeds travel? (4 points)

3. Why is it good for seeds to travel? (2 points)

4. What does *travel* mean? (1 point)

5. Give a sentence using the word *travel*. (1 point)

Total no. words: 23   Accuracy:
  No. words correct: 90% (21) [2]
  No. errors: 95% (22)
Reading time (wpm):   Comprehension score:

Autumn is a busy time
in the north.
Autumn is harvest time.
Potatoes are dug in autumn.
Corn is picked in autumn.
Many crops are being harvested.[3]

[1] *My Weekly Reader*, vol. 39, ed. 1, p. 3, Oct. 2–6, 1961.

[2] The figures in parentheses are the number of words correct to make 90 and 95 percent accuracy.

[3] *My Weekly Reader*, vol. 31, ed. 2, p. 1, Sept. 18–22, 1961.

Second Grade: "Autumn's Harvest Time"
Questions:
1. What are these sentences about? (2 points)

2. What kind of a time is autumn in the north? (1 point)

3. What is dug in autumn? (1 point)

4. What is picked in autumn? (1 point)

5. Why is autumn a busy time? (2 points)

6. What does *harvest* mean? (1 point)

7. Use *harvest* or *harvested* in a sentence. (2 points)

Total no. words: 27	Accuracy:
No. words correct:	90% (24)
No. errors:	95% (27)
Reading time (wpm):	Comprehension score:

The U.S. Army has been buying dogs. The dogs are German shepherds. The Army needs 200 dogs. The dogs will help to guard top-secret Army camps.

The Army tests the dogs before buying them. Army dogs cannot be afraid of noise. They must be smart and able to obey orders.[4]

Third Grade: "Dogs Guard Army Camps"
Questions:
1. What are these paragraphs about? (2 points)

2. How many dogs does the Army need? (1 point)

[4] *My Weekly Reader*, vol. 31, ed. 3, p. 13, Sept. 25–29, 1961.

3. What kind of dogs does the Army buy? (1 point)

4. What must the dogs be able to do? (2 points)

5. Why does the Army need dogs? (1 point)

6. What does *guard* mean? Give a sentence using the word *guard*. (1 point)

7. What does *top-secret* mean? (1 point)

8. Use *top-secret* in a sentence. (1 point)

Total no. words: 51	Accuracy:
No. of words correct:	90% (46)
No. errors:	95% (48)
Reading time (wpm):	Comprehension score:

> A giant, four-engine airplane swoops low over a burning forest in California. A "water bomb" drops from the plane. Soon, the roaring blaze is out.
> A helicopter flies slowly over a newly cut forest in Minnesota. As the helicopter moves, it leaves behind a trail of small seeds.[5]

Fourth Grade: "How Airplanes Help"
Questions:
1. What are these paragraphs about? (2 points)

2. What does the airplane drop on the burning forests? (1 point)

3. How do helicopters plant new forests? (2 points)

4. What does the "water bomb" do? (2 points)

[5] *My Weekly Reader*, vol. 43, ed. 4, p. 1, Sept. 25–29, 1961.

5. What does *swoop* mean? (1 point)

6. Use *swoop* in a sentence. (2 points)

Total no. words: 49   Accuracy:
  No. of words correct: 90% (44)
  No. errors: 95% (47)
Reading time (wpm):   Comprehension score:

> The big jet screeches as its engines turn. It takes off with a roar and climbs swiftly into the sky.
>
> Inside the plane, the passengers hear only a muffled sound of the jet's powerful engines. The takeoff is so gentle that travelers may not even know when the plane lifts off the ground. The jets fly at from 450 to 600 miles an hour. Travelers can go from New York to Chicago in two hours. They can travel from coast to coast in five to six hours.[6]

Fifth Grade: "Facts about Jet Planes"
Questions:
1. What are these paragraphs about? (2 points)

2. What sound does the big jet make when its engines begin to turn? (1 point)

3. How fast do jets fly? (1 point)

4. How long do jets take to go from New York to Chicago? (1 point)

5. How long do jets take to go from coast to coast? (1 point)

6. Why is it so quiet inside the jet? (2 points)

[6] *My Weekly Reader*, vol. 44, ed. 5, p. 1, Nov. 27–Dec. 1, 1961.

7. Give an example of a *screech* and a *muffled sound.* (2 points)

Total no. words: 87   Accuracy:
  No. words correct: 90% (78)
  No. errors: 95% (82)
Reading time (wpm):   Comprehension score:

> Kruger Park is a wild animal preserve. The fence around the park will keep the animals in and unlicensed hunters out. The fence is one of the steps being taken to protect wild life in African countries.
> Africa's wild life has been disappearing at an alarming rate. One wild-life expert says it is possible that all large animals will be gone from the continent within the next ten to twenty years.[7]

•

Sixth Grade: "Protection of Wild Life in Africa"
Questions:
1. What are these paragraphs about? (2 points)

2. Where is Kruger Park? (1 point)

3. Why is there a fence around the park? (2 points)

4. Why are steps being taken to protect wild life in Africa? (2 points)

5. In how many years may all large wild animals be gone from Africa? (1 point)

6. What is a wild animal preserve? (1 point)

7. What is a continent? (1 point)

Total no. words: 69   Accuracy:
  No. words correct: 90% (62)
  No. errors: 95% (66)
Reading time (wpm):   Comprehension score:

---

[7] *My Weekly Reader,* vol. 16, ed. 6, p. 1, Oct. 2–6, 1961.

Administration of the IRI

To be of practical value to teachers, a reading inventory should be so designed that it can be administered and scored quickly and easily. Both teacher and student will find the administering of the test more convenient if each paragraph is printed on a card for the student and on a separate sheet for the teacher that contains space for recording the student's errors in oral reading and answers to the comprehension questions. Since the individual reading inventory is used as a clinical rather than as a psychometric device, the teacher may reword the questions if he thinks the student knows the answer but is puzzled by the form of the question.

The oral reading of the paragraphs may be preceded by a brief preliminary conversation to explain the purpose of the inventory and to put the student at ease. The teacher may also give a test of knowledge of spoken words, such as the Gates Oral Vocabulary Test, or a test of word recognition, such as the Wide Range Achievement Test (Jastak, 1946) to ascertain the level of paragraph difficulty at which to begin. It is better to begin testing at too low rather than at too high a level, because the student's success in reading fluently and comprehending fully the easier paragraphs gives him confidence in his ability to read the more difficult ones.

As the student reads each paragraph orally, the teacher indicates his errors and jots down his responses to the questions. Usually the teacher tells the student a word on which he pauses for about five seconds or when he asks for help. When the same word recurs in the paragraph, the teacher can see how the student attacks a word when he meets it the second time. His failure to recognize it a second time time is counted as another error. The teacher may aid the student's comprehension by asking what the word might mean in the sentence. Inequality of response from paragraph to paragraph is to be expected. This may be partly due to unequal interest in or degree of familiarity with the topics. When the paragraphs become very difficult, the examiner may ask the student just to pick out the words he knows. He stops before the situation has become distressing.

If time permits, the teacher may learn more about the student's reading process by asking him about his method of reading, for example, how he got the meaning of some of the difficult words and why he had difficulty with others.

After the first oral reading the student may be asked to read the same paragraphs silently and then reread them orally. His improvement in pronunciation and comprehension is then noted. Improvement in comprehension may be due to his having the questions in mind as he rereads the paragraphs.

Asking the student to recognize and recall words that begin and end with the same sound as the stimulus word gives further understanding of his phonic ability, speaking vocabulary, and "divergent thinking."

The following responses were made by a ten-year-old boy (Johnny, of course!) when he was asked for: (1) words that begin with the same sound as

can	king, cook
saw	see, so, salt, said

and (2) words that end with the same sound, that rhyme with

can	ban
keep	sleep, peep
pig	mig, lig

At this point the teacher said, "What does *lig* mean?" Johnny replied, "That gets me, too." Teacher: "You made it up, didn't you? We call it a nonsense syllable. It has no meaning. You have a very good ear for sounds."

Asking a student to read a portion of a play or conversation in a story will yield further indication of his ability to read for meaning with proper phrasing and expression.

Reading aloud to the student other paragraphs beginning at or a little below his oral reading frustration level and testing his comprehension of them will show any discrepancy between his auditory comprehension and his instructional level of oral reading (see Chapter 11).

Administering a timed silent reading test composed of similar paragraphs will make possible a comparison between a child's silent and oral reading proficiency.

Instruction may be interwoven with testing in administering the individual reading inventory. If the teacher gives instruction or suggests exercises to correct difficulties as they are recognized, the student has immediate incentive to work on them.

From these procedures the teacher may select a pattern appropriate for his students. Even a recording of a student's response to one or two paragraphs has diagnostic value.

Recording of students' responses

After obtaining the student's responses on the IRI form, the teacher may record the errors and other kinds of responses to the graded paragraphs (see Checklist, page 200). The number and kinds of errors usually increase as the paragraphs increase in difficulty.

CHECKLIST FOR RECORDING PERFORMANCE ON ORAL READING PARAGRAPHS

Name_____Grade_____Date_____

Paragraphs	Rating on given paragraph level						General impressions
	I	II	III	IV	V	VI	
Word attack: Refuses to attempt unknown words							
Omits words or parts of words							
Inserts words							
Guesses at words:							
Makes sense							
Does not make sense							
Repeats words or parts of words							
Reverses letters or words							
Spells out words							
Sounds out words laboriously							
Recognizes beginning sound							
Mispronounces the whole word							
Recognizes other sounds and tries pronunciation							
Checks pronunciation with meaning in sentence							
Uses structural parts							
Uses combination of methods							
Phrasing: Reads in thought units							
Poor grouping							
Word-by-word reading							
Monotone							
Ignores punctuation							
Posture: Good							
Book too close							
Book too far							
Finger pointing							
Speed, wpm:							
Comprehension: Main ideas identified							
Details							
Inference							
Vocabulary							
Comparison between oral and silent reading Comprehension: Little or no difference							
Silent reading slightly superior							
Silent reading twice as good as oral							
Little or no improvement in oral reading							
Grade levels: Independent							
Instructional							
Frustrational							
Capacity 75% comprehension or better							
Listening comprehension							
No better than reading							
Slightly better							
Much better							

To obtain a qualitative impression of the student's reading performance, the teacher may note the pattern of errors in word recognition and the quality of comprehension—whether the student answers questions briefly or at length, in his own words or those of the book; whether he reports accurately what the author says or makes up stories and inserts information that was not in the paragraphs.

From the information recorded on the reading inventory sheet, the teacher may estimate the student's reading level and capacity. The characteristics of these levels have been described by Betts (1957) as follows:

1. *Independent reading level*

   Not more than one word recognition error per 100 words.

   Comprehension of at least 90 percent.

   Reading well phrased, natural intonation.

   Freedom from tension and anxiety.

2. *Instructional reading level*

   Not more than one word recognition error per 20 words.

   Comprehension of at least 75 percent.

   After silent study reads the passage in conversational tone with proper phrasing and without tension.

3. *Frustration reading level*

   Errors and refusals to attempt to read difficult words are numerous, as many as 10 percent of the running words.

   Comprehension is less than half of what is read.

   Tension, distractability, withdrawal from task.

4. *Probable reading capacity level*

   The most difficult paragraph on which the student can comprehend at least 75 percent when it is read aloud to him; he can pronounce and use properly many of the words and language structures in the selection.

The percentage of accuracy and comprehension for the independent, instructional, and frustration levels of reading is set rather arbitrarily at different levels by various people. More important than estimates of reading level is the diagnostic information which leads directly to improvement of reading.

On the independent level the student can do much supplementary reading for enjoyment and information. On the instructional level he can read challenging material with some instruction and guidance from the teacher. Subjecting students to books on their frustration level tends to perpetuate errors and cause dislike of reading.

Interpretation

The information obtained incidentally or systematically in giving the individual reading inventory lends itself to interpretation and application. The following are a few suggestions:

WORD CALLING   Word callers, who read with apparent fluency but little or no comprehension, need to focus their attention on meaning rather than on pronunciation. They need exercises in reading directions to which they will respond by action.

WORD RECOGNITION   Difficulty in word recognition may stem from a hearing loss. The examiner may check for a possible lack of auditory acuity by saying something in a low voice when the student is not looking at him. If the trouble stems from the student's inability to associate printed symbols with sounds, the need for a phonic inventory is indicated. Quite frequently an individual may be able to recognize the sounds of letters in words but be unable to pronounce the word correctly. Some students are able to recognize only the initial sound of a word; from this they guess at the meaning. They need frequent, systematic application of word recognition skills when they meet unfamiliar words in their reading.

CRITICAL READING AND THINKING   A discrepancy between the student's abilities to answer factual questions and those requiring more thought may be due to lack of practice rather than lack of ability. In the individual interview, when encouraged to think and guided in the process, many students show latent ability.

WORD MEANING   In recording substitutions, it is important to note what kinds of words are substituted. The student who substitutes *scurried* for *scampered* in the sentence "The squirrel scampered" shows that he is reading for meaning, whereas the student who reads "a bowl of soap" for "a bowl of soup" shows lack of concern for content.

MENTAL ABILITY   The individual inventory situation, if supplemented, as it usually is, by the teacher's information about the children in his class whom he already knows very well, yields clues that help the teacher interpret a student's mental ability. A student's superior mental ability may have been suppressed by his deprivation of intellectual stimulation in infancy and childhood, by anxiety, by fear, or by other environmental factors.

ATTITUDES AND EMOTIONS From observation of the individual's personal appearance and behavior, his friendliness or unfriendliness, his social poise or embarrassment, his enthusiasm or indifference, the teacher may gather something about his attitudes. For example, John had experienced several failures and was resentful about them. In his words, the art teacher was "crazy"; the shop teacher was "an old guy, quite crazy, too." In a class for slow learners, the other boys called him "the genius" because his mother had insisted on his going into the high school academic course; she was determined that he would eventually go to college. He stopped going to church and Sunday school because he was called upon to read aloud. Hints of his subsurface hostility, which came out in the IRI, were explored further through daily observation.

Another boy, who gave many indications of anxiety and apathy, was asked what was his favorite activity; he replied, "Going to bed." The fact that he was blocked on the easiest paragraph but later read a harder one fairly fluently showed that he could perform more efficiently after he realized that the situation was nonthreatening.

Signs of tension such as nail biting or twisting and turning in the seat may be readily observed. It is also interesting to see how an individual responds to increased difficulty and what happens when he moves from a satisfying to an unsuccessful experience.

INTERESTS Students usually express their interests freely in the individual reading situation. For example, one boy spoke with enthusiasm of the wonderful time he had had on a New England farm during the summer. During the winter he spent much time watching TV.

Recommendations

Recommendations based on the individual reading inventory, plus all the other information available about the student, should be highly personal and build on assets. Among general recommendations frequently growing out of an individual inventory are the following:

1. Continued efforts in school to give the student the experience of success in reading. In every class, skillful instruction along the specific lines indicated by the diagnosis can lead to improvement.

2. Provision of suitable reading material; even "baby books" are sometimes recommended for emotionally disturbed children who

have a need to live again through the baby stage. These books have therapeutic value in addition to increasing the child's reading fluency. Older students who are eager to read better often will accept beginner books if they are convinced that this is the path to improvement.

3. Analysis and correction of underlying factors and environmental conditions that may be preventing progress. Among these are psycholinguistic deficiencies, the influences of a disadvantaged home background, and lack of intellectual stimulation.

4. Analysis of the reading tasks into sequential steps by which all may learn.

5. Referral to a counselor who can find resources for widening the individual's school activities and interests, provide supporting counseling, and adjust the school program to meet his need. Sometimes it is desirable that the student be given a change of class or course. If the parents refuse to consent to the change, they must assume responsibility if the student continues to fail in his present course or if his reading problem becomes aggravated.

6. Work with parents when there is clear evidence that home conditions are continuing to prevent reading improvement. With adolescents whose parents have confirmed unrealistic attitudes and ambitions, it is sometimes possible to help the child change his attitude toward the home situation so that it does not continue to interfere with his progress.

7. Referral to a child guidance or mental hygiene clinic if the problem is primarily emotional.

STANDARDIZED READING TESTS

Oral reading tests

As suggested in Chapter 4, oral reading tests, informal or standardized, are the core of appraisal procedures in the primary grades. One of these tests is included in any thorough diagnosis of reading difficulties.

Several standardized oral reading tests are available, such as:

1. Gray Oral Reading Test by William S. Gray, for grades 1 to 8, two forms. The Bobbs-Merrill Company, Inc., Indianapolis, 1963. The original oral reading test was a pioneer in the field. It has been widely used and recently revised to include questions to check the student's comprehension of each paragraph.

2. Leavell Analytical Oral Reading Test by Ullin W. Leavell, for grades 1 to 10, Forms A and B, time fifteen to twenty minutes. Educational Test Bureau, Minneapolis, 1952–1953.

3. Gilmore Oral Reading Test by John U. Gilmore, for grades 1 to 8, Forms A and B, time fifteen to twenty minutes. Harcourt, Brace & World, Inc., New York, 1952.

It is important not only to know the response a student makes, but also to know how he arrives at it, e.g., how he tries to identify a certain word, why he substitutes one word for another, etc. Such understanding may be gained by asking him occasionally to think aloud as he attacks an unfamiliar word.

Standardized diagnostic reading tests

More detailed information about a student's reading proficiency and difficulties may be obtained from a number of diagnostic reading tests. The Durrell Analysis of Reading Difficulty Test (1937–1955) includes a set of both oral and silent reading paragraphs. As in the individual reading inventory, the student continues with the graded series of paragraphs until he reaches his frustration level. With the stories the teacher may orient the reader to the story as he does in teaching story material. For example, he may say, "This story is about a boy. It tells what happened on a weekend trip. Let's see what happened." In testing comprehension, the teacher may ask the pupil to tell in his own words what the author said: "You read the story to yourself. When you've finished it, put your book down, and then instead of asking you questions I'll ask you to tell the story." Many students can answer questions better than they can tell the story. This may be because they have had more practice in answering questions than in organizing the ideas they gain from reading. They need the clues that questions give. The Durrell test also gives information about listening comprehension, phonetic analyses, and quick recognition of words.

Other standardized tests help to determine students' need for instruction and practice on specific word attack skills. Among such tests are those by Gates and McKillop, Diagnostic Reading Tests (Teachers College Press, New York, 1962); Bond, Clymer, and Hoyt, Silent Reading Diagnostic Tests (Lyons and Carnahan, Chicago, 1955); (see the Appendix for more detail).

TESTS OF CORRELATES OF READING ABILITY

Recently several very important tests for the clinical analysis of correlates of reading ability have been developed.

The De Hirsch battery was selected experimentally (De Hirsch, Jansky, and Langford, 1966) from thirty-seven tests of many facets of perceptual-motor and oral-language organization initially administered to kindergarten children. The predictive index that was finally developed consisted of ten tests that measured eye-motor coordination as evidenced by the child's use of his pencil, visual-motor tasks, auditory discrimination, word fluency as indicated by the child's dictated stories, ability to categorize, reversals, word matching, word recognition, word reproduction, and human figure drawing.

The battery being developed by Wepman and his associates will include the Wepman Auditory Discrimination Test, the Chicago Visual Discrimination Test published by the University of Chicago Press in 1967, and other instruments for assessing factors related to success in reading.

The Illinois Test of Psycholinguistic Abilities (ITPA) (Kirk and Mc-Carthy, 1961) is unique in its systematic measurement of the reading process from "intake"—visual impression of the printed words—to "output" —verbal or motor response to the printed material. Expressed in the form of a profile, it is a unique approach to differential diagnosis of the reading process. The ITPA includes tests of auditory and visual reception, association, vocal expressive and motor expressive abilities, sound blending, perceptual speed, visual closure, and visual discrimination. These are important perceptual, linguistic, and cognitive abilities related to language and reading. Deficiency in any one of them may block the reading process.

Recognizing that the experimental form of the ITPA was incomplete, Kass (1966) supplemented it with tests of (1) visual closure measuring ability to complete a picture lacking in some detail, (2) ability to blend separate sounds into words, (3) ability to draw the way out of a maze, (4) memory for simple geometric designs, and (5) ability to quickly discriminate details that differentiate one word from others. (More detail about these and other clinical instruments is given in the References at the end of this chapter and in *Diagnosis and Treatment of Reading Disability in American Education,* Indiana University Press, Bloomington, Indiana, 1969.)

In addition to these predictive batteries used in clinical diagnosis, there are a number of separate tests of visual-motor ability and of auditory and visual perception which reading teachers can learn to administer and interpret. Among these are the Wepman Test of Auditory Discrimination (1958) and the Marianne Frostig Developmental Test of Visual Perception (1961). The Wepman test is most useful for detecting the lack of auditory discrimination needed for success in reading. A reading teacher can administer it in a few minutes. The Frostig test is more elaborate and requires more training. The results of research concerning its value in predicting success in beginning reading are somewhat inconclusive. Used in the first grade, it identifies many children who may have reading difficulties because of visual perception and related correlates.

The Minnesota Percepto-diagnostic Test (1963) is a test of directional orientation consisting of six gestalt designs to be copied. The only scoring criterion is the degree of rotation of the copied figure away from the orientation of the original. It purports to distinguish organic, primary, and secondary reading disability as defined by Rabinovitch (1959). In using the test, the examiner must decide whether the case is primarily a reading or an emotional problem.

The Bender Visual-Motor Gestalt Test, often referred to as the Bender-Gestalt, was developed in 1938 and revised by Lauretta Bender in 1946. Other persons have made revisions for different purposes and have called it by slightly different names. In addition to detecting deficits in graphomotor skills which are related to perceptual retardation and reading disability, the Bender-Gestalt as administered by a clinical psychologist with experience in using this test may yield clues of neurological disorganization or dysfunction.

The best way to become acquainted with any of these tests is to send for a sample set. Before giving the test, one must study the manual thoroughly and practice the procedure described. The ITPA Bender Visual-Motor Gestalt, and, to a lesser extent, the Frostig and the Wepman require special training.

RELATIVE CONTRIBUTION OF STANDARDIZED TESTS AND INFORMAL PROCEDURES

One wonders whether the diagnosis of a student's oral reading might not be accomplished as well by having him read sample passages from books of different levels of difficulty as by a standardized oral reading test. The most direct way of determining whether a child can read a given book on the independent, instructional, or frustrational level is to have him read a short passage from it. Observing the child as he reads aloud, the teacher finds errors as they occur. Each hesitation, each omission, each reversal raises questions about its cause.

Many of the activities commonly carried on in kindergarten and the primary grades give practice in and clues to prerequisites of success in learning to read. Difficulty in auditory perception, discrimination, and memory can be detected by the teacher through a child's response to questions or his attempt to retell a story. Following the text in a book while he listens to a recording of it will help him to listen better, and he will gradually gain understanding from the oral presentation alone. Putting together jigsaw puzzles and identifying details and relationships in pictures will give the child practice in spatial relations and visual perception and will disclose his difficulties. Just asking him to describe objects that he has seen on the way to school is a form of visual decoding beginning with the child's concrete experiences.

Similarly, identifying form and texture and practice in reproducing certain shapes on paper will make the child more proficient in this sensory avenue.

If a student is slow in associating what he hears with what he sees, and if he has difficulty organizing his separate perceptions into categories and concepts, he may be given many experiences of this kind. He may also be confronted with many little problems to solve in his own life and in the stories he reads. The "what might have happened if . . ." approach can be applied to social studies and science as well as to fiction.

Closely related to associating things heard or discussed is the ability to make visual-motor associations. If a child has difficulty in seeing that two things, such as a hand and a glove, go together, he can improve this ability by a number of matching games, noting objects that do not belong together as well as those that go together and telling why.

Childern should have more opportunity to express ideas vocally than is permitted in many classrooms. If a child has marked difficulty along this line, the teacher may first ask him merely to supply the rhyming word at the end of the second line of a poem or to fill in a missing word or a missing part of the story. The teacher can devise a number of interesting closure exercises. Eventually children will be able to retell the whole story or describe a personal experience in proper sequence. Conversation stimulates and builds up the child's ability to express what he has heard, read, and seen.

Children who have difficulty in writing or other aspects of motor coordination are easily identified. Improvement in motor coordination, hand coordination, and eye-hand coordination can be achieved through a graded series of imaginative physical activities. Specific practice in speech and in the use of hands may be given through hand puppets.

Since sequential memory is closely related to success in ability to learn to read, children should have many experiences and games that give practice in identifying and remembering sequence of letters in words, the home telephone number, the route they had taken on a trip, the order of events in the plot of a story, and the like. The teacher or students may cut apart comic strips or a cartoon series for practice in rearranging the pieces in a meaningful sequence.

During any instructional period, diagnosis, instruction, and practice can thus be combined. Another valuable diagnostic contribution of such a period is the insight that the teacher can gain into the student's learning capacity. After he has been given instruction in paragraph comprehension, for example, the teacher can note how quickly he "catches on." One boy who was unable to get the main idea of the first paragraph he read could give the main idea and supporting details of comparable paragraphs after he had had instruction in how paragraphs are built. The surest test of a student's learning ability is whether he learns when he has been given the best possible instruction.

CONCLUDING STATEMENT

The reading inventory is the simple procedure of asking a student to read aloud a series of graded paragraphs. If time permits and the need is indicated, the analysis of the student's oral reading may be supplemented by other techniques suggested in this chapter.

Interpretation may be based on fairly objective evidence of proficiency in word meaning and word recognition, or it may involve inferences derived from subtle clues of mental abilities, attitudes, and emotions.

Diagnostic information obtained from the individual reading inventory may be used immediately to help an individual student; it may be tabulated for the whole class as a guide to group instrution; it may be used to show trends in the development of a student's reading over a period of time. The important thing is that such information should be *used*.

When a reading problem does not respond to this first level of diagnostic techniques, it is necessary to try to detect underlying visual-motor, perceptual, and conceptual correlates and more pervasive mental abilities such as memory, reasoning, and attention. Specific remedial exercises similar to, but not identical with, those included in the tests may be used to build up areas in which deficits have been identified.

SUGGESTED PROBLEMS: PRACTICE AND DEMONSTRATION

1. Build up a file of reading tests including samples of each, the accompanying manual, and the articles and pamphlets describing its construction and use. Include also a copy of the appraisals of the test from Buros's latest *Mental Measurements Yearbook* and from other sources.

2. Select and administer one standardized oral reading test and one diagnostic test to a child. Record, score, interpret, and make tentative recommendations on the basis of the information thus obtained.

3. Give a demonstration of the individual reading inventory for teachers in your school.

4. Construct an individual reading inventory using paragraphs from the books you will expect pupils in their elementary or secondary school classes to read.

5. Use the McCullough Word Analysis Tests, grades 4 through college (Ginn and Company), to obtain information on each type of word recognition skill.

6. How might the individual reading inventory be adapted for use by classroom teachers? When would they have the time to give it to each pupil individually? How could they secure sufficient privacy?

7. What should a teacher do with a fourth-grade pupil who reads silently with adequate comprehension but makes many errors in pronunciation when reading orally?

REFERENCES

AUSTIN, MARY C., and others: *Reading Evaluation*, The Ronald Press Company, New York, 1961.

BENDER, LAURETTA: *Bender Visual Motor Gestalt Test*, American Orthopsychiatric Association, Inc., New York, 1938–1946.

BETTS, EMMETT A.: *Foundations of Reading Instruction*, American Book Company, New York, 1957.

Bond, Clymer-Hoyt Silent Reading Diagnostic Tests, Lyons and Carnahan, Chicago, 1955.

Botel Reading Inventory, Follett Publishing Company, Chicago, 1961. *Guide to the Botel Reading Inventory*, Follett Publishing Company, Chicago, 1961.

DE HIRSCH, KATRINA, JEANNETTE JANSKY, and W. S. LANGFORD: *Predicting Reading Failure*, Harper & Row, Publishers, Incorporated, New York, 1966.

DURRELL, DONALD D.: *Durrell Analysis of Reading Difficulty*, grades 1–6, one form for individual administration in grades 1–6, time 30–90 minutes, Harcourt, Brace & World, Inc., New York, 1937–1955.

FROSTIG, MARIANNE, D. W. LEFEVER, and J. WHITTLESEY: "A Developmental Test of Visual Perception for Evaluating Normal and Neurologically Handicapped Children," *Perceptual and Motor Skills*, 12:383–394, June, 1961.

GATES, ARTHUR I.: *Gates Reading Diagnostic Tests*, rev. ed., grades 1–8, time 60–90 minutes; Teachers College Press, Columbia University, New York, 1953.

JASTAK, JOSEPH: *Wide Range Achievement Test* and *Manual*, Wilmington, Del., 1946.

JOHNSON, ELEANOR: *Phonics Inventories*, published periodically in *My Weekly Reader*.

KASS, CORRINE E.: "Psycholinguistic Disabilities of Children with Reading Problems," *Exceptional Children*, 32:533–539, April, 1966.

KIRK, SAMUEL A.: *The Diagnosis and Remediation of Psycholinguistic Disabilities*, The University of Illinois Press, Institute for Research on Exceptional Children, Urbana, 1966.

——— and J. J. MC CARTHY: "The Illinois Test of Psycholinguistic Abilities: An Approach to Differential Diagnosis," *American Journal of Mental Deficiency*, 65:399–412, November, 1961.

LAIRD, J. T., and G. B. FULLER: *Minnesota Percepto-diagnostic Test, Journal of Clinical Psychology*, Brandon, Vt. 1962–1963.

STRANG, RUTH: *Diagnosis and Treatment of Reading Disability in American Education*, Indiana University Press, Bloomington, 1969.

WEPMAN, J. M.: *Wepman Auditory Discrimination Test*, Language Research Associates, Chicago, 1958.

Winter Haven Lions Club: *Perceptual Forms Test*, ages 6–8.5, Winter Haven Lions Research Foundation, Inc., Winter Haven, Fla., 1955–1963.

SUGGESTED READINGS

BOND, GUY L., and MILES A. TINKER: *Reading Difficulties: Their Diagnosis and Correction*, Appleton-Century-Crofts, Inc., New York, 1957.

BRUECKNER, LEO J., and GUY L. BOND: *The Diagnosis and Treatment of Learning Difficulties*, Appleton-Century-Crofts, Inc., New York, 1955.

BUROS, OSCAR (ed.): *The Fifth Mental Measurements Yearbook*, The Gryphon Press, Highland Park, N.J., 1959.

Durrell Analysis of Reading Difficulty, rev. ed., Harcourt, Brace & World, Inc., New York, 1955.

FERNALD, GRACE M.: *Remedial Techniques in Basic School Subjects*, McGraw-Hill Book Company, New York, 1943.

GATES, ARTHUR I., and ELOISE B. CASON: "An Evaluation of Tests for Diagnosis of Ability to Read by Phrases or Thought Units," *Elementary School Journal*, 46:23–32, September, 1945.

Gates-McKillop Reading Diagnostic Tests, grades 1–8, two forms, time 60–90 minutes, Teachers College Press, Columbia University, New York.

HARRIS, ALBERT J.: *How to Increase Reading Ability*, 4th ed., David McKay Company, Inc., New York, 1961.

HILDRETH, GERTRUDE: *Teaching Reading*, Holt, Rinehart and Winston, Inc., New York, 1958.

MC CARTHY, J. J., and S. A. KIRK: *Illinois Test of Psycholinguistic Abilities*, Institute for Research on Exceptional Children, University of Illinois, Urbana, Ill., 1961.

——— and ———: *The Construction, Standardization, and Statistical Char-*

acteristics of the Illinois Test of Psycholinguistic Abilities, The University of Illinois Press, Urbana, 1963.

———— and J. L. OLSON: *Validity Studies on the Illinois Test of Psycholinguistic Abilities*, The University of Illinois Press, Urbana, Ill., 1964.

MONEY, JOHN, and GILBERT SHIFFMAN (eds.): *The Disabled Reader: Education of the Dyslexic Child*, The Johns Hopkins Press, Baltimore, 1966.

Monroe Diagnostic Reading Examination, grades 1–6, one form, time about 45 minutes, C. H. Stoelting Company, Chicago.

MONROE, MARIAN: *Growing into Reading*, Scott, Foresman and Company, Chicago, 1951.

RABINOVITCH, R. D.: "Reading and Learning Disabilities," in S. Arieti (ed.), *American Handbook of Psychiatry*, vol. 1, Basic Books, Inc., Publishers, New York, 1959, pp. 857–869.

SCHONELL, F. J.: *The Psychology of Reading*, Oliver & Boyd Ltd., London, 1961.

SMITH, HENRY P., and E. V. DECHANT: *Psychology in Teaching Reading*, Prentice-Hall, Inc., Englewood Cliffs, N.J., 1961.

SPACHE, GEORGE: *Diagnostic Reading Scales*, grades 1–6, one form, time less than 45 minutes, California Test Bureau, Del Monte Research Park, Monterey, Calif.

WEENER, PAUL, LOREN S. BARRITT, and MELVYN I. SEMMEL: "A Critical Evaluation of the Illinois Test of Psycholinguistic Abilities," A Response: James J. McCarthy, *Exceptional Children*, 33:373–384, February, 1967.

Chapter Eleven

INDICATORS OF READING POTENTIAL

For many years the oral reading test, the silent diagnostic reading test, and the individual intelligence test formed the backbone of diagnostic procedure. As the complexity of the reading process has received increasing recognition, the need for teachers' observation and a combination of other diagnostic instruments has become apparent. But no entirely satisfactory method of diagnosing reading potential has yet been found.

In the past, reading potential was considered to be almost synonymous with intelligence as measured by intelligence tests. Now, reading potential has been shown to be dependent not only upon cognitive abilities such as perception, memory, and reasoning, but also upon linguistic, auding, and other more intangible factors such as concentration, attention, motivation, attitudes, values, and the self-concept.

RELATION BETWEEN READING AND INTELLIGENCE TEST SCORES

Since reading, broadly defined, and intelligence have so much in common, intelligence tests cannot be counted on to predict reading potential. According to Guilford's analysis of intelligence (1959), the processes characteristic of intellectual activity are also characteristic of reading: (1) "cognition"—recognition or discovery of units, classes, relationships, systems; (2) memory of what is recognized; (3) "divergent thinking," which involves fluency and originality in dealing with words, ideas, and relations; (4) "convergent thinking," which leads to the right or best answer; and (5) evaluation, which includes critical thinking, the making of inferences, and the drawing of generalizations and conclusions.

213

Of the three kinds of intelligence described by P. E. Vernon (1958)—
Intelligence A, which reflects the quality of the nervous system; Intelligence B, which is the result of the interaction between Intelligence A and the environment; and Intelligence C, which consists of samples of Intelligence B—only Intelligence A can be considered a possible cause of reading deficiency. Only Intelligence C is at present measured by intelligence tests.

The relation of intelligence test scores to reading achievement varies somewhat with the individual's IQ level. The curves of intelligence and of reading as measured by tests are usually quite similar for students with IQs of 90 to 110. Students with IQs above 110 who have not been intellectually stimulated often do not read up to their mental capacities, while those with IQs below average, if given special instruction, may read from one-half to two years above their tested intelligence.

The relation between reading achievement and intelligence test scores also varies according to the child's stage of reading development. In beginning reading, Durrell and his associates (1958) reported that a "high mental age does not assure a high learning rate in beginning reading" (p. 24). According to other research also there is a closer relationship with auditory and visual perception than with intelligence as measured at this stage. It is quite understandable that skill in associating the visual symbol with the spoken word may be determined more by previous experience in visual and auditory discrimination than by intelligence. But when recoding (associating sound with printed symbol) becomes subordinate to comprehending sentences and paragraphs, the need for intelligence becomes greater.

The relation between intelligence test scores and reading achievement also depends on the tests used. Not recognizing the limitations of tests, some reading teachers, on the basis of intelligence test scores, have tried to set specific reading goals by making a reading expectancy chart for each student. This reading expectancy chart is based on the relation between the student's mental age as determined by an intelligence test and his reading grade. For example, if J. B.'s chronological age is 15 years 7 months, his IQ 71, his mental age 11 years 1 month, and his present reading grade score 2.8, his reading expectancy would be 4.5; that is, he may be expected to learn to read fourth-grade books. Similarly, tables of academic expectancy have been used to call attention to the reading performance that might be expected of slow-learning or mentally deficient children and the difficulty which they might have with beginning reading.

These expectancy figures, if used at all, should be based on nonverbal intelligence tests and supplemented by information about other circumstances that may affect the individual's reading expectancy, such as bilingual background, emotional disturbance, and physical defects. Although such an expectancy chart is delightfully definite, its value is questionable. Kirk (1962), who has worked extensively with mentally deficient children, has become very cautious in predicting reading achievement from mental age. Two children with the same mental age may have very different mental abilities and reading abilities.

ACADEMIC EXPECTANCY: READING GRADE LEVELS

CA	IQ 50–59	IQ 60–69	IQ 70–75	IQ 76–85
6.0–6.6	Readiness	Readiness	Readiness	Readiness
7.0–7.6	Readiness	Readiness	Readiness	Readiness
8.0–8.6	Readiness	Readiness	1	1
9.0–9.6	Readiness	1	1	1, 2
10.0–10.6	Readiness	1	2	2
11.0–11.6	1	2	2	3
12.0–12.6	1	2	3	3, 4
13.0–13.6	1	3	3	4
14.0–14.6	2	3	4	5
15.0–15.6	2	4	4, 5	5, 6
16.0–16.6	2	4	5	6

A low IQ may indicate that the individual has difficulty in orienting himself to the symbolism expressed in language. It has also been suggested than an extremely high verbal IQ may be accompanied by too great a preoccupation with words and a neglect of the learning that should accrue from life experience. In some cases, the same conditions that are causing the reading difficulty may also be depressing the intelligence test score.

INTELLIGENCE TESTS

Intelligence tests have been the most important instrument used in predicting an individual's ability to make progress in reading. They have been used to answer the teacher's question, "Can we expect more of this student, or should we accept his present reading performance as the best he can achieve?" However, skepticism about the value of intelligence tests in the diagnosis of reading difficulty has been growing. Experts in testing are constantly warning us against the overinterpretation and misinterpretation of intelligence test scores.

Causes for caution

There are many reasons why we should be cautious in using intelligence tests to predict reading potentiality.

1. Intelligence tests are not a sure measure of innate ability to learn. They represent "developed ability." They measure the results of the interaction between the individual's heredity and his environment. It has recently been shown that malnutrition and lack of intellectual stimulation in the first years of life limit the development of the brain and central nervous system. Reading achievement also affects group test results. The poor reader is penalized on the verbal parts of the test. The fact that his store of information is limited by the small amount of reading he has done also works against him. Recognizing their inability, some severely retarded readers mark the items at random; they do not even attempt to answer them.

2. Intelligence tests show how an individual is functioning at present, at the time when he is taking the test.

3. An individual's intelligence test scores fluctuate from test to test. They vary with the type of test used and with the interval that has elapsed between testing. Children may change more than 15 IQ points between the ages of three and ten. During the elementary school years only about half the children tested may maintain the same score; half of the remainder may show a rising IQ trend, a few may show a falling trend, and about a third will show irregular growth curves. IQs have been reported to fluctuate by as much as 40 points for one reason or another. The reliability of intelligence tests is too low for individual diagnosis.

   A given IQ should be interpreted as a distribution, a range or band, not as a point. For example, a reported IQ of 90 may actually be anywhere from 80 to 100, or even from 75 to 105. If a student obtains an IQ of 125 on the California Test of Mental Maturity, his actual IQ may be somewhere between 115 and 135. (For a discussion of the *standard error*, "a calculated estimate of the amount of this variation," see Cronbach, 1960.) A difference of at least 15 IQ points is necessary before one can generalize about the comparative intelligence of individuals. When several successive IQ scores are available for an individual on *the same test*, an average of the scores is generally more reliable than a single score, but IQ scores from different tests should never be averaged.

   In view of the unreliability of tests and the probable error of the difference between the results of two tests, we must question the assumption that a mental age a year higher than the reading age indicates reading potential. Winkley (1962) suggested that a discrepancy of two stanine points between the measure of mental potential and the measure of achievement, supplemented by the judgment of perceptive teachers, is a useful indication of reading potential. At some intelligence levels we cannot be sure that a difference between mental age and reading age of less than seventeen months is not due to chance variation (Woodbury, 1963).

4. It must also be recognized that intelligence tests may have a serious lack of validity, especially above age thirteen. After all, any test is bound to be a fairly crude measure of something as complex as intelligence. At best it can only sample a small portion of the abilities that constitute intelligence broadly defined.

5. We may also make errors in interpretation if we fail to take into account the student's cultural background and home environment. Intelligence tests have been criticized with respect to their suitability and predictive validity for Negro and other groups having cultural backgrounds different from those on which the tests were standardized. The two main contentions are (*a*) that certain test items or types of items tend to be biased for racial and cultural subgroups, and (*b*) that predictions of academic success for the subgroups are consistently too low. An experiment reported in *ETS Developments*, vol. 14, November, 1966, did not find support for either of these criticisms with respect to the Scholastic Aptitude Test. It is quite possible, however, the habits, attitudes, and values more common in some cultures than in others influence both reading and intelligence test results. The so-called culture-fair or culture-free tests are attempts to measure native intelligence uninfluenced by specific cultural factors. This view subtly implies that intelligence is native, innate, and limited to a certain amount irrespective of the environment; it strengthens the concept of a given amount of inherited ability, rather than the broader view of intelligence as elaborating itself through environmental influences.

6. Proficiency in language is another factor that should be considered in interpreting intelligence test scores. It is well known that children from non-English-speaking homes and other environments which offer little stimulation and opportunity from the earliest years to explore, listen, talk, and receive answers to their questions are likely to be retarded in language development. This is another reason why test results should always be interpreted in the light

of the student's particular cultural background and educational experience.

7. Practice and coaching may raise intelligence test scores (Vernon, 1954). A student who has had no previous experience in taking standardized tests is penalized in comparison with a student of equal ability who has become "test wise." However, it is one thing for a student to score high because he has had stimulating teachers and curricula, and quite another thing for a student to score high because he has had specific practice or coaching. The latter has strictly limited effects.

The dangers of prediction or prognosis based on testing should be recognized. An individual's progress is impeded by limited expectations. To label an individual as a "slow learner" or an "underachiever" may set inappropriate minimal goals for teacher and student. The teacher's expectation has been shown to influence students' potential achievement. The emphasis on testing, therefore, should be on diagnosis rather than on prediction; on improving reading abilities rather than on determining reading status or level. Long-term prediction is impossible without knowing the future conditions under which the individual will live. Moreover, mental abilities develop in the process of learning; more advanced achievement is built on earlier foundations. Like physical development, reading achievement depends largely on environmental conditions. Especially "with the seriously disadvantaged, diagnosis and treatment are infinitely more important than the misplaced emphasis on testing and prediction" (Hamburger, 1965, p. 76).

Group intelligence tests

The group verbal intelligence test is useful as a predictor of academic achievement, but not as a means of estimating reading potential. In a verbal form of a group intelligence test, the correlation between the intelligence test and the reading test is so high (in relation to the reliability of each) that the differences arise primarily because of errors of measurement in the two tests.

Group intelligence tests, such as the Davis-Eells Games (1953), that require no reading may be more effective than other tests in measuring certain kinds of intelligence but less effective in predicting academic success. Some intelligence tests that involve little or no reading are described in the Appendix.

There is some value to measures of difference between nonverbal IQ and reading. If the nonverbal form of an intelligence test is used, the differences between mental ability and reading achievement are probably a little more meaningful but still unreliable enough to call for *very* tentative interpretation. Thus a child whose reading score is low relative to his nonverbal (or at least nonreading) IQ probably has problems specific to the mechanics of reading and is likely to respond to remedial reading. A child low on both types of tests has a more general intellectual deficit that would probably be less responsive to instruction in reading. However, approximately half of the backward readers eight to fifteen years of age studied by Lovell, Gray, and Oliver (1964) had average or better-than-average nonverbal reasoning scores. As children grow older, it becomes increasingly difficult to distinguish between potentially good and poor readers. As many as three-fourths of the students one year or more below their mental age in reading may be of at least average intelligence.

It therefore seems unwise to label students as "slow learners" or "under-achievers" or to deny them opportunity in special reading classes on the basis of group tests of intelligence. Some children read better than could be expected from their mental test scores; others fail to read up to expectation even under the best instruction.

Conversely, lack of reading ability affects individual scores on intelligence tests. Neville (1965) found that poor readers in the fifth grade scored higher on individual intelligence tests requiring little or no reading than on group tests; the average readers, about the same on both types of tests; and the good readers, as high or higher on the group intelligence test. A reading grade of 4.0 seemed to be "a critical minimum for obtaining a reasonably valid IQ for children in intermediate grades" (Neville, 1965, p. 260).

Individual intelligence tests

The two most widely used individual intelligence tests—the Stanford-Binet and the Wechsler Intelligence Test for Children (WISC)—both measure ability to concentrate, to comprehend and remember directions, to criticize and correct one's responses, and to understand words and pictures referring to familiar experiences. But the results of these two tests are not interchangeable.

In general the WISC scores, on the average, are around seven points lower than those obtained on the Stanford-Binet for the same individuals. The highest IQ obtainable on the WISC is 155; on the Stanford-Binet it is over 200.

The Wechsler verbal scale is more closely related to the Stanford-Binet than is the performance scale. Including as it does many verbal tasks, the Stanford-Binet tends to underestimate the intelligence of poor readers. Unlike the Stanford-Binet and the Wechsler verbal scale, the Wechsler performance scale depends very little on schooling. If an individual scores fifteen points or so higher on the performance scale than on the verbal, a language handicap is indicated which may be due to a foreign language background, limited education, or hearing loss. If any of these handicaps can be overcome, the prognosis for improvement in reading is favorable. But if the specialized verbal aptitude is innate, the reading retardation may be more difficult to eradicate. A much higher score on the verbal than on the performance scale may be due to an overcautious, careful way of working. A discrepancy of 20 points or more between scores on the two scales suggests possible emotional disturbance. The performance scale may indicate practical adjustment, while the verbal scale usually gives a better prediction of educational achievement. However, no single interpretation can be made for any verbal performance pattern; interpretation remains in the realm of supposition.

In brief, retarded readers tend to score higher on the performance section of the scale than on the verbal section. This may be due to an inherent lack of verbal ability; to environmental, emotional, or other factors that have interfered with the acquisition of verbal ability; to differences in ability to handle abstractions; or simply to failure to learn to read. We should remember, however, that on the WISC the nonverbal IQ generally runs higher than the verbal.

The diagnostic value of the individual intelligence test has been increased by its clinical use as advocated by Vernon (1937, pp. 99–113), Wechsler (1958), Rappaport (1950), and others. By studying the nature of errors and correct responses, the reading clinician may infer some of the individual's underlying mental abilities.

In intelligence tests as well as in reading tests, the total score may be misleading; the strong points may balance out the weak points. For example, an IQ of 105 does not truly represent the mental potential of an individual who scored very high on several subtests and almost zero on one or two others. The profile of subtests on the WISC, showing the ups and downs in performance on different tasks, has more diagnostic significance than the total score. Study of the subtest responses of poor readers on the WISC may give clues to lack of mental abilities that may be related to their reading achievement.

One possible explanation of unequal performance on the subtests is individual differences in the ability to handle abstractions or remember associations—abilities that are indispensable to reading success. The poor reader tends to approach a reading situation as though it were a matter of manipulating concrete entities. The good readers have the ability to use abstractions and to retain what they have learned (Brooks and Bruce, 1955). This ability is represented to a greater extent in the performance tests than in the verbal.

Tentative interpretations of the possible significance of the subtests of the WISC are given on pages 222–223 in the detailed analysis of the WISC scores reported for one reading case.

Many studies have been made of the relation of the WISC subtest scores and reading disability (Neville, 1961; Graham, 1952; Coleman and Rasof, 1963; Sawyer, 1965; Paterra, 1963). In the verbal section, the below-average readers tend to score significantly lower than the above-average readers on the subtests related to school learning, namely, information, arithmetic, and coding or digit span. The digit symbol subtest is often their lowest subscore within the performance group. A low score on this test may reflect inability to concentrate, fluctuations in attention, and moodiness—characteristics often observed in poor readers and intensified, perhaps, by anxiety in the test situation. On the arithmetic subtest, boys tend to score higher than girls.

The unsuccessful reader's highest scores on the performance section tend to be in tests that are manipulative, namely, picture arrangement, block design, and object assembly, and sometimes picture completion. They tend to approach a learning situation in a concrete manner because of their inability to handle abstractions. An analysis of items in the picture completion test of the Wechsler Adult Intelligence Scale (WAIS) suggests that three conditions may be operating here which observation has shown enter into serious reading problems. One is inability to make contact with the reading task, or "impaired contact with reality." The second is "maintenance of perspective," and the third is "awareness of uncertainty," a mental state in which the individual "may suspect a correct answer without having the confidence to guess it overtly" (Saunders, 1960, pp. 146–147). Factors such as these sometimes partially explain an individual's puzzling success or failure in a reading situation.

None of these interpretations, however, has been definitely established. At present they are impressions to be considered along with the accumulated information from all relevant sources.

Further analysis of the individual's responses on the vocabulary tests may yield additional diagnostic value. For example, his verbal fluency, the extent of his vocabulary, and the way in which he defines a word are significant. The vocabulary section of the WAIS is designed especially to elicit responses colored by personal factors.

The relation of WISC subtests and reading scores varies with different populations. For example, a group of bilingual sixth-grade children were higher in coding and arithmetic than a comparable group of unilinguals, whereas the unilinguals were higher in information and vocabulary (Ekwall, 1966). The bilinguals needed to build background of information through pictures, films, field trips, and easy reading materials.

WECHSLER INTELLIGENCE SCALE FOR CHILDREN *

Verbal IQ:	108	Classification: Average, Superior, Bright,
Performance IQ:	122	Normal (Wide range in subtests makes
Full-scale IQ:	116	general classification misleading.)

IQ range, verbal scale: 75 (information) to 138 (comprehension)
IQ range, performance scale: 100 (object assembly) to 135 (picture arrangement) †

Subtest	IQ level	Classification	General significance of subtest
Subtest Scores, Verbal Scale			
Information	75	Borderline	Measures background of general information; memory development and functioning; "intellectual ambitiousness." Reflects educational and cultural environment and background. Score will suffer from educational and cultural deprivation.
Comprehension	138	Very superior	Measures practical common sense; good judgment; understanding of everyday social situations; acceptance of conventional standards of behavior; stable emotional balance.
Arithmetic	100	Average	Measures powers of arithmetical reasoning; concentration; attention. Reflects reaction to time pressure, long- and short-term memory of computational processes.
Similarities	131	Very superior	Measures logical thought processes; intellectual maturity; ability to handle abstract ideas, to see relationships, to form concepts, to generalize.

* Analysis reported by Dr. Dorothy Withrow, psychologist, Philadelphia Reading Clinic.

† Measurements are approximate and relative, rather than exact and absolute. The last five subtests, constituting the performance scale, show reaction to time pressure and practice effect of previous testing, as well as the impaired functioning sometimes caused by emotional disturbance. This is less true of the verbal subtests.

WECHSLER INTELLIGENCE SCALE FOR CHILDREN (Continued)

Subtest	IQ level	Classification	General significance of subtest
Vocabulary	106	Average	Measures many of same mental processes that are measured by information and similarities. Also serves to suggest level of auditory comprehension. Score not likely to be depressed by emotional disturbance, but will reflect educational and cultural deprivation.
Digit span	94	Average	Measures powers of attention; concentration; retention for immediate recall when stimulus is auditory. Reflects behavior during a learning situation.

Subtest Scores, Performance Scale

Picture completion	128	Superior	Measures alertness to environment; ability to note detail and to distinguish essential from nonessential detail. Involves visual perception; minimum of verbalization.
Picture arrangement	135	Very superior	Measures "social good sense"; ability to see cause and effect relationships, to figure out chronological sequence, and to note significant detail. Involves visual perception; minimum of verbalization.
Block design	121	Superior	Measures ability to analyze, to synthesize, and to copy, using abstract designs as patterns. Involves visual perception, visual-motor coordination, no verbalization.‡
Object assembly	100	Average	Measures ability to analyze and to synthesize, using concrete, relatively familiar material; also reflects ability to see relationship of whole to part of whole, to visual-

‡ Block design score correlates highly with general mental ability and may indicate disturbances in the higher perceptual processes.

WECHSLER INTELLIGENCE SCALE FOR CHILDREN (Continued)

Subtest	IQ level	Classification	General significance of subtest
			ize or "anticipate" whole from part. Involves visual perception, visual-motor coordination, no verbalization. An "easy" subtest; low correlation with general mental ability. Subjects with reading disability often have trouble.
Coding	128	Superior	Measures ability to associate a digit with a meaningless symbol; to "learn" when stimuli are visual and kinesthetic. Furnishes clues to subject's ability to use left-to-right progression in reading and writing and ability to concentrate. Subjects with reading disability often have low scores. Involves visual perception, visual-motor coordination, no verbalization.

Insights gained through observation

Tests cannot supplant the perceptive teacher or clinician. In a series of interviews, the teacher can obtain a fairly accurate impression of the student's ability to remember and to see relations, his use of words, his quickness to learn, his ability to follow directions and to solve practical and theoretical problems. In his daily contacts with the teacher, the student reveals these and other indications of mental ability. The teacher also has the advantage of possessing background information that helps him to interpret his observations.

If the prospect of taking an intelligence test looms as a threat to the retarded reader, it had better not be given. There is danger in damaging the student's self-esteem, which is so important a factor in the efforts he puts forth to improve his reading. A youngster in the fourth grade who was having trouble with his reading, when asked by the teacher how he felt about his reading, replied, "If I could just get my reading, I'd 'preciate myself more."

Use of intelligence tests

Despite criticism, the individual intelligence test remains a useful tool in the appraisal and diagnosis of reading. The mental age is a measure of mental maturity; the IQ, an indication of rate of mental development. The total score is useful in indicating the individual's present overall capacity to think, to act, and to deal purposefully and effectively with his environment. The subtest scores and the observations made during the individual testing give clues to the nature, and sometimes the causes, of the person's reading difficulties.

In general, an individual intelligence test should be given when (1) the individual's group test scores seem inconsistent with his performance or with the teacher's estimate of his intelligence and achievement and (2) when a teacher is uncertain about whether an individual student has unrealized potential reading ability or is doing the best he can.

The teacher may request an individual test from the school psychologist on a form such as the following:

Name of pupil_____Date of birth_____Grade_____

Previous test results:
    Name of test   Date given   Results

Health record:

Teacher observations:
    Pupil's attitude toward himself, toward others, and toward reading
    Books he can read independently
    Books he cannot read without frustration

Teacher's questions about pupil:

The examiner should return the teacher's report with this additional information:

Name of test_____Date given_____By_____

Observation of pupil during test:

Interpretation of test results in detail:
    General level of ability
    Mental abilities in which pupil scored relatively high _____
_____, relatively low _____
_____, significance of these results
    for reading _____

Answers to teacher's specific questions:

Suggestions for helping pupil improve his reading:

The examiner should supplement the written report with a teacher conference in which they discuss the findings and make recommendations.

If the psychologist spends time in giving individual intelligence tests, he should take enough additional time to see that the test results are used to help both teacher and student.

When a parent asks point blank what his child's IQ is, what should the reading teacher say? If the teacher is trained in test interpretation, he can point out to the parent the implications of the test and describe the different kinds of learning ability it measures. The amount of interpreted information that the teacher gives would differ with different parents in the same way that a physician gives a detailed diagnosis to one patient but not to another; it is an individual matter. The only blanket rule is this: Give only as much information as is likely to be used for the good of the student.

It is important that the teacher use the test results to help the student think about his strengths and limitations, emphasizing what he *can* rather than what he *cannot* do. Together they can suggest books that the student can read independently with enjoyment and outline the progress in reading that he may be expected to make. In this discussion the teacher avoids labels and tries to correct wrong impressions of the nature of intelligence which the student may have acquired previously. The teacher need not mention specific scores in order to help the student arrive at an accurate concept of his ability. An intelligence test is not just a test of the student's ability to learn; it also indicates something about what he has already learned and what he needs to learn. Intelligence is educable.

In his study of WISC subtests related to reading achievement, Ekwall (1966) suggests practice to improve the underlying mental abilities in which an individual may be deficient. For example, if a student is low on the information subtest, he may be encouraged to observe more accurately, remember, and report on his daily experience in and outside of school. Practice in understanding and using good judgment may include analysis of everyday social situations concretely described or presented in role-playing or dramatic form. Memory and concentration, which are involved in many of the subtests, can be trained by listening to directions and carrying them out correctly, dialing telephone numbers, solving oral arithmetic problems. Fun with secret writing codes gives practice in perceiving unfamiliar symbols, associating them with their meaning, and writing them for others to decipher.

TESTS OF LISTENING COMPREHENSION

The degree of comprehension that the individual shows in answering questions on a passage or on paragraphs of graded difficulty that are read to him is one indication of his potential for further reading development. There are also standardized listening comprehension tests such as:

1. Brown-Carlsen Listening Comprehension Test, grades 9 to 13, two forms, time about 50 minutes, Harcourt, Brace & World, Inc., New York, 1953–1955

2. Diagnostic Reading Tests, Section II, Comprehension: Silent and Auditory, Forms A, B, C, D, rev. 1957, The Committee on Diagnostic Reading Tests, Mountain Home, North Carolina

3. Listening comprehension section of the STEP tests, two forms on each of four levels, Educational Testing Service, Princeton, New Jersey, 1956–1959

Using these standardized tests, the teacher can compare the individual's ability to comprehend when he listens and when he reads similar material silently.

The relationship between comprehension when listening and when reading varies with the difficulty of the material. As reading material becomes more difficult, individuals tend to do better in reading than in listening. Moreover, listening skills can be improved by instruction. This fact makes them less valuable for prediction because some individuals will have had more incidental instruction than others.

The correlations between tests of reading and of listening comprehension are substantial but still low enough to indicate deviations in many individual cases (Cleland and Toussaint, 1962, pp. 228–231). The following correlations show the relation of listening to reading and to intelligence as measured by certain tests:

Test	*Correlation*
STEP Listening Comprehension with Gates Reading Survey	.6679
STEP Listening Comprehension with Stanford-Binet	.6349
STEP Listening Comprehension with Durrell-Sullivan Reading Capacity	.7030
SRA Primary Mental Abilities (PMA) with Stanford-Binet	.7239
STEP and PMA with reading	.7564
STEP and PMA with American School Arithmetic, the highest correlation	.7852

Other studies have shown coefficients of varying magnitude. Duker (1965) reported a central tendency of .57 in coefficients.

If the student's STEP reading percentiles and his listening comprehension percentiles show a difference as great as three stanines in favor of listening comprehension, we may assume that he would have the ability to comprehend verbal material if he did not have a reading difficulty. Students with relatively high listening comprehension scores are most likely to profit from reading instruction. In general, prognosis for improvement in reading is good (1) when a student's listening comprehension is 75 percent or better, (2) when he is able to relate to his life experiences the information he gains through listening, and (3) when he can use in his conversation vocabulary and language structure that are as mature as those in the passage that is read to him.

OTHER INDICATORS OF READING POTENTIAL

Other factors significant for reading achievement are not measured by intelligence or by listening comprehension tests. Some of these are language factors measured by the ITPA (see Chapter 10). A child deficient in auditory or visual decoding, association, encoding, or automatic-sequential abilities might have adequate measured intelligence but poor reading ability. For such a child, intelligence test scores are unlikely to indicate reading potential. Using the ITPA profile as a diagnostic guide, the teacher might reinforce the child's special strengths and give specific instruction on the deficient areas. One reason why students fail is because they have avoided activities requiring the abilities in which they are deficient. If these underlying mental abilities are developed, improvement in reading performance could be expected.

There are also personality factors that may indicate reading potential. It seems paradoxical that tests designed to measure intelligence should sometimes be used to give indications of emotional difficulties and that the Rorschach, a measure of personality, should sometimes be used to detect potential mental ability. Although a test should be used for the purpose for which it is primarily designed, we are justified in making use of any supplementary clues that it may yield. A Rorschach given by an adequately trained Rorschach clinician to a retarded reader sometimes yields valuable information about potential intelligence that is not revealed by the usual intelligence test, which measures *functioning* intelligence (see Chapter 13). The following types of response to the Rorschach ink blots may indicate potentially adequate mental ability: the tendency to see wholes rather than parts or trivialities; and the tendency to see precise, relevant, and reasonable resemblances in the forms suggested by the ink blots.

THE CASE STUDY APPROACH

The case study synthesizes information on many abilities, attitudes, and conditions that may contribute to reading achievement. For example, both feeling and thinking affect reading development. They are interwoven; together they influence reading achievement. According to Piaget,

> There are no acts of intelligence, even of practical intelligence, without interest at the point of departure and affective regulation during the entire course of action; without joy at success or sorrow at failure. Likewise, at the perceptual level we have affective motivations. What we perceive is a function of attention regulation, which is pretty much motivation by needs and interests (1962, p. 130).

If enough were known about the child's developmental history, intelligence, language ability, personality factors, and environment, it would be easier to judge whether he was achieving as well as could be expected.

CONCLUDING STATEMENT

It is desirable but difficult to ascertain a student's reading potential. It cannot be derived from group verbal intelligence tests although, being based on his past achievement, they may predict the student's probable future school achievement. If the group test includes a nonverbal section, a large discrepancy in favor of the nonverbal suggests possible reading potential. As scores on individual intelligence tests are less affected by reading proficiency, they give a better indication of reading potential than do the group verbal tests. A large discrepancy between the Wechsler verbal and the performance scales in favor of the nonverbal gives a still better estimate of reading potential. Other nonlanguage intelligence tests are also useful for this purpose. A discrepancy of two stanine points between the measure of mental potential and the measure of reading achievement, supplemented by the judgment of the teacher, is a simple estimate of potential reading ability.

The value of even determining reading potential might be questioned. If such prediction assumes a given amount of mental ability, it would tend to perpetuate the status quo of the individual and leave no room for expectation of higher levels of performance.

The diagnostic, rather than the predictive, value of tests should be emphasized. By recognizing strengths and weaknesses in mental abilities that underlie success in reading, instruction can be given that will make potential ability a reality.

SUGGESTED PROBLEMS: PRACTICE AND DEMONSTRATION

1. Observe a demonstration of the WISC or the Stanford-Binet test with a dull and with a bright child. Note the differences in the two children's responses to the same mental tasks. Record your impressions of the children's attitudes and personality traits.

2. Write a thorough review of the literature on several of the specific topics indicated by the main headings of this chapter.

3. If detailed scattergrams of WAIS or WISC are available, repeat Graham's study of unsuccessful readers.

4. On the basis of all the information available about students in one of your classes, make a prediction of each student's reading scores at the beginning of the year. Compare your predictions with the actual scores obtained at the end of the year, and try to ascertain reasons for marked discrepancies between your predictions and the students' achievements.

5. Appraise various methods that have been proposed for predicting potential reading ability.

6. On what bases could students in a class set realistic reading goals for themselves?

7. What are some of the factors that might cause a discrepancy in predictions of reading potential based on individual intelligence tests? On listening comprehension tests?

REFERENCES

ABRAMS, ELIAS N.: "Prediction of Intelligence from Certain Rorschach Factors," *Journal of Clinical Psychology,* 11:81–83, January, 1955.

BROOKS, HAROLD F., and PAUL BRUCE: "The Characteristics of Good and Poor Readers as Disclosed by the Wechsler Intelligence Scale for Children," *Journal of Educational Psychology,* 46:488–493, December, 1955.

CASSEL, RUSSELL N., and GENEVIEVE HADDOX: "Comparing Reading Competency with Personality and Social Insight Test Scores," *California Journal of Educational Research,* 12:27–30, January, 1961.

CLELAND, DONALD L., and ISABELLA H. TOUSSAINT: "The Interrelationships of Reading, Listening, Arithmetic Computation, and Intelligence," *The Reading Teacher,* 15:228–231, January, 1962.

COLEMAN, JAMES C., and BEATRICE RASOF: "Intellectual Factors in Learning Disorders," *Perceptual and Motor Skills,* 16:139–152, February, 1963.

CRONBACH, LEE J.: *Essentials of Psychological Testing,* 2d ed., Harper & Row, Publishers, Incorporated, New York, 1960.

Davis-Eells Test of General Intelligence or Problem-solving Ability, grades 1, 2, 3–6, one form, time 30–35 minutes, Harcourt, Brace & World, Inc., New York, 1953.

DEVINE, THOMAS G.: "Reading and Listening: New Research Findings," *Elementary English,* 45:346–348, March, 1968.

DUKER, SAM: "Listening and Reading," *Elementary School Journal,* 65:321–329, March, 1965.

DURRELL, DONALD D. (ed.): "Success in First Grade Reading," *Journal of Education,* 140:1–48, February, 1958.

EKWALL, EDWARD E.: "The Use of WISC Subtest Profiles in the Diagnosis of Reading Difficulties," unpublished doctoral dissertation, University of Arizona, Tucson, 1966.

GRAHAM, E.: "Wechsler-Bellevue and WISC Scattergrams of Unsuccessful Readers," *Journal of Consulting Psychology,* 16:268–271, August, 1952.

GUILFORD, J. P.: "Three Faces of Intellect," *American Psychologist,* 14:469–479, August, 1959.

HAMBURGER, MARTIN: "Measurement Issues in the Counseling of the Culturally Disadvantaged," in *Proceedings of the 1964 Invitational Conference on Testing Problems,* Educational Testing Service, Princeton, N. J., 1965, pp. 71–81.

KIRK, SAMUEL A.: *Educating Exceptional Children,* Houghton Mifflin Company, Boston, 1962.

LOVELL, K., E. A. GRAY, and D. C. OLIVER: "A Further Study of Some Cognitive and Other Disabilities in Backward Readers of Average Non-verbal Reasoning Scores," *British Journal of Educational Psychology,* 34:275–279, November, 1964.

MC DONALD, ARTHUR S. (ed.): "Research for the Classroom: Reading Potential, Appraisal or Prediction?" *Journal of Reading,* 8:115–119, November, 1964.

MC LEOD, JOHN: "Reading Expectancy from Disabled Learners," *Journal of Learning Disabilities,* 1:97–105, February, 1968.

NEVILLE, DONALD: "Comparison of WISC Patterns of Male Retarded and Non-retarded Readers," *Journal of Educational Research,* 54:195–197, January, 1961.

———: "The Relationship between Reading Skills and Intelligence Scores," *The Reading Teacher,* 18:257–262, January, 1965.

———: "Learning Characteristics of Poor Readers as Revealed by the Results of Individually Administered Intelligence Tests," in *Vistas in Reading,* J. A. Figurel (ed.), *Proceedings of the International Reading Association,* vol. 11, 1966, 554–559.

PATERRA, MARY E.: "A Study of Thirty-three WISC Scattergrams of Retarded Readers," *Elementary English,* 40:394–405, April, 1963.

PIAGET, JEAN: "Affectivity and Intelligence," *Bulletin of the Menninger Clinic,* 26:130, May, 1962.

RAPPAPORT, DAVID: "The Studies of Diagnostic Psychological Testing," *Journal of Consulting Psychology*, 12:1–3, January–February, 1948; also "Diagnostic Testing in Psychiatric Practice," *Bulletin of New York Academy of Medicine*, 26:115–125, 1950.

SAUNDERS, DAVID R.: "A Factor Analysis of the Picture Completion Items of the WAIS," *Journal of Clinical Psychology*, 16:146–147, April, 1960.

SAWYER, RITA I.: "Does the Wechsler Intelligence Scale for Children Discriminate between Mildly Disabled and Severely Disabled Readers?" *Elementary School Journal*, 66:97–103, November, 1965.

VERNON, P. E.: "The Stanford-Binet Test as a Psychometric Method," *Character and Personality*, 6:99–113, December, 1937.

———: "Practice and Coaching Effects in Intelligence Tests," *The Educational Forum*, 18:269–280, March, 1954.

———: "Education and the Psychology of Individual Differences," *Harvard Educational Review*, 28:91–104, Spring, 1958.

WECHSLER, DAVID: *The Measurement and Appraisal of Adult Intelligence*, 4th ed., The Williams & Wilkins Company, Baltimore, 1958.

WINKLEY, CAROL K.: "Building Staff Competence in Identifying Underachievers," in *The Underachiever in Reading*, H. A. Robinson (ed.), Supplementary Educational Monograph no. 92, The University of Chicago Press, Chicago, 1962, pp. 155–162.

WOODBURY, CHARLES A.: "The Identification of Underachieving Readers," *The Reading Teacher*, 16:218–223, January, 1963.

SUGGESTED READINGS

ANASTASI, ANNE: *Testing Problems in Perspective*, American Council on Education, Washington, D.C., 1966.

BURKHOLDER, RACHEL B.: "The Improvement in Reading Ability through the Development of Specific Underlying or Associated Mental Abilities," unpublished doctoral dissertation, University of Arizona, Tucson, 1968.

BURT, CYRIL: "The Gifted Child," general introduction in *The Gifted Child*, *The Yearbook of Education*, Harcourt, Brace & World, Inc., New York, 1962.

CLYMER, THEODORE: "What Is 'Reading'?: Some Current Concepts," in *Innovation and Change in Reading Instruction*, Sixty-seventh Yearbook of the National Society for the Study of Education, part 2, The University of Chicago Press, Chicago, 1968, chap. 1.

COLEMAN, HOWARD M.: "Visual Perception and Reading Dysfunction," *Journal of Learning Disabilities*, 1:116–123, February, 1968.

DEVINE, THOMAS G. "Reading and Listening: New Research Findings," *Elementary English*, 45:346–348, March, 1968.

DUNN, J. A.: "Inter- and Intra-rater Reliability of the New Harris-Goodenough Draw-a-Man Test," *Perceptual and Motor Skills*, 24:269–270, February, 1967.

DURKIN, DOLORES: "Children Who Learned to Read at Home," *Elementary School Journal*, 62:15–18, October, 1961.

FROSTIG, MARIANNE, and PHYLLIS MASLOW: "Language Training: A Form of Ability Training," *Journal of Learning Disabilities*, 1:105–115, February, 1968.

GOINS, JEAN TURNER: *Visual Perceptual Abilities and Early Reading Progress*, Supplementary Educational Monograph no. 87, The University of Chicago Press, Chicago, 1958.

HAGIN, ROSS A., ARCHIE A. SILVER, and MARILYN K. HERSH: "Specific Reading Disability: Teaching by Stimulation of Deficit Perceptual Areas," in *Reading and Inquiry*, J. Allen Figurel (ed.), *International Reading Association Conference Proceedings*, vol. 10, Newark, Del., 1965, pp. 368–370.

HOLMES, JACK A.: "Factors Underlying Major Reading Disabilities at the College Level," *Journal of Genetic Psychology*, 45:3–97, 1954.

ORR, DAVID B., and WARREN R. GRAHAM: "Development of a Listening Comprehension Test to Identify Educational Potential among Disadvantaged Junior High School Students," *American Educational Research Journal*, 5:167–180, March, 1968.

RIEBER, MORTON, and MARCELEETE WOMACK: "The Intelligence of Preschool Children as Related to Ethnic and Demographic Variables," *Exceptional Children*, 34:609–614, April, 1968.

ROBECK, MILDRED C.: "Intellectual Strengths and Weakness Shown by Reading Clinic Subjects on the WISC," *Journal of Developmental Reading*, 7:120–129, Winter, 1964.

ROBINSON, H. ALAN: "Reliability of Measures Related to Reading Success of Average, Disadvantaged, and Advantaged Kindergarten Children," *The Reading Teacher*, 20:203–209, December, 1966.

SIEGEL, IRVING, and FRANK HOOPER: *Logical Thinking in Children; Research Based on Piaget's Theory*, Holt, Rinehart & Winston, Inc., New York, 1967.

STRANG, RUTH: "Relationships between Certain Aspects of Intelligence and Certain Aspects of Reading," *Educational and Psychological Measurement*, 3:355–359, 1943.

———: "A Dynamic Theory of the Reading Process," *Merrill-Palmer Quarterly*, 7:239–245, October, 1961.

———: *How to Help Your Child Develop His Potentialities*, E. P. Dutton & Co., Inc., New York, 1964.

THURSTONE, THELMA GWINN: *Your Child's Intelligence: A Briefing for Parents*, National Education Association, Washington, n.d.

VERNON, PHILIP E.: "The Relation of Intelligence to Educational Backwardness," *Educational Review*, 11:7–15, 1958.

———: *Intelligence and Attainment Tests*, University of London Press, Ltd., London, 1960.

———: "The Determinants of Reading Comprehension," *Educational and Psychological Measurement*, 22:269–286, Summer, 1962.

Chapter Twelve

INTERVIEW TECHIQUES

The interviewer has this advantage over the physical scientist: He can obtain information from the person as well as about him. Furthermore, the student's analysis of his reading problem is often sound; the parents' comments, often enlightening. A skillful interview is the surest means of gaining information and insights from both parents and students. It is also an effective way for the student to gain self-insight. The interview is not only two-way communication, but also two-way enlightenment. It is a joint quest for solutions to students' reading problems.

Interviews with parents give glimpses of parent-child relations and specific information about the student's characteristics, habits, and home environment. Interviews with children and young people may be primarily exploratory, definitely diagnostic, or essentially therapeutic. Most often they are for the purpose of giving individual instruction in reading, although every interview combines diagnostic, instructional, and therapeutic elements in varying proportions. Insights gained by the student are put immediately to work.

BACKGROUND NEEDED

In working with complicated reading cases, the interviewer needs to understand the personal and environmental factors that may influence reading achievement. Among these are early developmental history; physical defects, especially hearing, vision and speech impairments; attitudes and behavior of parents, siblings, friends, and teachers toward the child; his attitude toward other people, whether confident, trusting, dependent,

235

withdrawn, aggressive, or fearful; his attitude toward school activities, toward reading in general, and toward his specific reading problem; his reading and other interests, school achievement, mental alertness; parents' and teachers' expectations of him that influence the appraisal of his own learning and his academic aspirations and goals (see Chapter 8).

The interviewer also needs to know the duration of the reading problem and the kind and amount of special help that the student has been given by private tutors or in psychological clinics or welfare agencies.

If the interviewer has in mind these correlates of reading difficulties, he will be alert to items mentioned by parent or child that might be of central importance. Successful interviewers prefer to let the interviewee take the lead; they listen and respond appropriately. They are relaxed and not disturbed by silences. To obtain essential information, they do not bombard the parent or child with a staccato sequence of questions. But, if the client fails to mention anything that seems to be of special importance, the interviewer will attempt to uncover critical issues by posing appropriate questions.

The interviewer's evaluated experience helps him to recognize typical responses, clues to motives and behavior, and the interplay of antecedents and consequences. The experienced interviewer, by comparing an interviewee's responses with sequences of behavior that he has observed in other students, is better able to interpret in the individual case.

PREREQUISITES TO COMMUNICATION

An interview differs from a conversation in that it is purposeful; it is a conversation with a purpose (Strang, 1949). The interviewer should have some goals or objectives in mind to guide his thinking. Otherwise his questioning will be random and may have a desultory effect that is disappointing to the parent or student. One mother said indignantly, "I made a real effort to come for this interview and went to the expense of hiring a babysitter. And all I've learned is that 'Jimmy is a nice boy.' " It is most important that the interviewer maintain a sensitivity to the way the interviewee is thinking and feeling.

Inexperienced interviewers who have become enthusiastic about the so-called nondirective approach often merely parrot what the person has just said. This practice may annoy or otherwise disturb the interviewee. He may think, "What's wrong with the way I said it?" Skillful, accurate reflection of feeling, on the other hand, helps the client to understand himself better and gives him confidence in the interviewer's insight.

To be sure that he has heard correctly, the interviewer may from time to time reflect the person's thoughts or feelings. He may ask, "Is this what you meant?" "Am I seeing it your way?" "Am I right about this?" "You feel . . . ?" In this way the interviewer checks his understanding of what the person is trying to communicate. The person may correct, confirm, or modify the interviewer's initial impression.

Interviewing requires mutual understanding. The interviewee will not make the effort to communicate his thoughts and feelings unless he expects them to be understood. Sometimes language is a barrier; words have different meanings to different persons, depending upon their experience. As one boy said to his counselor, "Miss S, when my generation uses certain words they don't mean what your generation means." To one parent a "reading problem" may mean a serious handicap; to another it may indicate a minor inconvenience. To one parent an IQ may mean predetermined success or failure in life; to another it may be merely "another one of those school ratings."

It is often hard for children and parents to understand the interviewer's language, especially if he talks psychological jargon or pedagese. In talking with parents the interviewer should avoid technical words unless they are clearly explained. On the other hand, he should not talk down to parents or children, nor should he use slang or other expressions that might cast doubt on his professional competency.

The interviewer should also avoid wordiness—a common fault. The listener gets lost in a morass of unnecessary words. We should all cultivate the art of not saying everything.

Listening is both an art and a skill. It is perhaps the most neglected aspect of interviewing. Listening is not just keeping still. It is giving wholehearted attention to what the other person is saying—and feeling, insofar as feelings can be inferred. Some interviewers have the art of making the interviewee feel as though he were the most important person in the world for the moment; this manner assures him that what he is saying is worthy of the closest attention, that it will be accepted and held in confidence. Only then will he speak frankly.

Unless the interviewer can put himself in the place of the parent or the child and look at things from his point of view, unless he can enter the interviewee's psychological world, he will not be able to understand fully what he is saying and feeling.

THE INTERVIEW PLAN AND PROCESS

For any interview, the worker should make some preparation, a tentative plan based on his previous contacts with the client and on his reflective experience. On this basis he selects certain leads to take, certain questions to ask, certain reading material to have on hand.

He begins the interview with the most promising lead, often an open-ended question that invites the client to present himself and his reading problem in his own way. From then on he feels his way. He tries alternatives and notes how the client responds to them. Uncertainty does not disturb him; he welcomes it as an explorer does. He uses the feedback from his interview thus far (and also from his previous experience in interviewing) to go ahead along the same line or to take another tack. This is what I. A. Richards (1968) has called "feedforward." It may be a highly articulate process as in testing a hypothesis, or a barely recognized readiness to be guided by the client's comment or expressive movements. Sometimes the interviewer has something in mind to say but realizes that it is not just the right thing. So he pauses until he thinks of a response more in accord with the movement and purpose of the interview and with the interviewee's point of view.

"Rapport"—a word that is used so glibly—is a subtle thing. It has many components. One of these is the interviewer's confidence in his ability to help the student improve his reading. One teacher in his first interview with a nonreader said positively, "I know I can teach you to read." And he did. There are no formulas for building rapport, only sensitivity to the individual. The interviewer must feel his way, "listen with the third ear." The qualities of compassion, genuine concern, and respect for the individual are the basic aspects of a constructive relationship.

The interviewer should be cautious and tentative in his interpretations. He should learn to suspend judgment, to refrain from jumping to conclusions. The effect of excessive or premature interpretation may be to put the other person on his guard. He may feel, "This fellow knows too much about me." One emotionally disturbed boy said that the person he hated most was the psychologist because "he knows so much about me." It is often enlightening to ask the person to give his own interpretation of some statement he has made.

At the end of any interview, the client should have a feeling of satisfaction; he should feel that he has profited in some way from the experience.

The time element has important implications for the interviewer and the person interviewed. Both should be on time. If the student is late, he loses part of his allotted time. Habitually coming late often has diagnostic significance. If the interviewee comes early, he may be expressing anxiety or eagerness; if late, reluctance; if he is invariably on the dot, this may indicate some compulsive tendency.

Some interviewers take no notes but write up the important points immediately after the interview. Others will jot down key words and phrases during the interview to aid them in writing a fuller report later. Still others make a tape recording; this practice frees the interviewer to give his full attention to the client. It is extremely difficult for the interviewer to respond to the person whom he is interviewing and take notes at the same time. Later he will play back the interview to study what the client said, what he himself said, and what he might have said. He will also catch important points that may have slipped his memory. Recording also gives the interviewer the advantage of being able to say to the client later on, "You said this some time ago; how do you feel about it now?" As the interviewer studies the recording, he may note changing patterns or trends in attitudes and performance.

The practice of recording interviews is of special value to persons while they are learning the technique of the interview. They make tape recordings which they can play back, analyze, and discuss with their supervisor. In a reading clinic or center, however, where it is necessary to serve as many clients as possible, it is not feasible to keep verbatim records on each interview; there must be a balance between the time spent in appraising a client and the time spent in helping him.

The interviewer always asks the client's permission to make a recording or to take notes. At first, either form of record keeping may make the interviewee a little self-conscious; however, he soon learns to ignore it. Note taking stimulates some persons to think better; they may even ask, "Why don't you take notes? You may be missing important points." A response of this kind may indicate that the client is genuinely working on his problem with the interviewer.

Any notes or recordings are, of course, to be considered confidential; this fact should be made clear to the client.

SPECIAL PROBLEMS IN INTERVIEWING

If the person has difficulty talking, the interviewer may reflect his feeling by saying, "It's hard to know where to begin." Or he may ask if a few questions would help him to get started. If he gives only the barest answers to these questions, the interviewer may ask him to tell more or to explain a statement more fully. A nod or an expression of interest, such as "Yes, I see" or "That must have been difficult for you," conveys the idea that the interviewer accepts him and encourages him to continue. If he pauses, it is well to give him time to think the matter through. The interviewer should not get impatient or panicky if there is a silence. The interview time is the client's time to use as he wishes.

When the person interviewed talks about irrelevant things, it is usually better not to interrupt him. During the course of his random remarks he may contribute important diagnostic information. However, there are some parents and students who are compulsive talkers. They have rehearsed a sequence of thought many times and repeat it over and over like a broken record. Unless the interviewer interrupts the flow of reiterated grievances, they will make no progress in the interview.

When parents or students complain about other teachers, they create a situation that is hard to handle. When a student complains about a teacher, he may be encouraged to understand the teacher, to put himself in the teacher's place just as a teacher should do with a student.

Parents, too, have to realize that teachers are different; some are more skillful than others and have better personal relations with their students. The interviewer may point out that some teachers are better for certain students than for others. The very sensitive, overconscientious child needs a lenient teacher. The child of ability who is slipping into lazy habits needs a firm teacher who will hold him to appropriate standards of excellence. In the end, such a child will usually appreciate people who make him do what he can do.

It is usually better not to take sides with or against the student or parent about a person or an institution. If a mother complains about her husband's treatment of the child, the interviewer may show a sympathetic understanding of the situation, emphasize any positive aspect of it, and change the subject if necessary by asking a question about another problem. Contradicting the person or arguing with him often defeats the purpose of the interview.

In working with emotionally disturbed children, one must set limits and hold them firmly. The interviewer should remember that the child may be frightened by his own aggressiveness. Like other persons, the emotionally disturbed child needs to obtain an image of his most acceptable self, of the kind of person he can become. This goal is best achieved as the interviewer reflects his positive feelings and thoughts. For example, one child who was worried by the thought of being an adopted child made this comment at one point in the interview: "It [being an adopted child] doesn't matter." The reading teacher immeditaely picked up this positive insight and said, "You're right. It really doesn't matter. Your foster mother loves you very much."

One of the most difficult persons to interview is the student who conceives of himself as a person who cannot learn to read. He comes to the interview with a strong negative evaluation of himself. When asked about his previous instruction in reading, he insists that he "didn't learn nothing." He works halfheartedly on any method suggested or demonstrated by the teacher, almost as though he were trying to prove that he cannot learn to read. Later he may begin to think that he is as good as some others; as one nonreader said, "The other kids can't read neither." When he begins to take a more positive view of himself, the interviewer feels he is making progress.

INTERVIEWS WITH PARENTS

In interviews with parents the general goals are to help them and to get help from them in a mutual effort to understand the child and the conditions that are preventing him from realizing his potential reading ability.

Parents of children who are not realizing their reading potentialities are a valuable source of diagnostic information. Their contribution will supplement the school's factual information. They will give valuable clues about the causes of the child's retardation. Some of these causes lie in the reading habits of the family: there may be few books or magazines in the home or the parents may take a dim view of education in general and reading in particular. Skillful interviews elicit valuable understanding of parent-child relations as well as showing whether the parental attitude toward the child's reading is one of solicitude, anxiety, indifference, or annoyance.

Parents who write readily may give some of this information on a special record form prior to the interview. Reading centers and clinics have their own application blanks that ask for information on family background, education, reading history, and the child's present interests and activities.

The parent fills out the blank if the child is not able to do so. Sometimes parent and child fill it out together. When the child or young person himself writes the information requested, one gains additional information about his writing, spelling, vocabulary, and sentence structure as well as about his attitudes toward himself, toward school, and toward reading.

It is desirable to hold at least two parent conferences while working with a child. The first, at the beginning of a series of interviews, will give understanding helpful in working with the child. Another conference at the end of the series offers valuable opportunities to review progress and to work out the next steps. For example, in one windup conference the mother asked, "Do you think Helen had better stay in the eighth grade than go ahead to the ninth?" The interviewer did not fall into the trap of giving the mother advice when she was not really ready for it. Instead, he asked such questions as, "Why do you think it might be best for Helen to repeat the eighth grade?" "How do you think Helen would feel about staying in the eighth grade another year?" "What is her relationship with the teacher that she would have if she repeated the grade?" "Does she have many friends in her present class or are most of her friends neighborhood children?" "Is Helen more or less mature physically and socially than other children of her age?" These and other questions helped the mother to think through the problem herself. "Ask, don't tell" should be included in every interviewer's list of techniques.

Some parents come to the school voluntarily to talk with the teacher about their child's reading, usually to complain, sometimes to express appreciation. It was for the latter purpose that Mrs. L came to the school to see her son's young third-grade teacher, who was new to the school. Mrs. L first expressed her dissatisfaction that Billy had not made more progress in reading in the first two grades. She criticized the teaching methods that had been used there. She then told Miss J how pleased she was with his progress this year.

The role of the teacher in this interview was:

To show appreciation of the mother's interest in visiting the school

To listen intently to the mother's comments

To explain briefly her methods of work with Billy and give information the mother wanted

To reinforce the mother's positive feelings about Billy's progress and the school situation

To leave the way open for the mother to come in for another conference, if she wanted to come

Quite different was Miss J's role in the telephone conversation with Johnny's mother, who had been annoyed by reports of Johnny's bad behavior. Miss J permitted the mother to express her negative feelings about the school and the teachers. Then she tried several approaches which are usually effective:

She assured the mother that she had not singled out Johnny for exceptional treatment but was having conferences with all the parents and that she had not been influenced by the other teachers' unfavorable comments about Johnny.

As a new teacher she appealed to the mother for help and expressed respect for the mother's superior knowledge of her own child.

She showed consideration for the mother by offering to have the conference at a time convenient to her, either at home or at school.

She pointed out that they were both concerned primarily with helping Johnny.

Despite the teacher's efforts to establish a friendly relationship, the mother persisted in her attitude and refused to make a definite appointment for a conference. In view of the intensity of the mother's attitude, Miss J should have accepted her feeling for the time being and ended the phone call sooner than she did. At another time the mother might have been in a more receptive mood. Then, Miss J and the mother could explore various possible causes of the child's reading difficulty: his physical condition, his social relations, parental attitudes toward the child and toward reading, family conditions such as methods of discipline that might be related to the child's reading development, competing interests and activities, and previous reading or other special instruction.

The interview may begin with an unstructured question that invites the parents to present the problem or explain the situation in their own way. From then on the role of the interviewer is to encourage them to continue thinking about the problem, ask for clarification of some of their remarks, and express sympathetic understanding and appreciation of their efforts.

The following excerpts from an intake interview with a parent illustrate the technique of exploring, without probing, a number of factors that may be related to the child's reading problem.

MOTHER: Billy's teacher suggested that I bring him here because he isn't learning to read. As perhaps you know, he's eight years old and only in the second grade. I'm so worried about him. You said in your letter that you wanted to see me first. I'd be only too glad to answer any question you want to ask me.

WORKER: Well, tell me a little more about his difficulty.

M: Well, he's a perfectly normal child, I'm sure, but he just can't seem to master reading. Sometimes he can read a little, but then he seems to forget everything. He makes friends and isn't nearly as shy as I am.

W: In what way has he shown his lack of shyness?

M: Well he speaks to people easily. He has recited in front of people at Sunday School, and he'll play the piano in front of people. . . . I allow him to make his own friends. He has some nice playmates in the neighborhood and a few nice ones at school. His teacher says he has picked nice friends. I let him have his friends in for meals.

W: Will you tell me what you've already done about his reading?

M: We've tried to teach him at home, both his father and I. His father is an office manager now, but he used to teach.

W: How long have you been helping him at home?

M: Ever since he started to school until last spring. We stopped then because he was getting very nervous.

W: How did he show his nervousness?

M: He was restless and fiddled around. That's his trouble. His mind is on other things. It's the same way at school. I don't know exactly what to think about his school.

W: Will you tell me more about it?

M: Well, it's a progressive school and the progressive methods just haven't taken with him. He started in a private kindergarten and went into this school in the first grade. The very first term he wasn't promoted, but the school wasn't worried about that. They just thought he wasn't ready for reading and would be happier with the other group. He had to *repeat* the first term of the second grade too. He should finish the second grade this year, but I don't see how he can if he doesn't learn to read.

W: You say his mind is on other things. Do his teachers say he is restless in school?

M: I've wondered if the accident he was in might have had something to do with it.

W: What was the accident?

M: He was in an auto accident with his father and had his head cut. We've had five x-rays and they say he's all right. He began skating a couple of weeks ago and seems to be doing very well. He seems to try hard with his reading. I really don't know what to do.

W: You've tried very hard to be helpful to him. . . .

M: My father lived with us until last year. He died last year. He was an invalid for several years before he died.

W: That must have been very difficult for you.

M: (much disturbed): It was very hard. I nearly went to pieces afterwards.

W: It was a long period of strain. Was he difficult to handle?

M: Yes, he had heart trouble and it was very hard to keep him quiet. He wanted to run my household just the way he used to run his own; he wasn't able to do it. I had to handle him very carefully so as not to get him excited.

W: It must have made it harder, too, in your handling of Billy.

M: Yes, he spoiled him very much, and before his illness Billy was crazy about him. Toward the last, though, he was so irritable that that Billy didn't like him so much. He'd say cross things to Billy's friends when they came to our house. He was a very fine man though. He was a minister. He came from an old New England family and had a fine education and always did excellent work in school, but he thought that character was more important than education. He often said it was better to be good than learned.

W: What did you think it would be best to tell Billy when you bring him in?

M: I'll tell him that I'd like to have you people here see how well he can play. I won't tell him it is for reading because I'm afraid it will make him feel inferior.

W: Do you think that he would like to come here to play?

M: He'd love the idea.

W: Instead of bringing him in to see how well he can play, I think it would be better just to say it's a place where children often come to play. We might leave it that way for the present until we find whether it's better to approach the reading directly or indirectly. We may find later that it's better to explain the real reason. When would you like to bring him in? Does Billy have any special things some afternoon he wouldn't like to miss? It will work out much better if it's an afternoon when he isn't giving up something he likes.

M: No, I don't think it makes any difference to him. Would Thursday be all right for you?

W: That would be a very good time. Suppose we make it Thursday afternoon for the present. I can't tell you now how long it will take. It's not possible to do that until we know Billy better. Sometimes it takes quite a long time, and perhaps later we might want him to come more often than once a week. Would it be possible to bring him oftener if that seemed advisable?

M: I'd be glad to bring him whenever you say, for I am so anxious about his reading. We've tried to help him but don't seem to be able to.

W: Well, you are helping him by bringing him here and we'll need your help right along. You have helped today a great deal.

In this conversational type of client-centered exploratory interview the worker obtained information about Billy's reading difficulty as the mother saw it and a number of other factors that might be related to it. The interviewer's technique was to encourage the mother to speak freely and frankly and to clarify any points that seemed to be significant. Without apparent probing the interviewer introduced other aspects that might have a bearing on the mother and appreciation of her effort to obtain help on Billy's reading problem in its early stages.

Some of the many kinds of significant information elicited in parent interviews are illustrated by the following excerpts from interview reports:

PHYSICAL CONDITIONS In elementary school Bill was often ill and his attendance was necessarily poor. Thus an initial lack of reading skills may have affected his whole history and contributed to the personality difficulty which seems to have blocked any remedial efforts.

PARENT-CHILD AND FAMILY RELATIONS Trouble between the parents began when one girl was a baby, when the father first came home from the army from overseas experience. The parents are now separated.

Ted's father has very little use for him and seldom associates with him. Ted seeks adult male companionship elsewhere. His brother is a very fine student and very ambitious; he goes to high school and holds down two jobs. Ted is very proud of him, but the brother has always called Ted stupid. The mother has tried to stop this practice; she expresses great concern for Ted and wants to do all she can to help him.

A twin brother gives Don much competition. The brother is capable, enthusiastic, and Don has always "let brother do it." Brother reads well; Don was retained in first grade while brother passed.

PARENT'S DESCRIPTION OF THE CHILD The mother feels quite strongly that Sally is capable of better work at school than she is doing. She characterized her daughter as "boy crazy" and not very willing to study at all. She does no free reading, has poor concentration span, and did not want to come to the clinic for help.

ATTITUDE OF PARENT TOWARD CHILD The mother indicated her fears for the boy, and stated that regardless of how hard she worked to support him, he did not appreciate it. She added that both she and the older sister tried to help him with his reading, but that he was so stupid they lost patience with him. She said that he was a healthy child who suffered from occasional colds, that he had many personal friends, and that he was satisfied to go through junior high school accumulating a report card full of F's "just like in the lower grades."

She brought up the subject of his irresponsible attitude at home, his laziness when asked to help around the house, his constant bickering with the older sister. She added that it was her plan to "get him through ninth grade" so he could enter the auto mechanics course in a nearby senior high school, but she was afraid he was "too dumb to make it."

SCHOOL RELATIONS Ellen never liked school, even when very little. She completed the third grade at public school without being held back, even after the illness of the previous year. Did well that year although she was behind in reading. Got good school reports, liked the teacher that year.

Paula suffered from going to a part-time school when the schools were overcrowded. She went only half days in the early grades. She "freezes" on tests.

Each bit of information should be interpreted in the light of other knowledge about the individual and used to suggest the kind of experiences he seems to need. With adolescents it may be more effective to try to help them understand and accept the faults in themselves and their parents that they cannot change.

INTERVIEWS WITH STUDENTS

Exploratory interview

In the first contact, exploration is mutual. It is natural for a student to be reticent at the beginning of the first interview. He wants to find out what kind of person the interviewer is, whether he can be trusted, and whether the interviewer is willing to work with a person like him. The reputation that the interviewer has built up with other students helps this student decide whether he can talk frankly, freely, and easily to him.

The interviewer should always know the person's name and something about his present dissatisfaction with reading. He does not begin by asking, "What's your name?" and "What is your problem?"

There are many ways of conducting first interviews with students. The application blank or cumulative record often gives clues to the best approach to use and areas to explore or avoid. With some, a visual screening test may be a good initial approach; with others, it may be better to try an informal conversation, a basic vocabulary test, a chance to choose a book to read from among several of different levels of difficulty, or a reading game. With a little boy who was antagonistic to reading, the interviewer spent most of the first period letting him construct a model car. This pleasant experience established a friendly relationship and an appreciation of his need to learn to read directions. Whatever the approach, the interviewer will be sensitive to the individual's response.

The interviewer will have certain objectives for the interview but will not insist on fitting it into a preconceived frame. During the conversation he will obtain information about the student's attitudes toward reading, his ability to learn, his word attack skills, and other factors contributing to his success or failure.

In each interview it is important to give the student some experience of success and then ask him to summarize the procedures by which he attained it. If instruction is given, as indicated by some difficulty detected in the diagnostic procedure, the student will feel he has learned something, and the interviewer can see how well the student profits by instruction.

After the interview the interviewer may ask himself such questions as:

Did I achieve my objectives?

What information did I obtain that will help me understand the individual's reading capacity, achievement, and difficulties?

At the end of the interview did the individual feel that something had been accomplished?

An exploratory interview with a nonreading student was described in some detail by Bullock:

INTERVIEW WITH CHARLES

This boy was an unprepossessing client of a welfare agency with a long record of truancy, referred to the worker for help in reading. Half an hour after the time for the scheduled interview, the worker had almost given up hope of seeing the boy when the secretary ushered in a sullen-looking boy of fourteen and a determined-looking girl of about seventeen.

WORKER: Are you Charles?

CLIENT: Yeah.

SISTER: And I'm his sister. He wasn't going to come, so I brought him.

C: I was too (savagely).

W: Well, anyway, thanks for bringing him. How old are you, Charles?

C: Thirteen.

S: He'll be fourteen next month.

W: I see. Well, tell me, why did you come here?

C: Oh, Mr. _____. What's his name?

W: Simpson?

C: He told me to come here for reading.

S: Every Monday he told him to come here. (Sister leaves.)

W: Well, now, why did Mr. Simpson tell you to come here?

C: I dunno. He told me to come here to learn, you know, both speaking and how to read.

W: I see. Have you been having trouble with both speech and reading?

C: Yeah. I have like hoarse, like a hoarse voice.

W: Yes? How did it happen?

C: I don't know.

W: Has it always been that way?

C: I have it for three years or four.

W: Three years or four. . . . Did you have a cold or get sick or something? Did that bring it on?

C: I had a cold and every time I talk I get a hoarse voice.

W: Well, how about reading?

C: I don't know how to read big words; I just know how to read four letters, three letter words.

W: Always had trouble?

C: Yeah. Since I started school.

W: What grade are you in now?

C: Seventh.

W: Seventh. Let's see, thirteen. . . . You missed one year somewhere. Which year was that?

C: Last year I was in the seventh, you know, I didn't go to school and I was used to play hooky and then I got back to the seventh again.

w: I see, last year. And how's your attendance been this year? A little better, or about the same?

c: Same.

w: About the same. Is it because you don't like school? Or are there things outside that you'd rather do?

c: School.

w: Tell me about school.

c: Like I don't know how to read, so the teacher gives us a test and I don't like to go when they give a test. Sometimes they give you a reading test and I don't know to do it, I just sit there.

w: I can see why you wouldn't like that. . . . Tell me some more about school.

c: I like to do arithmetic, but sometimes like when they give a test on arithmetic, they give like fractions and I don't know how to do that and I sit down, and then the teacher comes around and sometimes he hits me and sometimes scolds me.

w: Does that happen often?

c: Like sometimes when the class is reading, so the teacher tells me to read, and like I don't know how to read, he tells me, "What was you doing, playing?" And then he hits me. . . .

w: You like arithmetic. (C nods.) Because you can do it. Now, let's see. How do you feel about English?

c: No, I don't like that.

w: Why?

c: The teacher doesn't show you how to read. They just give you the book and then they tell you to read.

w: They just tell you to read. What sort of books do they give you?

c: Like fifth year books, you know, but they have big words, nine, eight letters, like that.

w: Some of the words are hard. Do they tell you what they are?

c: No.

w: Do you ask the teacher what the words are?

c: No. He says, "You should know."

w: Do your friends tell you?

c: Yeah, like if the teachers sees my friends tell me, the teacher comes over, you know, hits my friend.

w: Oh, for talking. That's too bad. . . . Well, how about social studies?

c: I don't like that either.

w: What is it about?

c: Anything like, you know, about Christopher Columbus and explorers and all that.

w: And what do you have to do in that class?

c: The teacher takes the book and writes, you know, on the board and then we take and copy it in the notebook.

w: You don't mind that as much as the other?

c: No, that I like, you know. I like to write. . . . (Bullock, 1956, pp. 45–49)

In this initial contact the interviewer presented himself as a sympathetic, understanding person and obtained a vivid impression of the boy's school experiences and extreme difficulty in reading. He did nothing to increase the boy's sense of failure. To nonreading students, tests are almost always a threat. To obtain some idea of their reading ability, one may start with familiar signs and directions and then proceed to paragraphs of gradually increasing difficulty. Instead of continuing to test up to the individual's frustration level, it is better to stop at the instructional level and teach the student how to overcome some specific difficulty that he recognizes.

More able learners may be encouraged to analyze their reading problem and suggest procedures that they think may be helpful. It is naturally difficult for them to detect emotional factors or personality traits that may interfere with their reading achievement.

Diagnostic interview

Although also somewhat exploratory in nature, the definitely diagnostic interview tries to assess more systematically many aspects of a student's reading. The interview may be presented to the student as an opportunity for him to explore his reading. An individual who talks freely will often answer many of the questions that the interviewer has in mind. If he does not mention them directly, the interviewer can often follow up on some clue the student has given and thus avoid abruptly asking for the information he wants. In this informal way, the interviewer may learn about intellectual, social, and emotional conditions that may be related to the student's reading and note any obvious visual or auditory difficulties.

By giving the student a book from which he can select a passage to read silently, the interviewer will gain information such as the following:

How does the student explore a book?

What kind of article or story does he select?

Does he pause to think after reading the title?

Does he vary his rate of reading with the kind of material and with his purpose?

Does he stop to think while reading it?

What did he get out of it? How well did he organize the ideas?

How accurate was his report? Was it appropriate to the nature of the article or story?

Did he relate it to other books he has read or to his experiences?

Questions about his reading interests grow naturally out of the article or story he selected.

If he is asked how he spent his time during the previous school day and over the last weekend, he may reveal much about his recreational interests, study methods, voluntary reading, friends, etc. (see the section on Daily Schedule in Chapter 5).

While the student is reading a short selection aloud or silently, the interviewer may elicit such comments as the following:

> I used to read good, but now I don't know what's happened to me. I used to like arithmetic, but now I'm lousy at it.

> I know what the words are, but I just can't get them out. When I run across words like that, I think of all kinds of words it might be and try the ones I think may be correct.

The instructional interview

In most successful interviews, instruction is interwoven with diagnosis from the beginning as in the following initial interview [1] with a fifteen-year-old boy from which excerpts are taken.

INTERVIEWER: (Since the interview was to be recorded, the interviewer explained the recording system and said they would both listen to the interview at the next meeting.) The first thing I'd like you to do, George, is to put your name on this sheet (application blank).

GEORGE: Right here?

I: Yes, right on top. (Client does this.) Okay fine. There are certain things I'd like to know about because this information from you will help me to help you. (Interviewer asks about school, whether he has had any help in reading before; he asks about the boy's outside work, future plans, and reading.) From the time you first began to read, what kinds of reading have you done? What kind of reading do you do outside of school?

G: Well, my aunt, she try to help me read. . . .

I: Have you done any reading of newspapers or magazines without anyone helping you?

G: No, I couldn't do that (pause). I know words like *it* and *these*. . . .

I: I see. You know little words but have trouble with other words.

G: Yes. . . .

I: What is there about reading that bothers you most?

G: Uh, I don't know.

I: Just can't put your finger on it?

[1] Interview conducted and recorded by Dr. Harold Cafone, Oakland University, Mich.

G: No, I just can't read.

I: Oh, I see. You mean you just don't know how to go about reading.

G: Yes.

I: You say your aunt helps you a great deal with your reading. What is it she does?

G: She tries to learn me how to spell words. . . .

I: What happens when you get a word wrong?

G: Well, when I spell it wrong she says, "Ooops, stop." And then I stop.

(Interviewer explores boy's interest in TV, shopwork, basketball, cars, and other interests.)

I: George, I have a couple of driving manuals here, and I was wondering if you would like to look at them. They have all the signs you see on the road. Do you know the signs?

G: I think I know the signs.

I: All right (turns to page with copy of road signs on it), take a quick look through these signs and tell me about any that you know.

G (points to sign with RR): Railroad crossing.

I: Yes, very good. If you're driving you'd better know that one, huh?

G (points to and identifies other signs correctly): Yield right of way.

I: Say, that's pretty good! Where did you learn *yield?* That's a rather hard word.

G: When my aunt and I are riding in the car and we come to a sign, if I don't know it she tells me.

I: Well, I think that's an intelligent way to learn some words. . . . The next time you see a word or words you don't know copy them, bring them in, and I'll teach them to you. You see, one of the problems in reading is to learn many words, just as you've learned "Yield right of way." You know those words. Those words are yours.

Now I'd like to do something with you. It's a sort of quiz. You'll not have to read any words; I'll read them to you and you try to show me that you understand what each word means. (Gave vocabulary section of the Stanford-Binet. He then spread out different kinds of reading material from which George was to select one to read.)

Well, George, have you picked out a book that you think you might like? (George had selected a first grade book. The worker asked him to read it aloud.)

G (reading): Let's . . . I don't know that word ("take"; the interviewer tells him the word). Let's take a ride on this tugboat. (He con-

tinued to read and stumbled over words like *painted* and *her*.)
(As soon as the boy's reading showed that the book was too
difficult, the interviewer changed the activity. He next presented twenty of the Dolch basic sight words on cards. The
teacher put the words George knew in one pile and those he
did not know in another.)

Knew these	Did not know these	Substituted these
into	under	mother
they	were	where
ran	wash	was
what	with	wait
you	laugh	look
new	find	with
	found	with
	gave	girls

I: George, while you're working with me, you'll be making mistakes. Making mistakes will be important in a way because they
will help me understand things you don't know, and I'll be
able to teach them to you.
(At this point the aunt came in for her interview.)

The interview with George showed a discrepancy between his present
reading performance and his mental ability as indicated by the interviewer's observation and by the vocabulary section of the Stanford-Binet
test. There was clearly educational deprivation, which was confirmed by
more information about the family and school background. Fear, anxiety,
extreme hostility toward the stepfather, and a self-concept of being "dumb"
which was reinforced by teachers, uncle, stepfather, and peers became
evident in subsequent interviews with George and his aunt.

There were a number of positive factors in this case. The boy got along
well with his classmates. He could relate to the worker. His intelligence
seemed to be average. When taught words he did not initially know, he
remembered them an hour later. He had learned a number of road signs
and enjoyed doing this. He began to see reading as something that had
meaning and use to him.

In this interview, instruction was interwoven with diagnosis. For example, the interviewer taught the Dolch words that George did not know,
and at the end of the interview tested him on them. This procedure gave
additional information on the boy's learning capacity.

In many ways the interviewer showed a positive regard for the boy:

He ensured initial success by beginning with road signs the boy knew.

He forestalled failure by telling him promptly any word he could not pronounce or did not understand.

He did not let him continue to struggle through a book too difficult for him.

He did not push him to say more about his feelings when he seemed reticent.

Another excellent feature of this interview was the accent on retrospection, e.g., "How did you know that word?" This procedure directed the boy's attention to the methods by which he had achieved success in word recognition and sentence reading. The attitude developed toward mistakes was especially important in this case since fear of failure was very strong.

Evaluation of student progress

In a series of interviews one should be able to observe movement in desirable directions. More expansive voluntary contributions on the part of an initially unresponsive person or an increase in initiative on the part of an immature youngster is usually a sign of progress. Greater enjoyment of reading, a growing list of words recognized at sight, and increased skill in comprehension are other indications of improvement. In one case, for example, during a semester in which the boy was interviewed once a week, the following changes were noted:

On the Iowa Silent Reading Test, an increase from the 26th percentile to the 61st percentile

Observed changes in attitude—less anxiety, greater composure, less self-depreciation, more confidence in several areas

Changes in approach to reading situations, greater eagerness to read, more voluntary reading

Day-by-day improvement in comprehension on reading exercises such as those in the Science Research Reading Laboratories

Extension of the areas in which the student is able to concentrate

Increasing ability to analyze the reading methods that brought him success and to use them in new situations

More ability to perceive the reasons for the mistakes he was making

Changes in the parents' understanding of and attitudes toward the boy

REFERRAL FOR SPECIAL SERVICES (Ephron, 1953)

A teacher working within the area of his competence often has a therapeutic effect; but when a child does not respond to or show improvement from individual counseling, it is the interviewer's responsibility to suggest the additional services that he needs. A reading teacher or specialist who is also trained in clinical psychology, or a psychologist who has had training in reading, can be very effective in working with reading problems complicated by emotional difficulties. The psychotherapeutic interview is the province of the specially trained person. If referral to a psychologist or a mental clinic seems necessary, the interviewer can help allay parental anxiety by offering information about the treatment process and ways to prepare the child for it.

CONCLUDING STATEMENT

The interviewer's aim is not merely to get information about the individual, but to help him understand himself, his reading development, and difficulties. Desirable changes produced in the student may be due partly to conditions inherent in the interview situation. The student has the exclusive attention of an interested adult. This one-to-one relationship makes it possible, as one youngster said, "to teach me what I need, not what everyone else needs." Without classroom pressures, the interviewer may be permissive or strict according to the individual's need. For example, he can accept the student without criticism and thus help him accept himself. The interview itself offers opportunity for the student to take initiative, make decisions, relate himself to another person, and learn how to learn.

Principles of learning can be applied more intimately in the interview than in group situations. The interviewer can respond appropriately to whatever the interviewee says or does. He can ignore responses that do not contribute to growth; he can reinforce any move in the right direction and make the individual aware of the kind of behavior that brings success. In brief, the interview should have an educational, a therapeutic, and a diagnostic value.

SUGGESTED PROBLEMS: PRACTICE AND DEMONSTRATION

1. Read several application blanks and cumulative records from a school. Discuss the possible significance of each item from the standpoint of the

student's reading performance. Show how the initial impression thus gained might be used in the first interview.

2. Read several recorded initial interviews. Begin with an interview by an inexperienced teacher and work up to more expert interviews. Discuss each from the standpoint of the student being interviewed, the understanding gained by the interviewer, and the specific points of interview techniques.

3. Invite a panel of parents to discuss before a group of teachers the kind of interviews they would like to have with teachers.

4. Read several different kinds of interviews, stopping at certain points to suggest responses you think the interviewer might have made. Then compare your suggested responses with the responses the expert interviewer actually made.

5. What might be the purposes of the initial interview?

6. What approaches might be most effective with different kinds of students and parents?

7. When and how might tests or inventories be introduced in a series of interviews?

8. Observe the following characteristics of an individual during an interview or individual testing situation:
   a. Personal appearance—signs of neglect of cleanliness, grooming; clothes extremely different from other people's of same age, old-fashioned, bizarre, etc.
   b. Posture and expressive movements—how he walks, stands, sits; fidgets, moves hands nervously, has nervous tics, mannerisms, etc.
   c. Habitual facial expression—sad, anxious, tense, cheerful, fatigued, etc.
   d. Ways of talking—rapid or slow, hesitant or fluent, long pauses, uncommunicative, etc.
   e. Quality of verbal expression and response—vivid, apt, picturesque or incoherent, dull; good vocabulary, meager vocabulary, etc.
   f. Attitude toward examiner or counselor—overdependent or hostile, suspicious, uncooperative or cooperative, self-centered or considerate, impatient, etc.
   g. Reaction to difficulty—immediate reaction to difficulty, effect of failure on some items of subsequent performance, rationalization or other mechanisms used to explain failure
   h. Reaction to success

REFERENCES

BULLOCK, HARRISON: *The Non-reading Pupil in High School,* Teachers College Press, Columbia University, New York, 1956.

EPHRON, BEULAH K.: *Emotional Difficulties in Reading*, The Julian Press, New York, 1953.

"Guidance: An Examination," a special issue, *Harvard Educational Review*, 32:373–501, Fall, 1962.

PALUCIOS, M. H., and others: "Predictive Validity of the Interview," *Journal of Applied Psychology*, 50:67–72, February, 1966.

RICHARDS, I. A.: "The Secret of 'Feedforward,'" *Saturday Review*, 51:14–17, Feb. 3, 1968.

STRANG, RUTH: *Counseling Techniques in College and Secondary School*, 2d ed., Harper & Row, Publishers, Incorporated, New York, 1949, chap. 5.

SUGGESTED READINGS

ANASTASI, T. E., JR.: "Basics of Good Interviewing," *Journal of College Placement*, 28:37–39+, October, 1967.

ASFOR, M. H.: "Reading Test or Counseling Interview to Predict Success in College?" *Journal of Reading*, 11:343–345, February, 1968.

FRANK, GEORGE H., and ANDERS SWEETLAND: "A Study of the Process of Psychotherapy: The Verbal Interaction," *Journal of Consulting Psychology*, 26:135–138, April, 1962.

HOWE, EDMOND S., and BENJAMIN POPE: "Therapist Verbal Activity Level and Diagnostic Utility of Patient Verbal Responses," *Journal of Consulting Psychology*, 26:149–155, April, 1962.

KENNEDY, DANIEL A., and INA THOMPSON: "Use of Reinforcement Techniques with a First Grade Boy," *The Personnel and Guidance Journal*, 46:366–370, December, 1967.

LOWRANCE, ROBERT BRUCE: "The Development and Application of a Method of Analyzing the Reading Interview," unpublished doctoral dissertation, Teachers College, Columbia University, New York, 1960.

MOORE, MARY R., and W. JAMES POPHAM: "Effect of Two Interview Techniques on Academic Achievement," *Journal of Counseling Psychology*, 7:176–179, Fall, 1960.

NELSON, RICHARD C.: "Elementary School Counseling with Unstructured Play Media," *The Personnel and Guidance Journal*, 45:24–27, September, 1966.

PALLONE, H. J., and F. R. DI BI BENARDO: "Interview Sequence in Relation to Counselor Verbal Mode, Client Problem-related Content, and Rapport," *Journal of Consulting Psychology*, 14:503–504, November, 1967.

QUAST, WENTWORTH: "The Bender Gestalt: A Clinical Study of Children's Records," *Journal of Consulting Psychology*, 25:405–408, October, 1961.

ROBY, D. L.: "Learning about Pupils: Non-test Tools and Their Uses," *Teachers College Record*, 31:65–66, December, 1959.

ROTH, ROBERT M., HANS O. MAUKSCH, and KENNETH PEISER: "The Nonachievement Syndrome, Group Therapy, and Achievement Change," *The Personnel and Guidance Journal*, 46:393–398, December, 1967.

VELDMAN, DONALD J.: "Computer-based Sentence Completion Interviews," *Journal of Counseling Psychology*, 14:153–157, March, 1967.

Chapter Thirteen

PROJECTIVE METHODS

Projective methods may furnish keys to some of the deeper determinants of reading development. They may give glimpses of potential mental ability, of a personality structure capable either of preventing or of promoting reading achievement, and of personal relationships that are influencing the individual's behavior for the better or for the worse. Projective methods are primarily concerned with the psychodynamics and the "idiodynamics" of personality. This is the unique contribution of projective techniques to the diagnosis of reading difficulties.

The special feature of projective methods is that they present an unstructured situation, i.e., a situation for which the individual has no ready-made or habitual response (Sargent, 1945; Shaffer and Shoben, 1956, pp. 334, 342; P. E. Vernon, 1964). The assumption is that the individual will "project" upon these materials his ways of thinking and feeling. Since he is usually unaware of how his responses will be interpreted, he is less likely to try to present himself in a favorable light as in other personality tests where the "right" response is more obvious. In projective techniques there are no right and wrong or predetermined responses. The stimuli, the setting, and the instructions are intentionally unstructured and ambiguous.

A wide range of materials can be used (Cronbach, 1960, pp. 574–575). The stimulus may take the form of clay or some other plastic material to be manipulated, cloud pictures, ink blots, pictures of people in ambiguous situations, single words, incomplete sentences or stories, play materials and puppets, drawing and painting, or other media. To these unstructured materials the individual makes his own unique response and thus reveals himself.

259

The fantasy material produced can be interpreted qualitatively, or classified and scored. The classification, scoring, and interpretation of responses take much longer than with psychometric tests, and the interpretation is far more subjective.

The results of projective techniques may give to a person with clinical experience insights that are useful in planning remedial work, in the day-by-day contacts with the individual, and in the evaluation of changes that have taken place in his attitudes and personal relationships. As with all the other techniques described in this book, the impressions gained from projective methods should be checked against all the other available information about the student.

PROJECTIVE METHODS ON THREE LEVELS

Projective methods may be classified on three levels according to the degree of specific clinical training required. The first involves life situations. Whenever an individual is confronted with a new problem, he reveals himself to some extent through his behavior. Observations such as a teacher might make over a period of time will show the individual's characteristic ways of coping with life situations. One child will be eager and curious, another suspicious and hostile, still another apathetic and withdrawn. Their casual comments may give some clues as to the motivations that lie behind their behavior and their relations with parents, brothers, and sisters.

The second level is more technical. On this level the reading teacher may use certain projective techniques with individuals or with groups. Examples are the incomplete sentence or story; the ambiguous picture; the draw-a- person, house, and tree technique; the three-wishes question; the question, "Who are you?" The teacher interprets the student's responses to any of these stimuli as he would interpret any other significant observed word or action. An experienced psychologist or psychiatrist might find deeper meaning in the responses.

The third and most technical level includes projective techniques such as the Rorschach (Rorschach, 1942; Sargent, 1945; Cronbach, 1960, pp. 562–565) and the Thematic Apperception Test (TAT) (Bellak and Bellak, 1949; Murray, 1943; Schneidman, 1949; Symonds, 1948; Cronbach, 1960, pp. 569–572; Mundy, 1966; Whiteley, 1966). These tests must be administered and interpreted by persons with a clinical background and special training in projective techniques. The reading teacher may request a clinical examination, including these projective methods, to elucidate questions such as these:

Is there a discrepancy between the individual's potential and his functioning capacity?

What possible personality factors may be interfering with better functioning?

How strong is his achievement motivation? Does he desire achievement to strengthen his self-esteem, to win approval and love, to compete successfully with a rival, or for some other reason?

If he shows little ambition, what values have replaced a desire for success?

Why does he lack creative energy? Is his creative energy being shunted off into blind alleys?

Are conflicts and tensions making it impossible for him to function effectively?

Is he insecure and depressed about his relations to others?

What treatment is indicated by the report on the projective methods?

The Rorschach is said to throw light on the personality structure and on the adaptations that the individual has made as a result of his interaction with his environment. The TAT supplements the Rorschach by showing the specific ways in which the individual's personality expresses itself in a number of imagined situations. By studying and comparing the individual's total responses to the Rorschach and the TAT, a perceptive clinician may arrive at a personality picture that suggests promising ways of dealing with the case.

Using the Holtzman Inkblot Technique (developed by Holtzman et al., 1961), Krippner (1966) compared the gains of twenty-four elementary school children during a five-week reading clinic with each of the twenty-two variables of the Holtzman Inkblot Technique. There were four significant correlations: with location (r: .57), shading (r: $-.60$), verbalization (r: $-.96$), and hostility (r: $-.65$). "Location," which indicated ability to break inkblots down into smaller fragments, might similarly help a child to analyze words and sentences. "Shading" generally has been associated with tactile satisfaction or manipulation, a lower order need that is not satisfied by the symbolic process of reading. "Verbalization" here relates to disordered thought processes and fantasies that might interfere with interpretation of reading material. "Hostility" is often associated with reading difficulties. This research illustrates how a projective technique could identify important factors that might be preventing an individual from making progress in reading.

EXAMPLES OF INFORMAL PROJECTIVE METHODS

The reading teacher may use a number of informal projective methods to supplement his observation of the student in groups and in interviews. Recognizing that he must have the student's interest and cooperation in order to get authentic results, he will present any of these stimulus situations on a voluntary basis. He will also be cautious in using any of these techniques in communities where parents object to the school's collecting any kind of personal data. In interpreting an individual's responses to these techniques, the teacher will also avoid delving into deeply hidden meanings.

Incomplete sentences

The following form of the incomplete sentence technique was prepared especially for reading cases (Strang and others, 1961, pp. 322–323):

Date _____ Grade _____ Name _____

Directions: Complete the following sentences to express how you really feel. There are no right answers or wrong answers. Put down what first comes into your mind. Work as quickly as you can.

1. Today I feel _____
2. When I have to read, I _____
3. I get angry when _____
4. To be grown up _____
5. My idea of a good time _____
6. I wish my parents knew _____
7. School is _____
8. I can't understand why _____
9. I feel bad when _____
10. I wish teachers _____
11. I wish my mother _____
12. Going to college _____
13. To me, books _____
14. People think I _____
15. I like to read about _____
16. On weekends, I _____
17. I don't know how _____
18. To me, homework _____
19. I hope I'll never _____
20. I wish people wouldn't _____
21. When I finish high school _____
22. I'm afraid _____
23. Comic books _____

24. When I take my report card home _____
25. I am at my best when _____
26. Most brothers and sisters _____
27. I'd rather read than _____
28. When I read math _____
29. The future looks _____
30. I feel proud when _____
31. I wish my father _____
32. I like to read when _____
33. I would like to be _____
34. For me, studying _____
35. I often worry about _____
36. I wish I could _____
37. Reading science _____
38. I look forward to _____
39. I wish someone would help me _____
40. I'd read more if _____
41. Special help in reading _____
42. Every single word is _____
43. My eyes _____
44. The last book I read _____
45. My mother helps _____
46. Reading in junior high school _____
47. My father thinks reading _____
48. I read better than _____
49. My father helps _____
50. I would like to read better than _____

These incomplete sentences have elicited from young adolescents responses such as the following:

Today I feel (good because we don't have any homework) (tired).

When I have to read, I (do something else instead) (make myself comfortable) (don't mind it).

I get angry when (my father insults me).

My idea of a good time (is going to a school dance) (is to do just what you want).

I wish my parents knew (me better) (I wasn't smart) (that I really love them) (that I try to do my best of everything) (what I really think about things).

I feel bad when (people make fun of me) (I'm not being noticed) (my mother goes away for a long time) (my mother makes me dance in front of her guests) (my mother hits me) (I get a low mark on a test).

I wish teachers (would keep their word more often) (had more sense of humor) (would make things just a little clearer) (were stricter, some of them).

To me, books (are O.K., though school books aren't as interesting as free reading books) (are a source of pleasure) (are fascinating) (carry me into places and relax me).

On weekends, I (hate to read) (like to play with my friends) (like to stay in bed) (like to go out with my family).

I wish people wouldn't (think I am stupid) (blame me for things I don't do) (start war) (persecute me so) (make fun of me).

I'm afraid (of poison spiders) (of high places) (of reading new words).

Comic books (are fun to read) (are fun but noneducational) (set me in a much happier mood) (are getting worse and worse every day).

I'd rather read than (write) (watch TV sometimes) (do math) (jump off Brooklyn Bridge) (go to bed) (go to the dentist).

I like to read when (I have around two hours spare time) (I have nobody to play with on a hot day) (I am bored) (the book is interesting).

I'd read more if (I had more free time) (my eyes were better) (the books were ones I picked) (I didn't watch television) (I was smarter) (I made myself read) (I wasn't made to read) (I could find better books).

In reading through an individual's responses, the teacher becomes aware of certain recurring themes which suggest dominant trends. Sometimes these relate to physical conditions such as feeling tired, "like to stay in bed," and would read more "if my eyes were better." Many responses relate to family relations: "My father insults me"; "I wish my parents knew that I really love them"; "My mother hits me"; "My mother goes away for a long time." The sentences relating specifically to reading often give insight into the individual's attitude toward books and reading and reveal some of the difficulties he is having. Information of this kind, in conjunction with classroom observation and the analysis of test results, helps the teacher to individualize his program of reading instruction.

Informal projective picture stories

Any picture that portrays some person with whom the individual can identify or some situation into which he can project himself is suitable for this purpose. Advertisements and cover pictures of popular magazines can be used effectively. The directions for responding may be as follows:

What do you think is happening in this picture? Who are the people? What are they thinking? How are they feeling? What do you think will happen next?

A seventh-grade teacher, Carrie E. Hammil, reported a response made by an Indian boy to this technique. The picture was a photograph of the Golden Gate Bridge in the fog, with a subdued sun like an immense full moon shining through the suspension cables. The class discussed the picture and suggested several topic sentences for a paragraph about it. Then each student wrote a paragraph about the picture. The Indian boy who wrote the following paragraph seemed rather dull in most of his work; he is much larger and somewhat older than his classmates. He speaks seldom; when he does, his voice is so low as to be almost inaudible. He sits hunched over his desk as though afraid of missing a word. Yet, at other times, he is apt to lose interest in what is going on and to begin disturbing his classmates. In this paragraph, unchanged in spelling and grammar, he revealed a previously unsuspected creativity and depth of thought:

> The fog maks the bridge look like it starts nowere and goes nowhere. It is almost like life wich ends and starts agen and we do not no wer it was befor it come to us or wat we was befor we come to live this time. If it was no foggie we culd no look at the sun. But wen it is fogie we can look at the sun and no burn our eyes maybe life is like that too. When we die is it fogie and we get to see wat the sun is?

This response to the picture has an almost Biblical, poetic rhythm and quality, and the analogy between something seen and something spiritual is unusual for a boy of this age. The philosophy of life, expressed spontaneously, is also unusual.

With sixth-grade children the self-concept as inferred from responses to a picture story test was more realistic than that derived from self-rating (Parker, 1966). In another study of preadolescent boys, projective techniques, self-rating, and multiple-choice pictorial tests were positively related to one another and to the teacher's rating of pupils' adjustment (Perkins and Shannon, 1965).

Children's own drawings and paintings

In another projective approach, the student draws his own pictures. The freest and most tension-releasing medium is finger painting. In finger painting the child freely applies pastelike colors with his fingers, hands, and even his arms to make any designs he fancies. From both finger painting and the more conventional spontaneous drawings and paintings of children the teacher may gain clues of personality traits from the choice of subject, the colors, the size of the figures, the lines and outlines (faint and weak or bold and strong), and other combinations of elements in the drawing.

In interpreting children's drawings, one must know about the situation in which the drawing was made and the child's own interpretation of it. The teacher should resist the temptation to read into them far more than is warranted. To safeguard against overinterpretation, he should check his ideas about the drawings with all the available information about the child.

The Machover draw-a-figure test (Machover, 1950) is a useful source of diagnostic information. In this test the child is asked to draw a picture of a person. In a modified form of the test, he may also be asked to answer such questions as these about the person he has drawn:

1. What is the person doing?

2. How old is the person?

3. What grade is this person in?

4. Is the person good looking?

5. What are this person's worst physical features?

6. What are this person's best physical features?

7. What are this person's best personal characteristics?

8. What are this person's worst traits?

9. What makes this person angry?

10. What makes this person happy?

11. Will this person marry?

12. What type of person will this person marry?

13. If this person were given three wishes, what would he wish?

In using this technique with nonreaders, the teacher can ask the questions orally and write the answers each student gives. One emotionally disturbed child drew a robot whose appearance was quite sinister. The fact that the child gave his own age as the robot's age suggests that he might be identifying with his drawing. His response to the question about three wishes indicated a type of emotional disturbance whose presence the interviewer was able to confirm after further work with him. The child's three wishes were (1) to rule the earth, (2) to be master on his planet, and (3) to have everything he ever wanted.

The draw-a-person technique has been used in combination with a self-portrait (Gillies, 1968) and with the interview (Veldman, 1967). It has also been extended to include drawing a family, a house, a tree. In the drawing of the family, primitive stick figures may suggest immaturity; aimless activity, such as figures shooting in all directions, may suggest personal or family disorganization; a mighty woman who towers over a puny father and a still more diminutive child may suggest a domineering mother—or rather a mother whom the child perceives as domineering. In drawing a house, some children carefully build a fence all around it, perhaps as an expression of a desire to be left alone. These and other interpretations are made *very* tentatively. They are valuable in alerting the teacher to certain kinds of behavior as he observes the child in his daily contacts at school.

CONCLUDING STATEMENT

Used as part of a clinical procedure or as one of many techniques of observation in the classroom, the projective methods may contribute to the understanding of the more subtle factors that are involved in reading cases. The contribution of projective techniques to the teaching of reading is limited by the diversity and the highly individual nature of the responses which are evoked by the individual's freedom to organize and respond to unstructured material in his own idiosyncratic way. Interpretation is to a large extent subjective and difficult to communicate. Experts differ in their interpretation of the same recorded responses; some tend to give stereotyped reports.

Despite these limitations, teachers and reading specialists may gain insight from the clinical records interpreted to them and from the informal samples of behavior—incomplete sentences and stories, drawings, daily activities—which they interpret as they do other observations of the children and adolescents. Inferences should not be drawn from separate items but from patterns of test responses interpreted in the light of all the available background knowledge about the individual.

SUGGESTED PROBLEMS: PRACTICE AND DEMONSTRATION

1. Take one or more of the simple projective tests to give you a feeling for the way individuals may be thinking when they are responding to such nonstructured or slightly structured tests.

2. Write your interpretations of the results of several projective tests obtained from children of different ages; compare them with those made by a clinical psychologist with special background in projective techniques.

3. Study a reading case in which results of the Rorschach and TAT tests were included. What contribution do the projective tests make to the understanding of the case? To what extent did the projective techniques reinforce impressions gained from other sources or add new understanding?

4. Examine a number of children's drawings, preferably in crayon, paint, or finger painting, and speculate about the characteristics suggested by the paintings. Compare your descriptions with known characteristics of the children.

5. Summarize pros and cons about the validity and reliability of projective techniques.

6. Make a study of the three-wishes technique or paintings by the same children over a period of years; compare these findings with their reading development.

7. Give the draw-a-figure test as described by Machover to a class of children and study its usefulness in understanding their reading problems.

REFERENCES

BELLAK, L., and SONYA S. BELLAK: *Children's Apperception Test*, C. P. S. Company, New York, 1949.

CRONBACH, LEE J.: *Essentials of Psychological Testing*, 2d ed., Harper & Row, Publishers, Incorporated, New York, 1960.

GILLIES, J.: "Variations in Drawings of a Person and Myself by Hearing-impaired and Normal Children," *British Journal of Educational Psychology*, 38:86–89, February, 1968.

KRIPPNER, S. R.: "Reading Improvement and Scores on the Holtzman Inkblot Technique," *The Reading Teacher*, 19:519–522, April, 1966.

MACHOVER, KAREN: *Personality Projection in the Drawing of the Human Figure: A Method of Personality Investigation*, Charles C Thomas, Publisher, Springfield, Ill., 1950.

MUNDY, J. M.: "Junior Children's Responses to the Murray Thematic Apperception Test and the Cattell Personality Questionnaire," *British Journal of Educational Psychology*, 36:103–104, February, 1966.

MURRAY, H. A.: *Thematic Apperception Test*, Harvard University Press, Cambridge, Mass., 1943.

PARKER, JAMES: "The Relationship of Self Report to Inferred Self Concept," *Educational and Psychological Measurement*, 26:691–700, Autumn, 1966.

PERKINS, CHARLES W., and DONALD T. SHANNON: "Three Techniques for Obtaining Self-perceptions in Preadolescent Boys," *Journal of Personality and Social Psychology*, 2:443–447, September, 1965.

RORSCHACH, H.: *Psychodiagnostics*, 2d ed., Verlag Hans Huber, Berne, Switzerland, 1942.

SARGENT, HELEN: "Projective Methods: Their Origins, Theory, and Application in Personality Research," *Psychological Bulletin,* 42:275–293, May, 1945.

SCHNEIDMAN, E. S.: *Make a Picture Story (MAPS) Test,* Psychological Corporation, New York, 1949.

SHAFFER, LAURANCE F., and EDWARD J. SHOBEN: *The Psychology of Adjustment,* 2d ed., Houghton Mifflin Company, Boston, 1956.

STRANG, RUTH, and others: *The Improvement of Reading,* 4th ed., McGraw-Hill Book Company, New York, 1967.

SYMONDS, P. M.: *Symonds Picture-story Test,* Teachers College Press, Columbia University, New York, 1948.

VELDMAN, D. J.: "Computer-based Sentence Completion Interviews," *Journal of Counseling Psychology,* 14:153–157, March, 1967.

VERNON, P. E.: *Personality Assessment, A Critical Survey,* John Wiley & Sons, Inc., New York, 1964.

WHITELEY, T. M.: "Method for Assessing Adaptive Ego Functioning Using the Thematic Apperception Test," *Journal of Experimental Education,* 34:1–21, Spring, 1966.

SUGGESTED READINGS [1]

ALEXANDER, THERON: "The Adult-Child Interaction Test: A Projective Test for Use in Research," *Monographs of the Society for Research in Child Development,* ser. 55, vol. 17, no. 2, 1952, Child Development Publications, Champaign, Ill., 1955.

EISERER, PAUL E.: "Group Psychotherapy," *Journal of the National Association of Deans of Women,* 19:113–122, March, 1956.

MOUSTAKAS, CLARK E.: "Frequency and Intensity of Negative Attitudes Expressed in Play Therapy: A Comparison of Well-adjusted and Disturbed Young Children," *Journal of Genetic Psychology,* 86:309, June, 1955.

[1] Research on projective techniques is being constantly reported. See "Projective Methods" section in recent issues of *Psychological Abstracts,* The American Psychological Association, Inc., 1200 Seventh St., N.W., Washington, D.C., 20036, for new information about interpretation at different age levels, variations and improvement in administration and scoring, predictive value, relationship of performance on the projective test to achievement and personality characteristics, and many other aspects.

Chapter Fourteen

INTERPRETATION, SYNTHESIS, AND TREATMENT

The process of interpreting and synthesizing case data goes on continuously as one works with an individual. As the teacher works with the student or the clinician works with the client, he gains increasing understanding of the reading process and sensitivity to the individual. As he learns more and more about the case, he constantly evaluates and reevaluates his diagnostic formulation. The process is somewhat comparable to making an oil painting: The initial sketchy outline is gradually filled in with details which are often painted over as the artist gains fresh insights.

Diagnostic understanding emerges slowly. It seems to proceed in an orderly way from examination of data, to interpretation, to formulation of hypotheses, to evaluation of these hypotheses, to recommendations growing out of this process (Koester, 1951).

The physician goes through similar steps in making a medical diagnosis (Ledley and Lusted, 1959). He first obtains facts from the patient's history, the physical examination, laboratory tests, and conversation with the patient. Second, he evaluates the relative importance of the signs and symptoms that he has noted. He then relates these combinations of signs and symptoms to certain diseases with which they are often associated. In addition to his objective evaluation, the physician also has a "feeling about the case" based on intuition gained from his experience and study. A combination of reasoning and "educated guessing" is involved in diagnosing and in determining treatment. In reading cases the individual can take much more responsibility for both diagnosis and treatment.

The dynamic aspect of the process is defeated if the worker attempts to make the person fit into a particular category or a preconceived theory. For example, one worker, who had the idea that sentence fragments indicated a schizophrenic tendency, interpreted the client's natural innovative verbal expression as pathological.

The reading clinician seeks to ascertain the client's general state of health as well as his specific difficulties. He tries to identify potential strengths. In his treatment of the case he capitalizes on the client's innate striving for wholeness and often finds that the individual, by strengthening and integrating the ego, is better able to overcome his reading difficulties. At the same time he tries to detect and remove whatever is causing an interruption of the normal learning process so that the client may resume learning.

The main goal of diagnosis is to help the individual to understand himself. Self-understanding and self-acceptance will ultimately give the client greater self-sufficiency in using his own resources to develop his reading potentialities.

SIGNIFICANCE OF ITEMS OF INFORMATION

Interpretation involves knowledge of the possible significance of each kind of diagnostic information.

Parents' name and residence

The parents' name often suggests a particular racial, religious, or national background which may be associated with certain cultural characteristics. However, the teacher or counselor should avoid jumping to the conclusion that any particular individual has the common attitude or characteristics of the group.

To one who is familiar with the community, the student's address is significant; it gives a clue as to the family's socioeconomic status and the cultural level of the neighborhood. Some children live in environments that not only fail to stimulate worthwhile reading interests but actually discourage intellectual pursuits.

Facts about the family

The marital status of the parents and the composition of the family raise questions that can only be answered by further study. For example, there is no conclusive evidence about the influence of a broken home. Its effect on the child depends upon a number of factors, such as the degree of antagonism between the parents and, in the case of death, whether the deceased parent suffered a prolonged illness. The low economic status of the family and certain parent-child and sibling relationships may markedly affect a child's reading development (see Chapter 8).

Similarly, in cases where the mother is employed outside the home, the effect of this circumstance depends on such factors as the age of the child, the financial need of the family, the kind of mother substitute provided, the parent-child relationships, the family's health, the attitude of the father toward the mother's working, and the mother's satisfaction in her work. Any disturbing family conditions may inhibit a child's desire to learn to read or decrease his interest in reading at a strategic time.

School marks

The cumulative record of the student's marks lends itself to various kinds of interpretation. Ups and downs suggest a degree of sensitivity to conditions in school or outside. High marks in mathematics and science and low marks in English and social studies often suggest a reading problem. The trend in marks is also important; is the student doing better or worse each year? The relation of the teacher's marks to the standardized test scores in the same subject is also enlightening. If the mark is higher than the score, this may indicate a great deal of home study or a personality that is pleasing to the teacher. A higher test score may indicate the reverse.

Intelligence test scores

As we have already noted in Chapter 11, a poor reader's scores on group verbal intelligence tests that require much reading ability do not give an accurate prediction of his learning capacity or reading potentiality. As presently constituted, group intelligence test scores largely reflect the individual's present attainment. Recognizing this, the teacher will not take a fatalistic attitude toward a low IQ. He will reserve judgment until he sees what progress the student makes under the best possible instruction. If he learns, fine; if he does not learn, the teacher will obtain additional diagnostic information that may suggest other methods and instructional materials.

Within the same IQ range, pupils show much variation in performance. Too often the teacher either expects these "slow-learning" pupils to do the impossible or does not expect them to do as much as they can. He needs (1) to know what they can learn and the methods by which they can learn, (2) to help them set appropriate curricular goals, and (3) to provide suitable instructional materials.

With children who show extreme distractibility, overactivity, general disorganization, and other signs of possible brain injury, the simple draw-a-person test and the Bender Visual Motor Gestalt Test in addition to the Stanford-Binet Individual Intelligence Test give much insight to the skilled clinician who has used this same combination of methods with many children.

Listening comprehension

The student's score on a listening comprehension test contributes much to the interpretation of his potential reading ability. If his listening comprehension is significantly higher than his reading comprehension of similar material, a favorable prognosis for improvement in reading is suggested. (See section on Tests of Listening Comprehension in Chapter 11.)

Results of reading tests

An analysis of the student's performance on reading tests, standardized and informal, survey and diagnostic, can be used to answer such questions as these: How does his reading achievement compare with his mental ability? What kind of books can he read independently; which would only frustrate his attempts to read them? Where does his difficulty lie—in inability to recognize instantly the Dolch basic vocabulary, to apply word recognition skills in solving unfamiliar words, to comprehend the author's literal meaning, to interpret, to make inferences and generalizations, to appreciate and use the material he reads?

The total score may be misleading. For example, of two pupils with the same total score, one may be high in vocabulary and low in comprehension; the other vice versa. Most reading tests measure only a limited type of comprehension in a limited range of content (see Chapter 7 and the Appendix).

The maximum of value from any reading test may be obtained by analyzing and discussing with the student the errors made and by asking him to try to describe the mental processes that led to success or to error.

DEPTHS OF INTERPRETATION

The levels of diagnosis described in Chapter 1 apply to the interpretation of case data. Some reading teachers will take a reading behavioral approach. Having noted lacks and errors in vocabulary, word recognition skills, sentence and paragraph comprehension, interpretation, and critical reading, they reinforce the individual's reading strengths and give practice and instruction to overcome his weaknesses and deficiencies.

Other reading teachers will focus their attention on possible causes of the reading difficulties, such as those described in Chapter 8. They too often spend time exploring conditions in the past that may explain but do not help remedy the present deficiencies.

Still other reading specialists, baffled by a child's persistent difficulty in basic word recognition, will explore certain perceptual-motor abilities, strength of closure, memory, concentration, and attention which, if specifically trained, may make the child's reading achievement possible.

The clinically trained reading specialist may trace the reading problem to deeper emotional difficulties and unconscious motivation. But having solved the emotional difficulty, he still has the problem of teaching specific reading skills. He does not always recognize that skillful teaching may have a therapeutic effect.

It has become popular to offer the diagnosis of "brain injury" to children whose severe reading disability cannot be traced to other causes. This tendency is unfortunate because the more subtle aspects of neurological dysfunction are exceedingly difficult to diagnose. A direct cause-and-effect relation of actual brain injury, independent of concomitant factors such as anxiety and distractibility, to reading disability has not been convincingly demonstrated.

EXAMPLES OF DIAGNOSTIC
SUMMARIES OF READING CASES

Accent on reading performance (Tanyzer, 1956)

Twelve-year-old John entered kindergarten at the age of four years nine months. During the spring of his year in kindergarten he scored as follows on the Monroe Reading Aptitude Test:

Part of test	Percentile
Language	85
Visual	42
Auditory	4
Motor	13
Articulation	19

The results on this test showed marked weakness in three prerequisites for success in beginning reading: auditory perception and discrimination, motor coordination, and accurate articulation. The Keystone Visual Screening Test showed good visual acuity and no eye defects. The speech consultant reported no hearing loss. Although John had a lisp and some difficulty with the s sound and with blends such as *thr* and *str*, he could produce sounds correctly if he observed and imitated the way the teacher produced them.

During his first year of school he was absent about one-third of the time. His teacher described him as "of average size, left-handed, right-eyed, babyish in speech, nervous during testing."

When John was in the sixth grade, his grade scores on the Iowa Silent Reading Test (elementary form) were:

Reading comprehension	3.0
Vocabulary	2.8
Total	2.9

At the same time his grade level on the Gray Oral Reading Paragraphs was 3.1.

Although he was reading, both silently and orally, three years below his grade placement, the results of the Durrell-Sullivan Reading Capacity Test (intermediate), which is composed entirely of pictures and uses the child's ability to understand spoken language as a measure of his capacity to read, indicated ability to understand spoken words and paragraphs beyond his age and grade placement. This high reading capacity was confirmed by the results of the Wechsler Intelligence Scale for Children:

Verbal IQ	134
Performance IQ	108
Full-scale IQ	124

Day-by-day observation confirmed the test estimates of John's mental ability. The teacher noted that he had an excellent listening and speaking vocabulary. He could solve verbal problems. He was alert and showed a wide range of interests including chess and space travel. These are not the traits or interests of a dull child. His low reading performance was obviously not due to lack of mental ability.

To ascertain more precisely the nature of John's reading difficulty, an analysis of his reading was made by means of other diagnostic tests and inventories:

Informal word recognition test

An informal reading inventory (see Chapter 10)

Informal tests of visual discrimination, visual memory, and speed of perception

Test of auditory discrimination

The Dolch Basic Sight Word Test

On the word recognition test John began to encounter difficulty on the first-grade level. When asked how he attacked a new word, he said he tried to "spell it out" or sound it out letter by letter. He could make sound-letter associations for initial consonants but was not sure of blends, especially when they came at the end of a word.

On the informal reading inventory he maintained 95 percent comprehension but made an increasing number of word perception errors through the fourth grade. On the fifth-grade level his reading became so labored that he was not asked to go on after the first two sentences. In twenty-five running words he made two repetitions, two hesitations, and four word perception errors. The following reading levels were indicated by the informal reading inventory:

Basal: First grade

Independent level: Second grade

Instructional level: Third grade

Frustration level: Beginning at fourth grade and definitely at the fifth

When selections on the fifth-, sixth-, seventh-, and eighth-grade levels were read to him, John showed excellent comprehension and eighth-grade capacity level, which confirmed the impression gained from the Durrell-Sullivan Reading Capacity Test and the Wechsler Intelligence Scale for Children.

It became apparent that, although John is a bright youngster with a high reading capacity, he has difficulty in associating sounds with symbols and has no system of figuring out unfamiliar words except by initial consonants and context clues.

An informal visual discrimination test revealed no difficulty in identifying printed symbols, in discriminating differences and similarities in letter and word forms, or in remembering a letter or word that he had just identified. He was also good on speed of perception.

The test of auditory discrimination did not confirm the results of the readiness test given in the second half of the kindergarten year. On an informal test of ability to associate a sound with its corresponding letter, John's performance was excellent on initial consonants, initial blends and digraphs, and on final consonants and blends. He was quite good at identifying the two words that rhymed in a group of three and excellent on auditory fusion and in hearing sounds at the beginning, end, or middle of words. In general, his auditory discrimination was surprisingly good.

Of the 335 words in the preprimer, primer, and first reader vocabularies, John recognized on the tachistoscope all but 11. His difficulty in pronouncing these seemed to be that he did not know the vowel principle involved in such words as *Jane, pets, hope, party,* and *tall.* Of the Dolch list, John missed 9 of the 220 words. Here again his difficulty seemed to be with the short vowel sounds.

Further study of his word attack skills indicated the need for specific instruction and practice with such blends and digraphs as *str, br, thr, tw, shr,* and *sw,* and with final endings like *ck* and *nk.* The vowels gave him the most trouble; short *e, o,* and *u* and the long vowels *e* and *o;* he found it hard to differentiate between the long and short vowel and vowel digraphs and diphthongs. He was quite unable to apply phonetic principles, although he knew several rules of syllabication.

To summarize: John has superior intelligence, good visual and auditory acuity, and no speech defect that might hinder his reading growth. Yet at twelve years of age he is reading on the third-grade level and his oral reading on material that is above fourth-grade level is characterized by many repetitions. The repetitions may represent the corrections he makes as he gets meaning from context clues, which is his best method of word attack. He also makes good use of initial consonants but encounters difficulty with certain blends and digraphs and with vowel sounds.

John's failure in reading seems to be the result of a combination of factors: a general immaturity; initially poor visual and auditory discrimination; prolonged absence from school during his first two years, which caused him to miss a great deal of beginning reading instruction; and insufficient and ineffective reading instruction as he progressed through the grades.

If the diagnosis of emotional and social factors had been as thorough as the diagnosis of visual and auditory discrimination, vocabulary, and word attack skills, specific emotional difficulties might also have been uncovered. It is not unrealistic to assume that seven years of failure in reading must have had some effect on John's attitude toward himself and his ability to read. However, he now seems to have a strong desire to read.

In working with John, it should not be difficult to give him practice in the specific letter-sound associations which, according to the diagnosis, are causing him difficulty. For example, the "Phono-Word Wheels" published by the Steck Company, Austin, Texas, are a useful device; and similar devices may be constructed by teachers and students to give specific practice in such consonant blends and digraphs as *str, br, thr, tw, shr, sk, sw, er, ser, wr, fr, shr, fl,* and *bl.* Other word games and practice exercises can be used in teaching the vowel sounds, vowel digraphs such as *ai, ow, ea, ai,* and *oa* and the vowel diphthongs *oo, au, oi, ou,* and *ow.* John should be given this practice in connection with words in which these sounds appear. He may join a small group of other children who are having similar difficulty for practice in these skills using games and exercises. The teacher may ask a good reader to serve as assistant instructor of this small group. When John meets unfamiliar words in his reading, he should be expected to apply his phonetic skills as needed to get their meaning.

Along with this specific practice, John should read beginners' books, such as the Miami Linguistic Readers (1965), which provide practice in the vowel sounds in an interesting context.

It would be well to have John do a certain amount of choral reading and dramatized reading which would help to develop thoughtful phrasing.

John may also be given opportunity to discover and apply the principles of pronunciation and syllabication that govern a large portion of words. For example, he is familiar with words such as *am, ham, sat, at, cat, mat.* He can note that each word has only one vowel at the beginning or in the middle and that in all these words the vowel has the short sound. He can then state the principle himself: When a word has only one vowel at the beginning or in the middle, the vowel is usually short. Experiences of this kind would help him discover underlying principles and spelling patterns. While acquiring these skills, John should become aware of the methods that resulted in success—of the strategies of learning. As soon as he has acquired the basic vocabulary and word recognition skills, he will be ready for instruction and practice in sentence and paragraph comprehension and other reading abilities needed on his grade level.

Much silent reading of easy, interesting material will help John develop smoothness, rapidity, and fluency; will decrease unnecessary vocalization; will reinforce the mastery of words and parts of words already learned; and will give him an opportunity to recognize new words.

While working with John, the reading teacher, without prying or probing, may get glimpses of emotional difficulty. For example, if John expresses anxiety about his mother's illness, the teacher may encourage him to talk about ways he can help at home. One of the best ways to relieve anxiety is to do something constructive about the anxiety-arousing situation.

In this case, since the central factor seemed to be failure to acquire basic word recognition and vocabulary skills, which in turn limited his comprehension of sentences and paragraphs, remediation consisted largely of instruction and practice in his specific reading deficiencies. The diagnostic procedures detected the specific reading difficulties; remediation attacked these directly. The reading teacher analyzed each specific task into steps by which John could achieve mastery of each skill in which he was deficient. For example, he needed to acquire the ability to identify, distinguish, recall, and apply the *tw* sound in words. Assuming that there were no serious deficits in auditory acuity, perception, discrimination, and memory, the analysis of this task might include these steps:

1. Recognize the *tw* sound in a key word (twins).
2. Identify the sound in other words in initial, medial, and final positions.
3. Distinguish the *tw* sound from other sounds in words.
4. Apply this knowledge to the pronunciation of new words in sentences.

The teaching procedure stemming from the analysis might be as follows:

1. The teacher pronounces the word *twins*, writes it, and calls attention to the *tw* sound.
2. John mentions any words he knows that have the *tw* sound; he also tells where the sound is located in the word.
3. The teacher adds other *tw* words to those John mentions.
4. She pronounces a number of words, some of which have the *tw* sound, some do not: *twin, twig, tell, twice, train,* etc. John tells which words have the *tw* sound and which do not.
5. He uses these words in sentences.
6. The teacher writes his sentences, underlining the *tw* in each word.
7. John writes these words on his vocabulary cards.
8. He substitutes the *tw* in words that he knows: *nice, twice; rice, twice.*
9. He writes and reads sentences that have *tw* words in them.
10. He reads sentences that have unfamiliar words with the *tw* sound.

This procedure may be used in teaching troublesome sound-letter associations to a whole class. John may not need all these specific steps. The teacher starts a little below the level at which the pupil is functioning at present and encourages him to go ahead as fast as he can with success. The pupil's success is rewarded by the teacher's approval and, more important, by his own satisfaction in the progress he is making. As he becomes more and more proficient in reading, he will obtain intrinsic satisfaction from the content of books he has learned to read.

Accent on attitudes

In the case of John, the discrepancy between his mental ability and his reading performance seemed to stem from inadequate instruction in basic reading skills. Accordingly the method was (1) to identify the specific reading behaviors that he needed to acquire, (2) to analyze the steps in learning each behavior, and (3) to develop appropriate teaching procedures.

In the case of José who was eleven years seven months old and in the sixth grade, the problem was different although the test results showed a similar reading level. On an informal reading inventory and on the Stanford Achievement Test his reading grade was 3.2; on the Gates Advanced Primary Reading Test, 4.9. If encouraged and prompted, he could apply his knowledge of consonant sounds, rhyming words, and syllables to reading material. He could use context clues and picture clues to get the meaning of unfamiliar words. He knew all of the Dolch Basic Sight Vocabulary in isolation and in sentences.

Although not scoring as high as John on intelligence tests, José's measured intelligence fell within the normal range. There were no health or vision problems noted on the medical record. He had missed only six days of schooling in five years.

José lacked facility in oral language. He came from a home where two languages were spoken and where the English that he heard was substandard. The Wepman Auditory Discrimination Test indicated inadequate development of auditory perception and discrimination. Yet José made few typical errors in pronunciation and did not speak with a heavy Spanish accent. He did have difficulty with sentence structure; his summaries and stories were poorly organized; they consisted of fragments of thoughts and repetitions. Any language situation seemed threatening to him.

His general lack of confidence was indicated by his frequent response, "I don't know," and by his uncertainty about the correctness of his answers. He seemed surprised when he made a correct response. Yet he was not easily discouraged or distracted when engaged in manipulative tasks such as constructing a model airplane.

There were a number of explanations for his feelings of inferiority and discouragement regarding himself and his reading. At home his mother often compared him with the older, academically successful brother. She was dissatisfied with his "average" school marks. For the current year his marks were below average in arithmetic and science, average in reading and English, superior in social studies and spelling. She forced him to read every day at certain hours. In the interview with the worker she said that her major concern was José's lack of interest in reading and that he does not read independently or enjoy reading. Another factor in his poor self-concept was his history of failure, which constantly reminded him that he was not living up to his mother's expectations.

Too often a case study neglects the assets of the client. In this case there were many:

Unusually good attendance at school

Adequate intelligence

Cooperative attitude and responsiveness to the worker and to the materials prepared for him

Ability to persist and avoid distraction when a task was meaningful to him

Capacity to learn and remember

Ability to relate and apply his knowledge and skills in new situations

The worker gained most of this understanding of José gradually while helping him to become a better reader. Two central factors in this case became obvious: the boy's oral language handicap and his negative attitude toward himself and toward reading. The worker tentatively planned her interviews with the improvement of speech and reading and the building of self-confidence in mind. It was important for José to acquire competence in the language arts and to experience success instead of failure.

Among the teaching procedures and materials employed to accomplish these objectives were the following:

Preparing reading material about things that interested him, e.g., "animal mysteries"

Using selections written on a difficulty level that would ensure success

Personalizing instruction by relating it to him and his interests, e.g., stories about his dog Fido

Introducing surprises which caught his attention and thus created an essential condition for learning

Using check marks, gifts of candy, and books to reinforce desirable behavior and reward progress

Giving practice in oral communication through games, puppets, dramatized reading

Providing a progression of learning experiences leading to mastery of each behavioral objective

Making charts that would show José his improvement graphically

Recording and playing back examples of his good sentences and organization of ideas in his summaries of stories

Relating his experiences at the reading center to his school work

Repeatedly asking him to summarize the processes that he used successfully in each reading task

Encouraging him to do as much independent reading as possible on his present level of difficulty

In this case the worker recognized José's deficits in oral speech, vocabulary, and word recognition skills and also his need for increasing his self-esteem. Especially in the early contacts she avoided the kind of pressure on reading that at home was beginning to cause José to resist reading. As his interest and confidence increased, the teacher gave him more systematic instruction in the skills in which José was deficient.

The case of John mentioned earlier illustrates the classic case study method in which the worker supplements information from available records by his own observation, interviews, and testing. After noting discrepancies between the client's capacity and performance level, the worker makes a thorough behavioral analysis of the reading problem. To obtain further understanding of the client's difficulties, he explores possible correlated or underlying conditions and characteristics often associated with reading disabilities. Out of this interpretation and synthesis of the data he formulates a diagnostic hypothesis that leads directly to remediation (Bateman, 1965). This behavioral approach in remediation focuses on improving the individual's reading performance by skillful instruction and psychologically designed reinforcement.

The case of José illustrates the diagnostic-teaching method. The worker gains understanding of the client simultaneously with the teaching-therapeutic process. His interpretation of the client's responses guides his next step. This is I. A. Richards' idea of "feedforward" (1968). This method actively involves the client; it explores his learning process with him. The worker is constantly making new and always tentative formulations. These lead immediately to whatever teaching procedure or instructional material seems appropriate.

NO TWO ALIKE

Each case is unique. The method of study, the diagnosis, the hypotheses, the treatment all form a different pattern for each individual.

In the case of Tom, a ten-year-old boy in the third grade, the worker through systematic instruction attempted to reeducate an otherwise well-adjusted child who was completely confused in his beginning reading. To accomplish this goal, the worker used the Kirk, Kirk, and Hegge *Remedial Reading Drills* published by the George Wahr Publishing Company, Ann

Arbor, Michigan. When he had obtained familiarity with the sounds, Tom practiced them in word families such as *s-at, r-at,* etc. In addition to the *Remedial Reading Drills,* word wheels or flip charts such as those published by the Webster Division, McGraw-Hill Book Company, New York; Science Research Associates, Chicago; and the Steck Company, Austin, Texas, relieved the more tedious drill.

Tom improved his sight vocabulary by noting likenesses and differences in words, and reading the Dolch basic vocabulary words in sentences. To continue the reading center instruction in his regular classroom, the worker provided Tom's regular teacher with the Sullivan programmed learning books with which Tom experienced immediate pleasure and success. The worker used the first book of the *Under Water Adventure* series, published by Harr Wagner Associates, as an opportunity to teach, reinforce, and apply word attack skills.

Each session also included the reading of directions for Tom to carry out in action. This procedure helped to build his concept of reading as useful and rewarding.

In the case of thirteen-year-old Sammy, the worker changed his treatment objectives as the client gained ego strength to attempt more difficult intellectual tasks. Sammy responded to the more rigorous program and experienced satisfaction in the use of his mental ability in aspects of reading that required more thinking and reasoning than did the earlier emphasis on simpler word recognition skills. However, the original hypothesis that his earlier concept of himself as worthless could be changed—and was changed—by the attention given him, success in simpler tasks, and primary reinforcement paved the way for receptivity to the more demanding program. The worker used instructional materials that were similar to those Sammy was having in his regular school work and analyzed each task into a series of learning steps. For example, in teaching vocabulary the worker taught the following steps:

1. Get a clear visual impression of the word.

2. Use his knowledge of phonics and structural analysis to pronounce it and/or get the meaning.

3. Use context clues to get its meaning.

4. Use the dictionary to obtain accurate definitions.

5. Choose definition that is appropriate in this particular context.

6. Write word on one side of a vocabulary card and divide it into syllables; on the other side, give definition and write sentence using the word.

7. Relate the word to other personal or learning experiences.

8. Compare word with other words already in his vocabulary—synonyms, antonyms, homonyms.

9. Categorize the word in a hierarchy of word values.

10. Use word in his writing and speaking.

In the case of Bert, a fourteen-year-old boy entering ninth grade, the worker, recognizing a reciprocal relationship between the boy's self-concept and his need to improve his reading, included both aspects in her treatment objectives. She concentrated on four objectives: to improve his self-concept, to increase his vocabulary, to improve his concentration and study skills, and to learn how to take a test.

During the interview the worker took advantage of any opportunity to reinforce a positive outlook toward himself. When Bert said he could not do the reading task presented, the worker analyzed it, gave him opportunity to do it, and praised him when he accomplished it. Her praise was always sincere and not indiscriminate. In each interview she gave him the opportunity to succeed.

The most successful procedure was a series of dialogues which she wrote relating to Bert, his interests, and the content of his school subjects. These improved his oral expression and confidence in himself. A "vocabulary bank" gave him concrete evidence of his progress. A chart for outside reading, on which he could record the number of words per minute, showed the gains he was making in speed of reading.

In the case of Marilyn, a fourteen-year-old girl in the eighth grade, it was necessary to give reading instruction as subservient to the girl's more dominant interest. She viewed herself as a person who could not read in a society where everyone can read—even her little brother! The worker's main objective, based on the information obtained before and during a series of interviews, was to help Marilyn see the need for and value in reading and help her build on the skills she already had acquired.

The general procedure that the worker used was to find reading materials of interest to Marilyn and use them as a basis for instruction and practice in word recognition skills, vocabulary building, oral reading. Together they analyzed recordings of Marilyn's oral reading and pointed out where pauses were necessary and showed how focusing on the idea of the passage increased fluency. They took turns reading lines of a story in *The American Girl* and enacted TV commercials and radio announcements.

Utilizing Marilyn's interest in modeling and fashions, the worker arranged with the mother for Marilyn to make a dress. To select a style she had to read pattern catalogs and then read the directions for making the dress. It was difficult reading and required periods of instruction on technical words, word recognition skills, and sentence and paragraph comprehension.

During this period the worker brought in stories in *Ingenue, Seventeen,* and *The American Girl* which gave additional practice on specific reading skills. Marilyn would take the magazines home to read. She asked her mother to subscribe for *Seventeen* which she particularly enjoyed.

As Marilyn gained reading proficiency, the worker helped her become aware of the skills she was learning. and of the new words she had acquired. At the end of the reading sessions, she had learned to read to get the information she wanted.

READING RECORDS

Records of student progress

If the reading teacher has obtained information about the student's reading achievement before beginning to work with him, the usual method of appraising his progress is to administer later a comparable form of the tests initially given and report the gains he has made. When appraisal is interwoven with instruction, the teacher may note progress by keeping a continuous record and chart. This might include a day-by-day graph of scores on comparable exercises, a growing list of words recognized at sight, reports of books read, and dated tape recordings of early and later oral reading. Unless adequate comprehension can be assumed, a record of speed alone has little significance. More useful is the record that shows rate of comprehension for materials of varying difficulty and of different types: study type, and free or recreational reading. These and other kinds of continuous records that show the ups and down of progress are enlightening to the student, the teacher, and the parent.

Records to guide instruction

The main purpose of records is to indicate treatment needed and to give continuity in working with a reading case. Before giving any tests, the reading clinician examines records already available. He resists the tendency to be unfavorably influenced by previous test results or comments. He does not jump to conclusions about the nature of the reading problem.

From the cumulative records in a school, he will obtain more or less information about the tests that have already been given, the pupil's achievement in different areas, and trends or fluctuations in performance over a period of years. As he obtains additional data, he may summarize whatever seems relevant to the case in the form of a checklist or a descriptive summary (see Chapters 3 and 10). Process as well as performance should be noted and recorded. There should also be blank space for comments that indicate dominant or central characteristics and conditions and that show relationships among them.

A descriptive summary is more functional than a checklist because it indicates interrelations among items and identifies items of central importance. At the end of every interview the worker should review new understanding gained; revise, if neccesary, previous hypotheses; and plan for the next session.

The case summary at the end of a period of treatment should include:

1. Identifying data
2. Description of client
3. Reading problem as presented by parent and client
4. Family composition
5. Summary of test results
6. Diagnostic formulation
7. Treatment
8. Prognosis
9. Recommendations to the school, parents, and client
   (Such a summary is essential for any follow-up or further work with the case.)

The diagnostic formulation made at any stage of working with the student is useful in giving the worker a sense of direction and an understanding of the reading difficulty and the conditions that seem to have caused it. Likewise the formulation enables the worker to give the individual practice and instruction that can be applied to his daily reading.

The diagnostic summary has certain limitations. It involves some degree of inference; it is never complete, and it should be constantly revised as new information is obtained. The limited diagnostic procedure may also fail to describe attitudes, values, and motivations that are basic to improvement in the individual's reading; for any given effect, several causes are possible.

Remedial procedures, like the diagnostic summary, cannot be determined once and for all. The reading teacher selects the most plausible method of treatment, tries it out, and acts in accordance with the results.

Most valuable is a case conference that includes not only the reading teacher but also the student's regular teachers, the principal, the school nurse, and others who may be helpful (Hocker, 1968). Such a conference is a learning experience, a form of in-service education for all the participants. The specialists learn what the teacher can and cannot do. The teachers gain understanding from the specialists' interpretations and recommendations.

CONCLUDING STATEMENT

Interpretation and syntheses of data are the most difficult steps in the diagnostic process. They involve an understanding of the possible significance of each item and ability to keep in mind related items and to organize them into patterns. From these patterns, one derives hypotheses from which the treatment of the case tentatively stems. These hypotheses are modified as new information and insights are gained in working with the case. Each reading case offers a unique creative experience to the teacher or clinician.

While not abandoning the established clinical procedure of analyzing the reading process, uncovering possible causes, then trying to synthesize the information collected and formulate hypotheses from this compilation of facts, might we not experiment with a more dynamic clinical method of studying students' reading? A proposed method would recognize the continuing development of the client's reading, his inner urge to improve, the environmental conditions that are inhibiting or facilitating improvement, and his interaction with the clinician and with other people in school and at home. The clinician would begin working with the reading problem as the client sees it and assist him through tests and interviews in clarifying it. He would teach the client methods of learning which he can apply to each reading task. He would try to change conditions that are inhibiting progress.

SUGGESTED PROBLEMS: PRACTICE AND DEMONSTRATION

1. Make a comprehensive diagnostic study of two children of different ages and reading problems, going through the process of interpretation and synthesis of the information obtained.

2. Read a number of different kinds of cases; first note the diagnostic information available, then formulate your own hypotheses and recommendations for treatment, and finally read the case as it was actually carried out.

3. Participate in a case conference on a reading problem involving an exchange of information and ideas among the various participants.

4. Make a cumulative reading record that you can use in your school or clinic situation.

5. Read some of the case studies reported in the Suggested Readings at the end of this chapter. Extract from them ideas concerning the significance and use of various kinds of diagnostic information.

6. Read Kirk's chapter in the report of the Annual Reading Conference (The University of Chicago Press, Chicago, 1962) for more detailed understanding of the idea of sequential diagnosis.

7. Summarize the values and the limitations of diagnostic summaries.

8. What applications of this chapter can teachers make to their work with reading problems within a class group?

REFERENCES

BATEMAN, BARBARA: "Learning Disabilities: Yesterday, Today, and Tomorrow," *Exceptional Children*, 31:167–177, December, 1965.

CAHOON, D. D.: "A Comparison of the Effectiveness of Verbal Reinforcement Applied in Group and Individual Interviews," *Journal of Counseling Psychology*, 12:121–126, Summer, 1965.

HOCKER, MARY ELSA: "A Case-study Approach to Reading Problems," *The Reading Teacher*, 21:541–543, March, 1968.

KOESTER, G. A.: "A Study of the Diagnostic Process," *Educational and Psychological Measurement*, 14:473–486, Autumn, 1951.

LEDLEY, ROBERT S., and LEE B. LUSTED: "Reasoning Foundations of Medical Diagnosis," *Science*, 130:9–21, July 3, 1959.

Miami Linguistic Readers, D. C. Heath and Company, Boston, 1965.

RICHARDS, I. A.: "The Secret of 'Feedforward,'" *Saturday Review*, 51:14–17, Feb. 3, 1968.

TANYZER, HAROLD J.: Case presented by Mr. Tanyzer in an advanced case study course at Teachers College, Columbia University, New York, 1956.

SUGGESTED READINGS

BALOW, B., and MARLYS BLOMQUIST: "Young Adults Ten to Fifteen Years after Severe Reading Disability," *Elementary School Journal*, 66:44–48, October, 1965.

DE HIRSCH, KATRINA: "Concepts Related to Normal Reading Processes and Their Application to Reading Pathology," *The Journal of Genetic Psychology*, 102:277–287, June, 1963.

FRIEDMAN, SYLVIA SCLAR: "Remedial Therapy with a Twelve-year-old Incarcerated Delinquent," *The Reading Teacher*, 19:483–489, April, 1966.

FRY, E.: "Reading Clinic Reports: Its Results and Methods," *Journal of Educational Research*, 52:311–313, April, 1959.

GLASS, GERALD G.: "Students' Misconceptions Concerning Their Reading," *The Reading Teacher*, 21:765–768, May, 1968.

JANSKY, JEANNETTE: "A Case of Severe Dyslexia with Aphasic-like Symptoms," *The Reading Teacher*, 15:110–113, November, 1961.

KANTROWITZ, VIOLA: "Bibliotherapy with Retarded Readers," *Journal of Reading*, 11:205–212, December, 1967.

KRESS, ROY: "Case Study of Reading Retardation: The Diagnosis and Correction," *Conference on Reading*, The University of Pittsburgh Press, Pittsburgh, 1960, pp. 75–91.

MAYHEW, LEWIS B.: "Critical Incidence Technique in Educational Evaluation," *Journal of Educational Research*, 49:491–598, April, 1956.

NEWMAN, RUTH, and others: *Technical Assistance in a Public School System*, School Research Program, P.H.S. Project OM-525, Washington School of Psychiatry, Washington, D.C., 1962.

OFMAN, WILLIAM, and MORTON SHAEVITY: "The Kinesthetic Method in Remedial Reading," *The Journal of Experimental Education*, 31:317–320, March, 1963.

ROBBINS, M. H.: "Case Study of a Retarded Child," *Education*, 82:230–231, December, 1961.

SHEPERD, GEORGE: "Reading Research and the Individual Child," *The Reading Teacher*, 21:335–342, January, 1968.

STRANG, RUTH: "Diagnostic Teaching of Reading in High School," *Journal of Reading*, 8:147–154, January, 1965.

"Symposium: Contributions to the Diagnosis and Remedial Treatment of Reading Difficulties," *British Journal of Educational Psychology*, 30:146–179, June, 1960; 31:79–105, February, 1961.

BRIEF DESCRIPTIONS OF A FEW TESTS FOR DIFFERENT PURPOSES ON DIFFERENT DEVELOPMENTAL LEVELS

A teacher may gain an understanding of students' reading development and difficulties by observing their responses to the teaching methods and materials that he uses day by day. Systematic observation procedures developed to evaluate children in natural settings could result in more meaningful educational appraisal than could be made from test results.

The teacher may supplement his day-by-day observation with informal group and individual tests. To obtain a basis for comparing his students' reading achievement with that of others of the same age or grade, he may use a standardized reading survey test. To help individuals learn more about their specific reading abilities, he may administer a diagnostic reading test. If a student continually fails to profit by the instruction, he may obtain clues to causes of the difficulty from the results on a test of psycholinguistic abilities. From an individual intelligence test he would gain understanding of the perceptual and mental deficiencies underlying success in reading. If progress in reading seems to be blocked by emotional difficulties, certain projective techniques may give clues to causes.

A pattern of diagnostic procedures will be suggested for each developmental period. The tests included are merely samples from among many others that might have been chosen. The items are arranged from the most informal to the most technical.

No list of "recommended tests" should be used without carefully considering the suitability of the test to the situation. Moreover, any such list soon becomes outdated.

Details regarding each test can be readily and fully obtained from the test manual, from the latest revision of Oscar Buros' *Mental Measurements Yearbook*, and from many sources such as the following:

291

ANASTASI, ANNE: *Testing Problems in Perspective*, American Council on Education, 1785 Massachusetts Ave., Washington, D.C., 1966.

BOND, GUY L., and MILES A. TINKER: *Reading Difficulties: Their Diagnosis and Correction*, 2d ed., Appleton-Century-Crofts, Inc., New York, 1967, pp. 529–537.

BUROS, OSCAR K. (ed.): *The Sixth Mental Measurements Yearbook*, The Gryphon Press, Highland Park, N.J., 1965.

CRONBACH, LEE J.: *Essentials of Psychological Testing*, 2d ed., Harper & Row, Publishers, Incorporated, New York, 1960, pp. 228–233.

DEUTSCH, MARTIN, and others: "Guidelines for Testing Minority Group Children," *Journal of Social Issues*, 20:129–145, April, 1964.

EBEL, ROBERT L.: "The Social Consequences of Educational Testing," *Proceedings of the 1963 Invitational Conference on Testing Problems*, Educational Testing Service, Princeton, N.J., 1964, pp. 130–143.

"Educational and Psychological Testing," *Review of Educational Research*, 38:1–110, February, 1968.

Let's Look at Children, Educational Testing Service, Princeton, N.J., 1967.

MONEY, JOHN: *The Disabled Reader*, The Johns Hopkins Press, Baltimore, 1966, pp. 402–407.

WEINER, BLUMA B.: "Assessment: Beyond Psychometry," *Exceptional Children*, 33:367–370, February, 1967.

WILSON, ROBERT M.: *Diagnostic and Remedial Reading for Classroom and Clinic*, Charles E. Merrill Books, Inc., Columbus, Ohio, 1967, pp. 230–236.

PRESCHOOL, KINDERGARTEN, AND FIRST GRADE:

Tests of Visual and Auditory Acuity

Observation of children's responses to informal exercises in auditory and visual perception, discrimination, memory, and sequencing, vocabulary, speech, etc.

"A Group Visual Perception Test for the Prediction and Diagnosis of Reading Ability," Marjorie K. Mertens, unpublished doctoral dissertation, University of Arizona, Tucson, 1968.

The *Peabody Picture Vocabulary Test*, L. M. Dunn, American Guidance Service, Minneapolis, 1959. For ages 2.5–8. It may be used with older children in the differential diagnosis of reading and speech difficulties. The only verbal direction is "Show me _____" (the word being tested). For preliminary appraisal this test can serve both as a substitute for the administratively more complicated WISC and as a test of the child's ability to recognize spoken words and their meaning.

The *Wepman Auditory Discrimination Test*, J. M. Wepman, Language Research Associates, 950 E. 59th St., Chicago, 1958. This test is an easy-to-administer method of determining a child's ability to recognize the fine differences that exist between the phonemes used in English speech.

Illinois Test of Psycholinguistic Abilities (rev.), Samuel A. Kirk and James J. McCarthy, Institute for Research on Exceptional Children, University of Illinois, Urbana, 1968. For ages 3–10, this test is a unique approach to differential diagnosis of the reading process from "intake" to "output." It is focused on the diagnosis of abilities underlying reading achievement. The results are presented in the form of a profile. (For detail on theory and use see *The Diagnosis and Remediation of Psycholinguistic Disabilities*, Samuel A. Kirk, The University of Illinois Press, Institute for Research on Exceptional Children, Urbana, 1966.)

To obtain an estimate of a child's mental maturity, the *Goodenough Draw-a-Man Test*, Harcourt, Brace & World, Inc., New York, has been used for many years. The child is asked to draw the best man he can. The carefully described scoring takes into account the basic structure of the figure drawn. A reliability of .84–.86 has been obtained for kindergarten children. Both the original form and the Harris revision of this test have moderate to good validity based on correlations with the WISC and Stanford-Binet.

The *Wechsler Preschool and Primary Scale of Intelligence* (WPPSI), published by The Psychological Corporation, 304 E. 45th St., New York, consists of a series of ability tests of various facets of a young child's intellectual competence. There are norms for eleven age levels at three-month intervals from ages 4 to 6½ years.

FIRST GRADE

Observation of children's responses to opportunities to browse in the book corner or library, their degree of interest, the kinds of books they select, their ability to recognize words or parts of the story, etc.

Observation of children's reading abilities, difficulties, errors, and learning capacity as shown in the reading periods.

The "Fresno Test" (see Ruth G. Jameson, "The Development of a Phonemic Analysis for an Oral English Proficiency Test for Spanish-speaking School Beginners," doctoral dissertation, University of Texas, Austin, 1966). The examiner presents the child with any provocative picture and asks him to tell a story about it. By analyzing the recording of this story, the examiner can learn a great deal about the child's fluency and accuracy in speaking, his language patterns, vocabulary, imagination, and ability to organize and relate ideas. The child may also reveal personality traits and family relationships. If the child is unable to tell a story about the picture, the examiner asks him just to tell what he sees in the picture. This is an effective, informal way of diagnosing the oral language proficiency of children from non-English-speaking or disadvantaged homes.

The *Wide Range Achievement Test*, Joseph Jastak and Sidney Bijou, Guidance Associates, 1526 Gilpin Ave., Wilmington, Del., 1965. This test covers a range from kindergarten to superior adult. It is widely used in psychological and reading clinics. It is easy to administer and correlates around .80 with other criteria of reading achievement—the Gilmore Oral Reading Test; Stanford Achievement Test, reading section; and teachers' ratings.

The *Metropolitan Reading Readiness Tests*, Gertrude Hildreth and Nellie Griffiths, Harcourt, Brace & World, Inc., New York, 1933–1950; kindergarten-grade 1; two forms. The reading readiness section includes tests of word meaning, sentence meaning, information, visual perception, number knowledge, visual perception combined with motor control, and a draw-a-man test. This test, administered to a group, identifies quite successfully children who have not acquired these prerequisites for success in beginning reading.

The *Durrell Analysis of Reading Difficulty* (new edition), D. D. Durrell, Harcourt, Brace & World, Inc., New York, 1955; grades 1–6. This individual test includes materials for individual diagnosis of oral and silent reading, listening comprehension, word recognition and analysis, spelling, and handwriting. The *Durrell-Sullivan Reading Capaicty Test* is a valuable addition. The detailed analysis of errors, as in most tests, is more useful for diagnosis and remediation than is the total score.

The *Lorge-Thorndike Intelligence Tests*, Irving Lorge and Robert Thorndike, Houghton Mifflin Company, Boston, 1954; kindergarten through high school. At the primary level the pupils respond to questions read by the teacher requiring verbal understanding and reasoning by marking the appropriate pictures.

The *Wechsler Intelligence Scale for Children* (WISC), D. Wechsler, The Psychological Corporation, New York, 1955; ages 5–15. This widely used individual intelligence test has high reliability. It yields a verbal, a performance, and a total IQ. Because no reading tasks are required, the student's intelligence score is not lowered by reading deficiencies. The WISC consists of twelve subtests which tap cognitive strengths that may underlie reading ability.

PRIMARY GRADES

Observation of children's responses in classroom situations (see Chapter 3).

Informal reading tests of oral and silent reading with different kinds of material.

Individual reading inventory (see Chap. 10).

Dolch Basic Sight Word Test, E. W. Dolch, Ginn and Company, Boston, 1942. This test presents the entire basic sight vocabulary of "220 service words" which make up 70 percent of first readers and 65 percent of second and third readers. It can be administered in groups or individually. By repeating the test on words that pupils have been taught, the teacher may obtain additional understanding of their vocabulary learning capacity.

Gray Oral Reading Tests, W. S. Gray (Helen M. Robinson, ed.), The Bobbs-Merrill Company, Inc., Indianapolis, 1963; grades 1–12; four forms. The examiner records eight types of errors as the student reads the carefully graded paragraphs aloud. Average intercorrelation among forms is .98. This is a test of oral reading only; comprehension is not considered in the scoring. (Some teachers prefer the Gilmore Oral Reading Test, Harcourt, Brace & World, Inc., New York, because it places emphasis on comprehension as well as on rate and accuracy of oral reading.)

The *Stanford Achievement Test* (1964 edition), Truman Kelley, Richard Madden, Erie F. Gardner, and Herbert C. Rudman, Harcourt, Brace & World, Inc., New York; grades 2–3, 4–6, 7–9; three to five forms. This is a series of achievement tests; three of them—word meaning, paragraph meaning, and word study skills—are directly concerned with reading. At each level the paragraph-meaning section begins with simple sentences and progresses to longer and more difficult paragraphs. In each paragraph one to four words are omitted, to be replaced by one of the four possibilities suggested. It is a good example of the reading survey type of test.

The *Gates-MacGinitie Reading Tests,* Arthur I. Gates and Walter Mac-Ginitie, The Psychological Corporation, New York, 1965; grades 1, 2, 3, 2–3; three forms. This test is a more recent attempt to measure primary reading abilities.

The *Gates-McKillop Reading Diagnostic Tests* can also be used at this level. Teachers College Press, Teachers College, Columbia University, New York; grades 1–8; two forms. Materials are provided for individual diagnosis of difficulties.

INTERMEDIATE GRADES

Continued observation of students in reading situations.

Informal tests of paragraph comprehension.

Group informal reading inventory (see Chapter 7).

The *McCullough Word-Analysis Tests,* Constance M. McCullough, Ginn and Company, Boston, 1962; grades 4 through college. Tests I, II, III, and VI on initial blends and digraphs, phonetic discrimination, matching letters to vowel sounds, and dividing a word into syllables may be used with average fourth graders. Tests IV, V, and VII on sounding whole words, interpreting phonetic symbols, and dividing a word structurally into prefix, root, and suffix are useful for those who are on fifth-reader level. All tests may be used beyond fifth grade. This test may be used in groups or with individuals; it provides an extensive diagnosis of word analysis skills and is useful with older retarded readers.

The *Developmental Reading Tests, Intermediate Reading*, Guy L. Bond, Theodore Clymer, and Cyril J. Hoyt, Lyons and Carnahan, Chicago, 1955; grades 4–6. These tests appraise basic vocabulary, factual reading, reading to organize, evaluate, interpret, and appreciate.

Stanford Achievement Test for grades 4.0–5.4, Intermediate I Test; for grades 5.5–6.9, Intermediate II Test.

California Test of Mental Maturity; E. T. Sullivan, W. W. Clark, E. W. Tiegs, California Test Bureau, Monterey, Calif., 1957. A group test of intelligence for school age children. This test offers separate "language" and "nonlanguage" IQ, but these have little significance for estimating reading potential unless the difference is very large. There are subscores for memory, logical reasoning, and other mental abilities. The standardization of this test along with the reading test provides a comparison of the pupil's reading achievement scores with expectancy for his IQ level.

Progressive Matrices, J. C. Raven and H. K. Lewis, The Psychological Corporation, New York; ages 5½–11; age 9 upward. This test is unique in obtaining a nonverbal measure of reasoning ability, with special emphasis on spatial reasoning.

JUNIOR HIGH SCHOOL

Continued observation of students in reading situations, reading and discussing different kinds of material read for different purposes.

Informal silent reading tests in each subject (see *Making Better Readers*, Ruth Strang and Dorothy Bracken, D. C. Heath and Company, Boston, 1957).

Stanford Achievement Test. (To measure progress from year to year it is desirable to use the same test series.)

Sequential Tests of Educational Progress: Reading, many authors; four levels: grades 4–6, 7–9, 10–12, and 13–14; Cooperative Test Division, Educational Testing Service, Princeton, N.J., 1963. The abilities measured in this test give more attention to interpreting, summarizing, criticizing passages, and recognizing motives and the author's purpose than does the usual reading test. The selections have been geared to the interest level of many of the pupils in today's schools rather than to high literary quality.

SENIOR HIGH SCHOOL

Continued observation of students in reading situations.

Informal silent reading tests in each subject.

Reading Comprehension: Cooperative English Test, Cooperative Test Division, Educational Testing Service, Princeton, N.J.: grades 7–12, Cl; grades 11–16, C2; four forms. Measures vocabulary, speed, and level of comprehension.

Sequential Test of Educational Progress (STEP).

Iowa Tests of Educational Development, E. F. Lindquist and Leonard S. Feldt, Science Research Associates, Chicago, 1942–1959; grades 9–13. These tests measure reading in social studies, natural sciences; literary material, as well as understanding of social concepts, vocabulary in each field, and other abilities.

Cooperative School and College Ability Tests (SCAT), Educational Testing Service, Princeton, N.J., 1955; grade 4 to college. A verbal score measures vocabulary and reading comprehension; a quantitative score measures arithmetic reasoning and understanding of arithmetic operations; both measure school-learned abilities and predict academic success.

Culture-free Intelligence Tests, Raymond B. Cattell, Institute for Personality and Ability Testing, 1602 Coronado Drive, Champaign, Ill.; ages 4 to adult; 3 levels. A nonverbal test including matrices and other reasoning tasks, independent of language skill but not truly free of cultural influences. The IQs have a large standard deviation.

There are many other excellent tests designed to measure an individual reading performance, to show specific strengths and weaknesses, and to identify certain psychomotor, psycholinguistic, or more pervasive mental abilities that underlie successful reading.

NAME INDEX

SUBJECT INDEX

Ability, "developed," 216
Activities, record of, 99–101
American Foundation for the Blind, 172
American Journal of Mental Deficiency, 70
American Optical Company, AO Vision Screening Test, 171
American Optometric Association, committee on Visual Problems of Children and Youth, 169
Anxiety:
    associated with reading difficulties, 157, 158
    relief of, 279
Attention-distraction charts, 52
Attitudes, 280–283
    and reading ability, 16, 203
Auding (*see* Listening comprehension)
Audiometer, 184
Auditory acuity, tests of, 292–293
Auditory difficulties, 183
Auditory discrimination, 184–185, 277
Autobiography(ies):
    oral, 82
    reading, 18, 20, 82–91
        samples of, 86–89, 91
        and study of reading process, 91

Background, needed in reading cases, 235–236
Beginning reading, prerequisites for success in, 275
Behavior of students, recording of, 59–63
"Behavior modification," 157
Behavioral approach, 274, 283
Bender-Gestalt (*see* Bender Visual-Motor Gestalt Test)
Bender Visual-Motor Gestalt Test, 207, 273
Bilingual students, 89, 281–283
Biochemical factors, 185–186
Books:
    for beginners, 279

Books:
    choice of, as evidence of reading interests, 112–113
    selection of, and interest inventories, 118
Brain damage, 9, 183
Brain-damaged children, 152
"Brain injury," diagnosis of, 275
Brown-Carlsen Listening Comprehension Test, 227

California Test of Mental Maturity, 216, 296
Camera, eye-movement, 177–178
Case conference, 287
Case data:
    depths of interpretation, 274–275
    interpreting and synthesizing, 271
Case studies, 31, 93, 158
    diagnostic summaries, 275–283
Case study approach, 229
Cerebral dominance, disturbed, 181, 182
Charts of reading interests, 111
Checklist form of autobiography, 85
Checklists, 98, 114
    for recording observations, 59–62
Chicago Community Child Guidance Centers, 160
Chicago Reading Clinic, 171
Chicago Visual Discrimination Test, 206
Children's interests, studies of, 112
"Children's Vision and School Success," 169
Choral reading, 279
Class, reading ability, 139
Class discussion and study of the reading process, 90–91
Classroom situations, analysis of, 49–58
"Cloze" technique, 131
Coaching and intelligence test scores, 218
Communication, prerequisites to, 236–237
Comprehension:
    aided by interest, 108–109

Mental abilities, 202
  development of, 218, 226
  and reading potential, 14–15
  and reading proficiency, 156
Mental Measurements Yearbook, 291
Mental processes, understanding of, 81
Mentally retarded children, 71
Metrazol, 185–186
Metropolitan Reading Readiness Tests, 37, 40, 294
Miami Linguistic Readers, 279
Mind and body, close relation between, 186
Minnesota Percepto-diagnostic Test, 207
Motivations, 260
Motor coordination, 180–181
My Reading Design, 111
My Weekly Reader, 192
Myopia, 168

National Society for the Prevention of Blindness, 172
Nelson-Denny Reading Test, 89
Nervous system stimulants, 185
Neurological deficits:
  clues to, 57
  and severe reading disability, 152, 157, 181

Observation:
  in classroom, 47–65
  and detection of visual defects, 169
  in gathering information, 20
  during individual tests, 191–192
  limitations of, 48–49
  opportunities for, 49
  and reading interests, 110
  recording of, 59–63
  skill in, 63
  supplemented by tests, 291
  techniques of, 259–269
  training in, 48
  value of, 224
Observations:
  interpretation of, 62–63
  versus tests, 64
Oral reading:
  as diagnostic technique, 67–80
  in high school and college, 72–77
  individualized, 68–69
Oral reading tests, 204–205

Oral report periods in classroom observation, 50–51
Ortho-Rater, 171
Overreferral and visual tests, problem of, 172

Parent-child relations, 17, 235, 241, 246, 281
Parents:
  education of, 155
  interviews with, 235, 241–246
  and IQ information, 226
  and reading problems, 160–161
Peabody Language Development Kits, 185
Peabody Picture Vocabulary Test, 202
"Peep-hole" method of studying eye movements, 178–179
Peer relations, 17, 58
Perception:
  auditory, 154, 214
  visual, 152–154, 214
  and achievement in reading, 152
Perceptions determining behavior, 96
Perceptual Achievement Form Test, 181
Perceptual-conceptual continuum and reading potential, 15, 153
Perceptual-motor abilities, 152–154, 275
Perceptual speed, building of, 173
Personality:
  psychodynamics of, 259
  and values, clinical analysis of, 9
Personality development, related to interest, 107–108
Personality factors and reading potential, 228
Personality patterns, clues to, from reports of reading interests, 118
Personality problems and progress in reading, 156–157
"Phono-Word Wheels," 278
Physical factors in reading diagnosis, 16, 152, 167–190
Picture completion test, 221
Picture stories, informal projective, 264–265
Play periods, observation during, 55–56
Practice exercises, 278–279
Predictive index, 206
Preschool children, tests for, 292–293
Primary grades, tests in, 294–295
Prognosis based on testing, dangers of, 218
Programmed learning books, 284